AFGHANISTAN

D1728890

This book offers an overview of the formation of the Afghan state and of the politics, economic challenges and international relations of contemporary Afghanistan.

It opens with an account of some of the key features that make Afghanistan unique and proceeds to discuss how the Afghan state acquired a distinctive character as a rentier state. In addition, the authors outline a complex range of domestic and external factors that led to the breakdown of the state, and how that breakdown gave rise to a set of challenges with which Afghan political and social actors have been struggling to deal since the 2001 international intervention that overthrew the anti-modernist Taliban regime. It then presents the different types of politics that Afghanistan has witnessed over the last two decades; examines some of the most important features of the Afghan economy; and demonstrates how Afghanistan's geopolitical location and international relations more broadly have complicated the task of promoting stability in the post-2001 period. It concludes with some reflections on the factors that are likely to shape Afghanistan's future trajectory and notes that if there are hopes for a better future, they largely rest on the shoulders of a globalised generation of younger Afghans.

This book will be of interest to students and scholars in the fields of Middle East and Central Asian studies, international relations, politics, development studies and history.

Niamatullah Ibrahimi is Associate Research Fellow at the Alfred Deakin Institute for Citizenship and Globalisation at Deakin University, Australia.

William Maley is Professor of Diplomacy at the Asia-Pacific College of Diplomacy at The Australian National University, Australia.

THE CONTEMPORARY MIDDLE EAST
Edited by Professor Anoushiravan Ehteshami
Institute for Middle Eastern and Islamic Studies, University of Durham

For well over a century now the Middle East and North Africa countries have formed a central plank of the international system. **The Contemporary Middle East Series** provides the first systematic attempt at studying the key actors of this dynamic, complex, and strategically important region. Using an innovative common format – which in each case study provides an easily-digestible analysis of the origins of the state, its contemporary politics, economics and international relations – prominent Middle East experts have been brought together to write definitive studies of the MENA region's key countries.

Books in the series

Tunisia: Stability and Reform in the Modern Maghreb
Christopher Alexander

Libya: Continuity and Change
Ronald Bruce St John

Lebanon: The Politics of a Penetrated Society
Tom Najem

Libya: Continuity and Change 2nd Edition
Ronald Bruce St John

Morocco: Challenges to tradition and modernity 2nd Edition
James N. Sater

Tunisia: From stability to revolution in the Maghreb 2nd Edition
Christopher Alexander

The United Arab Emirates: Power, Politics and Policymaking
Kristian Coates Ulrichsen

Iran: Stuck in Transition
Anoushiravan Ehteshami

Israel
Ilan Pappé

Afghanistan: Politics and Economics in a Globalising State
Niamatullah Ibrahimi and William Maley

For a full list of titles: https://www.routledge.com/middleeaststudies/series/CME

AFGHANISTAN

Politics and Economics in a Globalising State

Niamatullah Ibrahimi and William Maley

LONDON AND NEW YORK

First published 2020
by Routledge
2 Park Square, Milton Park, Abingdon, Oxon OX14 4RN

and by Routledge
52 Vanderbilt Avenue, New York, NY 10017

Routledge is an imprint of the Taylor & Francis Group, an informa business

British Library Cataloguing-in-Publication Data
A catalogue record for this book is available from the British Library

Library of Congress Cataloging-in-Publication Data
A catalog record has been requested for this book

ISBN: 978-1-138-32063-5 (hbk)
ISBN: 978-1-138-32091-8 (pbk)
ISBN: 978-0-429-45300-7 (ebk)

Typeset in Bembo
by Lumina Datamatics Limited

On 17 August 2019, one of the authors took part in a conference at the Afghanistan Centre at Kabul University, timed to mark the 100th anniversary of Afghan independence. The majority of the speakers were young Afghan researchers who presented papers of outstanding quality, and at the end of the day, the participants adjourned for a convivial dinner at a nearby restaurant.

On the same evening, in a part of Kabul not far from the university, families and friends gathered to celebrate the wedding of a young couple, Mirwais Alani, 25, and Raihana, 18. The wedding invitations proposed a celebration 'with a world of hope and desire'. At around 11:40 pm, a suicide bomber detonated an explosive charge in the midst of the guests, killing 80 and wounding 180. The dead included 14 members of the bride's family.

Responsibility was claimed by the 'Islamic State' terrorist group, in pursuit of its fanatical hostility to Shiite Muslims. In a heartbreaking statement, Mirwais said 'I was supposed to return happy, but within span of two hours, they devastated my whole life. They devastated my life within seconds ... We had done nothing wrong to anyone, but our lives were devastated'.

In today's Afghanistan, hope and horror walk side-by-side. We dedicate this book to the innocent victims of terror in Afghanistan.

CONTENTS

LIST OF ILLUSTRATIONS

Tables

Figure

ACKNOWLEDGEMENTS

The generous assistance that we have received over many years from Afghan and non-Afghan colleagues has greatly aided our understanding of Afghanistan. It has indeed been so extensive that it would be invidious even to attempt to list those from whose insights we have benefited. They will know who they are, and will also know of our deep appreciation for their contributions. We, of course, remain exclusively responsible for the content of this study.

We particularly wish to acknowledge the support of colleagues at the Alfred Deakin Institute for Citizenship and Globalisation at Deakin University, and at the Asia-Pacific College of Diplomacy at The Australian National University, who staunchly supported our work on this book. We would also like to thank the splendid team at Routledge who commissioned it and then oversaw its production.

Gul Begum, Hazhir and Shahir Ibrahimi showed great patience towards a husband and father who was tied to a computer when he could have been doing other things. And Jean Maley, who died aged 98 in March 2019, was almost infinitely tolerant of a son who persisted in travelling to parts of the world which media stereotypes routinely suggested it would have been better to avoid.

Niamatullah Ibrahimi and William Maley
Melbourne and Canberra, September 2019

CHRONOLOGY

1747 CE	Birth of the Durrani Empire
1772 CE	Death of Ahmad Shah Durrani
1776 CE	Transfer of capital from Kandahar to Kabul
1839–42 CE	First Anglo-Afghan War
1879 CE	Second Anglo-Afghan War
1880 CE	Accession of Abdul Rahman Khan
1891–93 CE	Hazara Wars
1893 CE	Drawing of the Durand Line
1901 CE	Death of Abdul Rahman Khan and accession of Habibullah
1914–18 CE	Afghanistan remains neutral throughout the First World War
1919 CE	Assassination of Habibullah and accession of Amanullah
	Third Anglo-Afghan War and achievement of full independence
1919–29 CE	Decade of attempted reforms
1924 CE	Promulgation of first Constitution of Afghanistan
1926 CE	Title of ruler changed from amir to king (*Padshah*)
1929 CE	Forced abdication of Amanullah
	Emergence and overthrow of Habibullah Kalakani
	Occupation of throne by Nadir Khan
1933 CE	Assassination of Nadir and accession of Zahir Shah
1934 CE	Afghanistan joins the League of Nations
1935 CE	US-Afghanistan diplomatic relations established
1939–45 CE	Afghanistan remains neutral throughout the Second World War
1946 CE	Shah Mahmoud replaces Muhammad Hashim as prime minister
	Afghanistan joins the United Nations
1953 CE	Muhammad Daoud replaces Shah Mahmoud as prime minister
1953–63 CE	Daoud escalates the Pushtunistan dispute with Pakistan
1963 CE	Muhammad Daoud removed as prime minister

1964 CE	New constitution inaugurates 'Decade of Democracy'
1973 CE	Zahir Shah overthrown in a palace coup by Daoud
1973–78 CE	Republic of Afghanistan
1978 CE	Daoud overthrown and killed in a violent communist coup
1979 CE	Soviet invasion of Afghanistan and installation of Babrak Karmal
1979–80 CE	Major Afghan refugee movements to neighbouring states
1979–89 CE	War in Afghanistan between Soviet forces and *Mujahideen*
1986 CE	Replacement of Karmal by Dr Najibullah
1988 CE	Signing of Geneva Accords on Afghanistan
1989 CE	Completion of withdrawal of Soviet forces
1992 CE	Collapse of communist regime
1992–95 CE	Destructive battles for control of Kabul
1994 CE	Taliban emerge and occupy Kandahar
1995 CE	Taliban occupy Herat
1996 CE	Taliban occupy Kabul
	Dr Najibullah seized from UN office and killed
2001 CE	Assassination of anti-Taliban leader Ahmad Shah Massoud
	Al-Qaeda terrorist attacks and US overthrow of Taliban regime
	Bonn Conference on Afghanistan
	Establishment of Interim Administration under Hamed Karzai
2003 CE	Resumption of Taliban attacks from bases in Pakistan
2004 CE	Adoption of new Afghan Constitution
	Presidential election
2005 CE	Wolesi Jirga election
2009 CE	Presidential election
2010 CE	Wolesi Jirga election
	Collapse of Kabul Bank
2014 CE	Completion of withdrawal of most US and NATO forces
	Presidential election
	Establishment of 'National Unity Government'
2018 CE	Wolesi Jirga election
2018–19 CE	Negotiations between the US and the Taliban over Afghanistan

MAP

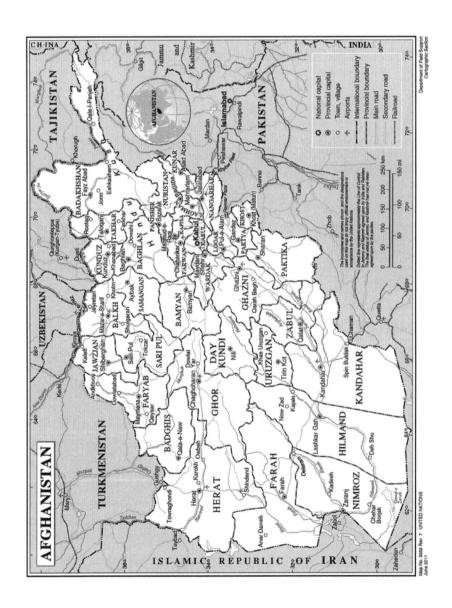

1

INTRODUCTION

More than 40 years have passed since a communist coup on 27 April 1978 tipped Afghanistan into an abyss of bloodshed and disarray, and a pervasive sense of uncertainty about the future continues to be a feature of the daily lives of many ordinary Afghans. Rarely has any single country been so continuously disrupted for so long. Yet at the same time, Afghanistan has been dramatically transformed since 1978 and has absorbed the effects of globalisation in an arresting fashion since the beginning of the twenty-first century. Many Afghans would leave the country if given the opportunity, and many have good reason to do so, but survey evidence suggests that a solid majority, some 58 per cent, would prefer to stay.[1] This alone should give pause to those who see Afghanistan as a disaster area with nothing whatsoever to recommend it. Any broad generalisations about Afghanistan have the potential to mislead. Afghanistan's story is much more complicated, and this book explores why this is the case. Four points of context deserve to be emphasised at the outset.

First of all, Afghanistan is a *complex* country. The borders of its landlocked territory have been largely defined since the late nineteenth century, but within those boundaries one can find desert plains, green valleys, and the rugged mountains that make up the so-called Hindu Kush, an offshoot of the adjacent Himalayas. This formidable terrain has shaped the development of Afghan society. No comprehensive census has ever been completed in Afghanistan, but the current estimate of its population stands at 32,225,560. The majority of the population, 71.3 per cent, still live in rural areas, many in small villages, although, as in many countries, Afghanistan's people are increasingly to be found in urban areas, where 24.1 per cent dwell (the remainder being nomads).[2] The population is overwhelmingly Muslim, but alongside the Sunni Muslim majority is a substantial Shiite minority, and amongst adherents of both of these components of Islam there are diverse forms of belief, worship and ritual to be found,[3] as well as an increasing number of people whose Muslim identity is mainly cultural rather than religious. There are also small communities of Hindus and Sikhs left in Afghanistan, although terrorist attacks have thinned their numbers in recent years.

The Afghan population is also ethnically diverse. The largest ethnic groups are the Pushtuns, Tajiks, Hazaras and Uzbeks, but more than 50 distinct groups have been identified,[4] and the exact numbers that the different groups comprise have been both a matter of contention for political reasons and also the subject of methodological debate, since ethnic identification is subjective rather than objective, and there are also Afghans whose parents and ancestors come from different groups. These factors help explain why social scientists increasingly shy away from simple ideas of 'identity', recognising that individuals may choose to identify themselves in different ways as circumstances change, and that in everyday life, people as a matter of course shift between different social worlds, often with considerable dexterity. This is particularly likely in perilous situations, where to be identified with particular groups may be a life-threatening development.

In addition, Afghanistan is linguistically diverse. In common with what has been experienced in many other countries, a grammatically easy language, namely, Persian, has become the *lingua franca* or *koine* of the country at the expense of other languages such as Pushto which are grammatically more complicated. As a result, a surprisingly large number of Afghans are bilingual or even trilingual, with English increasingly seen as the language to master if people are to move ahead. This diversity is not without its problems. Issues can arise over whether a tongue used by a particular group, such as Hazaragi amongst Hazaras, is a distinct language or merely a dialect of Afghanistan's Dari Persian, as well as over which languages should be recognised as official languages and which cannot aspire to such status.[5] On occasion such disputes can become the occasion for the airing of a much wider set of grievances, posing challenges both for political leaders and for those with an interest in the promotion of community harmony.

Afghanistan is frequently described as a 'tribal' society, but this label is liable to mislead. The very word 'tribe' is an English word and in recent years has been treated with considerable caution by anthropologists who have been increasingly alert to its colonial origins, and to the danger that its use will lump together quite diverse forms of social organisation. As Elisabeth Leake has put it, 'Colonial officials across empires constructed "tribes" to explain local relationships, to create leadership hierarchies, and to establish "stable, enduring, genealogically and culturally coherent units" that were easier to understand and thereby govern'.[6] It is also the case that social relations need not be arranged around lineages in the way that the idea of 'tribe' seems to imply. Amongst groups such as the Tajiks, the village provides a stronger basis for community than does the lineage. The term *qawm*, used quite frequently in Afghanistan to describe a social network, is considerably more elastic than the idea of the tribe, but more useful as a tool for making sense of Afghanistan's complexities.

Second, as a result of decades of war, Afghanistan is a *damaged* country. It was a very poor country even before the April 1978 coup and the Soviet invasion of Afghanistan in December 1979, but the events of the period since the late 1970s have greatly added to Afghanistan's difficulties. The mortality associated with war has been on a scale that boggles the mind. According to a (conservative) demographic study, between 1978 and 1987, unnatural deaths amounted to 876,825, or to put it another way, over 240 deaths every day for ten years straight.[7] This was undoubtedly the most lethal period in Afghanistan's recent history, but civilian casualties have continued to be a major blight well into the twenty-first century[8]; between the beginning of 2007 and the end of 2018, some 35,636 civilian deaths were recorded in United Nations data.[9] And these figures are only the tip of a very ugly iceberg. For every person killed, there are likely to be many more injured, maimed, disabled or traumatised, in a society which by virtue of its poverty is poorly equipped to cope with the enduring needs for assistance, both medical and psychosocial, that such victims of war have.

Afghanistan has also witnessed enormous human displacement. At the beginning of the 1990s, the Office of the United Nations High Commissioner for Refugees estimated that there were some 6.2 million Afghans living outside the country.[10] Refugee camps in Pakistan in the 1980s provided a support network for the Afghan resistance forces that were combating the Soviet Army in Afghanistan,[11] but as conflict dragged on after the completion in February 1989 of the Soviet troop withdrawal and the collapse of the Communist regime in April 1992, refugee camps also became breeding grounds for the anti-modernist Taliban movement. There have been refugee movements back and forth since then, but the Afghan refugee population long remained the largest in the world, and it took the massive outflows from Syria following the outbreak of the Syrian civil war in 2011 to displace Afghanistan from this unfortunate pedestal. In addition to refugee movements, Afghanistan has also witnessed very substantial internal displacement with all the consequences of social dislocation that flow from it.[12] The risk of forced migration of Afghans remains very high.

Human displacement has also contributed to a further form of damage, namely, the erosion of human capital as displaced persons have been detached from the environments in which they would have learned the kinds of skills necessary to function effectively within Afghanistan's economy. It is hard to learn to be a farmer when sitting in a refugee camp, since one loses access to the kind of practical knowledge that is central to the accomplishment of this kind of activity. Of course, Afghanistan also suffered enormous destruction to its infrastructure during the 1980s, and the continuation of conflict in the 1990s meant that far less 'reconstruction' took place than one might have hoped. To some extent that has changed since 2001, but as we shall see, the process of reinvigorating economic life in Afghanistan has faced considerable difficulties.

Third, unhappily for its people, Afghanistan is also a *strategically located* country. In the nineteenth century it was widely seen as a buffer state, physically distancing the expanding Russian Empire from the British Raj in India. Both the Russians and the British saw an interest in preventing Afghanistan from falling under the domination of the other and pursued various strategies designed to block any such outcome. During the First World War, Afghanistan maintained its neutrality, but its proximity to India meant that it was a focus of efforts by Wilhelmine Germany to boost Germany's influence, notably via a mission headed by Oskar von Niedermayer and Werner Otto von Hentig.[13] It was faced with similar efforts by Nazi Germany during the Second World War,[14] when Afghanistan once again adopted a neutral position. During the Cold War, it trod a delicate path, with both the United States and the Soviet Union supporting development projects in Afghanistan from which they clearly hoped to extract a degree of influence. But the vulnerability to which it was exposed by its strategic location became very clear with the Soviet invasion in December 1979, and although with hindsight it is clear that the Soviets' motives in entering Afghanistan were not geostrategic,[15] this was far from obvious at the time, and led to Afghanistan's becoming a theatre for contestation in what many came to see as a Second Cold War.

Afghanistan has also been seen as a crossroads, linking different regions of the world.[16] This is understandable in a cultural sense; Afghanistan's landscape is richly supplied with archaeological relics of the different civilisations that at various times have been present on its territory. This is surely one part of the country's fascination. But in a more concrete sense, it has also been viewed as an economic crossroads. This was most obvious in the late 1990s, when companies such as the US UNOCAL and the Argentinian Bridas competed for the opportunity to build resource pipelines – under Taliban protection – from Turkmenistan to the energy-hungry South Asian market. Nothing much came of the endeavour at the time,[17] but the hope has lingered on that a 'crossroads' role may prove Afghanistan's salvation.

The greatest problem of Afghanistan's strategic location, however, is that it has become a theatre for competition between regional rivals with an incentive to compete through proxy forces rather than direct confrontation. Afghanistan occupies a very uncomfortable seat. Whether one sees it as surrounded by distinct conflict spheres, or as a victim of multiple interlocking security dilemmas and strategic challenges,[18] it is unfortunately the case that the interests of its people in peace and stability have frequently been subordinated to the selfish interests of neighbouring countries to deny their rivals influence in Kabul and the territory around it. Thus, Afghanistan is not just haunted by its own immediate problems; it is also a victim of tensions between India and Pakistan that go back to the partition of the sub-continent in 1947 and are regularly refuelled by the Kashmir dispute.

Fourth, Afghanistan is a *romanticised* country. This may seem a quaint point to make, but how Afghanistan is seen in the wider world actually has important ramifications for how it will be treated. In Afghanistan's cultures there is of course much to celebrate, including a rich oral tradition, as well as literary, artistic and musical achievement.[19] There is in turn a developed and extensive scholarly literature dealing with Afghanistan's history, politics, societies and cultures,[20] and while some works from the nineteenth century now have a decidedly 'Orientalist' or 'colonialist' tinge, other work has been immensely instructive. But there is no doubt that in contrast to countries such as, say, Singapore, Afghanistan has been seen as markedly exotic. Tales from Afghanistan can be found in the poetry of Rudyard Kipling, who never once set foot in the country, and of Sir Henry Newbolt; and even the Sherlock Holmes stories of Arthur Conan Doyle contain references to Afghan wars. Older travel writings also tended to emphasise the esoteric at the expense of the mundane. The 1980s did not do much to overcome this problem; on the contrary, those years witnessed a revival of what one might call a 'war travel' genre, which in turn stimulated the information and propaganda departments of various resistance organisations that recognised that they had a constituency with which to deal. Some works on Afghanistan by authors with a strongly developed 'Lawrence of Arabia' complex still appear from time to time, and they have the potential to plant damaging stereotypes in the minds of outside observers and policymakers. The most important development countering these tendencies has been the emergence since 2001 of a vibrant community of young Afghan journalists and scholars whose work has transcended these stereotypes. Writings of high quality in both Afghan and European languages have emerged from their computers, the very technology itself pointing to major changes Afghanistan has undergone. These writings have helped to show that ordinary Afghans are not very different from ordinary people in most other countries; they simply face, on a daily basis, different challenges and different incentive structures.

This book cannot address all the complexities that flow from these issues of context, but it does set out to provide the reader with an overview of some of the key matters with which it is important to be familiar in order to make sense of the dramatic developments that from time to time put Afghanistan in the headlines. It opens with a discussion of state formation in Afghanistan. As we shall see, the Afghan state emerges through a complicated process which to a degree accounted for the character that it came to assume. Over time it developed into a 'rentier' state, dangerously dependent upon unstable sources of income. This unravelled after 1979, and, following a period of several decades during which the state became increasingly debilitated and disrupted, the 2001 intervention by the United States and its allies set the scene for the development of a new kind of state which increasingly assumed what we call a neopatrimonial character. The third chapter explores in detail the kind of politics that surfaced within this framework. Perilously for Afghanistan, institutional politics provided only a small part of the story, with network politics, warlord politics, contentious politics and identity politics all coming into play, within the context of ongoing insurgency. The fourth chapter examines some of the key challenges facing the Afghan economy, including the problem of dependence on foreign aid, the issue of how businessmen and entrepreneurs relate to the state, the challenges faced by Afghan agriculture in an environment in which opium cultivation is very profitable, and the whole issue of where Afghanistan's economic development fits into the wider world economy. This leads to the fifth chapter, which is concerned with Afghanistan's international relations. How Afghanistan fits into the world is important, since this shapes the opportunities it might be able to exploit. What Afghanistan can aspire to achieve is limited by the complexity of its relations: in its neighbourhood with Pakistan, India and Iran; somewhat more broadly with China and Russia; and at a greater distance with the United States. Nonetheless, globalisation has created new opportunities that Afghanistan never previously enjoyed, and from these one may derive a measure of hope for the future. A brief conclusion sums up some of the key lessons of the book.

Notes

1 See *A Survey of the Afghan People: Afghanistan in 2018* (Kabul: The Asia Foundation, 2018) p. 285.
2 *Estimated Population of Afghanistan 2019–20* (Kabul: Central Statistics Organization, 2019).
3 See Nile Green (ed.), *Afghanistan's Islam: From Conversion to the Taliban* (Oakland: University of California Press, 2017).
4 See Conrad Schetter, *Ethnizität und ethnische Konflikte in Afghanistan* (Berlin: Dietrich Reimer Verlag, 2003).
5 See Jonathan Pool, 'The Official Language Problem', *American Political Science Review*, vol. 85, no. 2, June 1991, pp. 495–514; David D. Laitin and Rajesh Ramachandran, 'Language Policy and Human Development', *American Political Science Review*, vol. 110, no. 3, August 2016, pp. 457–480.
6 Elisabeth Leake, *The Defiant Border: The Afghan-Pakistan Borderlands in the Era of Decolonization, 1936–1965* (Cambridge: Cambridge University Press, 2017) p. 9. See also Nivi Manchanda, 'The Imperial Sociology of the "Tribe" in Afghanistan', *Millennium: Journal of International Studies*, vol. 46, no. 2, 2018, pp. 165–189.
7 Noor Ahmad Khalidi, 'Afghanistan: Demographic Consequences of War, 1978–1987', *Central Asian Survey*, vol. 10, no. 3, 1991, pp. 101–126. By contrast, a plausible estimate of the total number of unnatural deaths for the 30-year period from 1989–2018, supplied by the Uppsala Conflict Data Program, Department of Peace and Conflict Research, Uppsala University, is 227,510, or on average fewer than 21 per day: https://ucdp.uu.se/#country/700
8 See Niamatullah Ibrahimi, 'When few means many: The consequences of civilian casualties for civil-military relations in Afghanistan', in William Maley and Susanne Schmeidl (eds.), *Reconstructing Afghanistan: Civil-military Experiences in Comparative Perspective* (London: Routledge, 2015) pp. 165–176; William Maley, *Transition in Afghanistan: Hope, Despair and the Limits of Statebuilding* (London: Routledge, 2018) pp. 169–185.
9 For an overview of UN data related to civilian casualties, see *Afghanistan: Protection of Civilians in Armed Conflict. Annual Report 2018* (Kabul: United Nations Assistance Mission in Afghanistan and United Nations Human Rights Office of the High Commissioner, February 2019).
10 See Rupert Colville, 'The Biggest Case Load in the World', *Refugees*, no. 108, 1997, pp. 3–9.
11 See Fiona Terry, *Condemned to Repeat? The Paradox of Humanitarian Action* (Ithaca: Cornell University Press, 2002) pp. 55–82; Sarah Kenyon Lischer, *Dangerous Sanctuaries? Refugee Camps, Civil War, and the Dilemmas of Humanitarian Aid* (Ithaca: Cornell University Press, 2005) pp. 44–72.

12 See Susanne Schmeidl, 'Internal displacement in Afghanistan: The tip of the iceberg', in Srinjoy Bose, Nishank Motwani and William Maley (eds.), *Afghanistan – Challenges and Prospects* (London: Routledge, 2018) pp. 169–187.

13 See Thomas L. Hughes, 'The German Mission to Afghanistan, 1915–1916', *German Studies Review*, vol. 25, no. 3, October 2002, pp. 447–476; Jules Stewart, *The Kaiser's Mission to Kabul: A Secret Expedition to Afghanistan in World War I* (London: I.B. Tauris, 2014).

14 See Milan L. Hauner, 'Afghanistan between the Great Powers, 1938–1945', *International Journal of Middle East Studies*, vol. 14, no. 4, November 1982, pp. 481–499.

15 For a more detailed discussion of Soviet motivations for the invasion, see William Maley, *The Afghanistan Wars* (New York: Palgrave Macmillan, 2009).

16 See Bernard Dupaigne and Gilles Rossignol, *Le carrefour afghan* (Paris: Gallimard, 2002).

17 See William Maley, 'The Perils of Pipelines', *The World Today*, vol. 54, nos. 8–9, August–September 1998, pp. 231–232.

18 For elaborations of these visions, see Kristian Berg Harpviken and Shahrbanou Tadjbakhsh, *A Rock Between Hard Places: Afghanistan as an Arena of Regional Insecurity* (London: Hurst & Co., 2016); Nishank Motwani, 'Afghanistan and the regional insecurity contagion', in Srinjoy Bose, Nishank Motwani and William Maley (eds.), *Afghanistan – Challenges and Prospects* (London: Routledge, 2018) pp. 219–240.

19 See Margaret A. Mills, *Rhetorics and Politics in Afghan Traditional Storytelling* (Philadelphia: University of Pennsylvania Press, 1991); Wali Ahmadi, *Modern Persian Literature in Afghanistan: Anomalous Visions of History and Form* (New York: Routledge, 2008); Mohammad Alam Farhad with Arley Loewen, 'Drawing back the curtain: Art and artists of Afghanistan', in Arley Loewen and Josette McMichael (eds.), *Images of Afghanistan: Exploring Afghan Culture through Art and Literature* (Karachi: Oxford University Press, 2010) pp. 251–261; Hiromi Lorraine Sakata, *Music in the Mind: The Concepts of Music and Musician in Afghanistan* (Washington DC: Smithsonian Institution Press, 2002).

20 For overviews, see Louis Dupree, *Afghanistan* (Princeton: Princeton University Press, 1980); Thomas J. Barfield, *Afghanistan: A Cultural and Political History* (Princeton: Princeton University Press, 2010); Robert D. Crews, *Afghan Modern: The History of a Global Nation* (Cambridge: Harvard University Press, 2015); Jonathan L. Lee, *Afghanistan: A History from 1260 to the Present* (London: Reaktion Books, 2018).

2

STATE FORMATION

In order to discuss state formation, it is necessary first to outline what one might mean by 'the state'. This is a rather more elusive undertaking than one might first think. When one is living in a country, it often seems easy enough to identify key state actors by symbolic markers – officials may wear uniforms to give them a distinctive appearance and may work in premises decorated with coats of arms or crests to highlight their special status. But these tell only a small part of the story. Non-state actors (for example, private security guards) can wear elaborate uniforms, and state officials (such as bureaucrats and secret police) can dress like their fellow citizens. Nor does the mere exercise of power by rulers necessarily imply the existence of a state. Historically, there have been diverse rulers whose power was not grounded in the existence or control of anything like what we would now call the state: conquest empires, and rulers within them such as Tamerlane, come immediately to mind,[1] as do 'city-states' of the kind that dwelt within walled fortresses in Central Asia.[2] And while Max Weber's famous definition of the state in terms of a monopoly on the legitimate means of violence is much cited, there is no shortage of weak states where both the capacities and the legitimacy of 'the state' are contested.[3]

Two distinct senses of the word 'state' need to be distinguished at the outset. First is what one might call the 'territorial state', a close equivalent of the word 'country'. Some 193 such 'states' are members of the United Nations (UN), and there is a rich legal literature on how such states emerge.[4] Afghanistan's standing as a 'territorial state' in this sense is completely uncontested. It has been a UN member since 1946, and its membership preceded that of the post-colonial states whose joining the UN from the 1950s onwards marked the first great wave in the expansion of international society. The second sense of the word 'state' is in a number of respects much more complex and contested. It refers to political and administrative structures domiciled *within* the boundaries of a 'territorial' state that perform a number of distinctive functions. In an influential study, Migdal has identified state functions as being to '*penetrate* society, *regulate* social relationships, *extract* resources, and *appropriate* or use resources in determined ways'.[5] He has also sought to distinguish different parts of the state: these he calls the *trenches*, consisting of 'the officials who must execute state directives directly in the face of possibly strong societal resistance'; the *dispersed field offices*, the 'regional and local bodies that rework and organise state policies and directives for local consumption, or even formulate and implement wholly local policies'; the *agency's central offices*, the 'nerve centers where national policies are formulated and enacted and where resources for implementation are marshaled'; and the *commanding heights*, the 'pinnacle of the state' where the 'top executive leadership' is to be found.[6] It will at once be obvious that the processes by which states form are likely to be ragged and fitful rather than smooth and linear, and historical analysis strongly supports this view.[7] Furthermore, while the metaphor of a 'social contract' has figured in political theory since the time of Hobbes, Locke and Rousseau, the empirical reality, thoroughly documented by Charles Tilly, is that state formation has been historically more associated with the deployment of superior force than with friendly agreement.[8]

The emergence of the state

History and mythology are easily blurred. There may or may not be substance in the depiction of the Pushtuns as descended from the Lost Tribes of the Israelites,[9] but a common myth of descent can be very important in the constitution of an ethnic identity.[10] Similarly, histories of state formation all too often contain substantial elements of myth, since a claim of responsibility for establishing a state in the past can easily be transformed into the claim of a right to control the state in the present or future. Afghanistan has witnessed the flourishing of diverse discourses about state formation,[11] and to survey them at this point would require many pages. In recent years, there have also been significant works of revisionist history and historiography by both Western and Afghan scholars that have contested in detail some of the more 'Orientalist' studies and 'understandings' of Afghanistan that have tended to minimise Afghan social and political agency.[12] Nonetheless, despite all these complexities, it is possible to offer, at least in skeletal form, a picture of how the Afghan state took shape.

As a clearly delineated territory with a centralised government, Afghanistan emerged during the reign of Amir Abdul Rahman Khan (1880–1901) in the last two decades of the nineteenth century. It developed as a culmination of two major socioeconomic and political processes: the decay and decline of traditional conquest empires that ruled the region for several centuries, and the subsequent advent of modern European colonialism. During the nineteenth century, the South and Central Asian regions were dominated by geostrategic rivalries between the British and Russian colonial powers. The rivalries that became known as the 'Great Game' marked the demise of traditional empires and the advent of colonial powers and new forms of social and political organisation.

During the first half of the century, the British Empire consolidated its hold over most of the Indian sub-continent, taking control of Sindh, Punjab and Peshawar and Kashmir. The Russians also advanced, southwards, extending their influence to the Oxus River by taking control of the historic cities of Bukhara, Samarkand and Tashkent and much of the rest of Central Asia. Afghanistan came to play the role of a 'buffer state' between the two major powers and was labelled as such by the British as early as 1883.[13]

The territory of what is now Afghanistan long made up simply a small part of the conquest empires that ruled the region for several centuries, and 'Afghanistan' as the name of the country was only formalised towards the end of the nineteenth century. Prior to the advent of colonial powers, much of the Muslim world was governed by large empires. Without clearly delineated boundaries, these empires did not 'rule' in any modern sense of term. The broader region encompassing modern-day Afghanistan was often identified as 'Khorasan'. Literally meaning 'land from where the sun rises', the region covered the space between the east of Persia and north of India.[14] The boundaries of Khorasan changed over time as the empires that ruled the region expanded and contracted. The area of Afghanistan played a pivotal role in the rise and decline of many of these powers in the region. Several of these empires were based in urban centres that became parts of Afghanistan. The Ghaznavid Empire, which dominated modern-day Afghanistan and much of the territory around it from 975 to 1187, was founded by Sebüktegin, a Turkish slave-warrior in the city of Ghazni in Afghanistan. Sultan Mahmoud Ghaznavi, Sebüktegin's son and successor, further expanded the empire beyond the Oxus River to the north, and into parts of Persia and western India, and played an important role in the expansion of Islam in these regions. Similarly, the Ghorid Empire was founded by Alauddin Husain in the middle of the twelfth century in Firozkoh, now in Afghanistan's province of Ghor. In 1150, Alauddin Husain overthrew the Ghaznavid rulers by conquering and plundering the city of Ghazni. The Ghorid dynasty also rapidly expanded its control to cover most of Afghanistan, north eastern regions of Persia and parts of India.

For most other conquerors, Afghanistan was a key transit route or a 'highway of conquest'[15] between the Central and South Asia regions and ancient Persia. Many of these conquerors originated from across the Oxus River. These included Genghis Khan in the thirteenth century, Timur, known as Tamerlane, in the fourteenth century, and Babur in the early sixteenth century. These conquerors displaced existing dynasties and established extensive empires. The most successful traditional empires relied on large armies and charismatic leadership provided by figures such as Mahmoud, Genghis Khan and Timur. Some of these empires were relatively stable and created conditions for a remarkable flourishing of commerce, arts and culture that endured over centuries. As historian Frederick Starr has argued, between the ninth and twelfth centuries, the Greater Central Asia region, including modern-day Afghanistan and China's eastern province of Xinjiang, was a major centre of the world's civilisation. During this period, the region developed significant urban areas, where trade flourished and rulers patronised the growth of an intellectual class that produced polymaths such as Abu Rayhan al-Biruni and Abu Ali al-Husayn ibn Sina, who were at the forefront of a wide range of scientific discoveries and intellectual currents. Highlighting the importance of cities to these developments, Starr describes the city of Balkh, currently in the province of Balkh in the north of Afghanistan, in the following terms:

> To appreciate Balkh's size, the citadel alone, called Bala Hisar, was twice the size of the entire lower city at Priene, a typical Hellenistic city on the Turkish coastline, and ten times the total area of ancient Troy. And the citadel comprises less than a tenth of Balkh's total area! Everything about Balkh exuded the immense wealth amassed from a booming agricultural sector based on wheat, rice, and citrus fruits; the manufacture of metal tools and ceramic housewares, turquoise gemstones, and fine leather goods; and from international trade that reached as far as India, the Middle East, and China. Indeed, Balkh was perfectly positioned along the main route across Afghanistan to India and westward to the Mediterranean.[16]

Besides Balkh, the cities of Herat, Ghazni and Kabul played central roles in these regional networks of trade and artistic, scientific and intellectual exchange. During the fifteenth and sixteenth centuries, under the Timurids, the city of Herat became a centre of art, culture and fine architecture.[17] Nonetheless, the flourishing of these centres of culture and civilisation followed the ebbs and flows of the major empires.

Beginning in the early sixteenth century, the territory of Afghanistan became a contested zone between the Safavid and the Mughal empires, which were based in Isfahan and Delhi, respectively. The Mughal Empire was founded by Zahiruddin Muhammad Babur, who was born in the Fergana Valley in Central Asia, but conquered Kabul in 1504 and Delhi in 1526. Babur and his successors gradually expanded the areas under their control to include nearly all of the Indian sub-continent. Even after conquering Delhi, Babur chose Kabul as his summer capital. In his memoir, Babur provided insights into the rich social and cultural diversity of Kabul. After identifying twelve separate languages that were spoken in the city, he concluded that 'It is not known if there are so many different peoples and languages in any other province'.[18] He also admired the city's fauna, gardens and climate and requested that his body be buried in Kabul. Babur's Garden remains a very popular place for residents of Kabul to spend a restful afternoon.

As the Mughal Empire under Babur's successors expanded in the Indian sub-continent and captured areas with more resources and population, Kabul assumed a peripheral role in the empire. Around the same time, the Safavid Empire gradually expanded its influence eastwards to include Herat and even extended its control over Kandahar by the mid-seventeenth century. However, the control of the Safavids over their easternmost territories remained fragile.

In 1709, a local rebellion in Kandahar led to the overthrow of the Safavid governor of the province. Mirwais Hotak, the leader of the uprising, laid the foundation for the first major Afghan monarchy. In its short lifespan, the Hotaki dynasty achieved remarkable successes. The Hotakis belonged to the Ghilzai Pushtun tribal confederation, which often competed with the Durrani Pushtuns for power and influence. In 1722, Hotaki forces even took control of Isfahan in Persia, but internal weaknesses and the rise of Nader Shah Afshar led to the defeat of the Hotakis in Persia and eventually the fall of Kandahar to the hands of Nader Shah in 1738. Nader Shah Afshar recruited into his army many local Afghans, particularly from among the Abdali tribes, who fought in his wars of conquests in the Indian sub-continent. In 1747, after Nader Shah was assassinated, Ahmad Shah Durrani, one of his Afghan military officers, founded the Durrani Empire in Kandahar. He changed the name of the Abdali tribes to Durrani (meaning 'pearl') to symbolise the economic and political privileges of the tribes. However, Kandahar and its surrounding areas did not provide the economic resources and revenues required for the maintenance of an empire.[19] To raise and maintain revenues, Ahmad Shah led ten major military campaigns to expand his power beyond Kandahar. Like previous conquerors of the region, Ahmad Shah focused his attention on the Indian sub-continent, to which he directed seven of his ten major military campaigns. By 1772, when Ahmad Shah died, his empire stretched from Mashhad in Persia to Bukhara in Central Asia to Delhi in India.[20]

Ahmad Shah was succeeded by his son Timur Shah, who moved the capital from Kandahar to Kabul. Timor managed to maintain the empire until his death in 1793, but he died without naming a successor from among the 32 of his sons who were alive at the time of his death. Timur Shah's death exposed a major weakness of the monarchy that resulted from persistent rivalries among numerous contenders for power from within the royal households.[21] What followed was a series of extremely violent battles for succession that gradually broke up the empire and dislodged the descendants of Ahmad Shah from the throne. Shah Zaman took the throne by overpowering his rivals, but was overthrown by his brother Mahmud Shah in 1800. He was captured while fleeing and then blinded and placed in prison in Kabul until his death in 1809.

By 1818, the violent rivalries among the competing sons of Timur Shah had effectively led to the disintegration of the Durrani monarchy. As a result, the Sadozai dynasty effectively lost their hold over power. The Sadozais belonged to the Popalzai tribe of Durrani Pushtuns, which had become the dominant tribe following the rise to power by Ahmad Shah in 1747. However, the Sadozais often ruled in a coalition with powerful families of the Barakzai tribe, which was also a large and powerful tribe within the Durrani Pushtuns. Members of the Barakzai tribe served as *wazirs* – in effect, ministers – under the Sadozai rulers. The weakening of the Sadozais' hold on power opened an opportunity for the Muhammadzai branch of the Barakzai tribe to make a claim to power.

In 1826, the Barakzai Dost Muhammad Khan took control of Kabul, from where he attempted to expand his control over the rest of the country. However, at this time, the expansion of the empire through traditional wars of conquest had become more difficult as much of the Indian sub-continent had fallen under the control of the British East India Company, which was concerned about the expansion of Russian influence in Central Asia. The story of British policy at this time is a notably complex one,[22] but these concerns helped raise the significance of Afghanistan for the British as a potential 'gateway' through which Russians could threaten India. Officials of the Company suspected that Dost Muhammad would not have the will or capacity to resist Russian encroachments. In 1839, Lord Auckland, the Governor-General of India, ordered several thousand British and Indian troops to invade the country, launching the first Anglo-Afghan War. Their objective was to overthrow Dost Muhammad Khan and install Shah Shuja as the ruler of Afghanistan. Shuja was one of the sons of Timur Shah and had occupied the throne in Kabul from 1803, but had fled to India after he was overthrown by Mahmud Shah in 1809. The British and Indian troops quickly seized control of Kandahar and Ghazni. In August 1839, the British forces took control of Kabul where they helped enthrone Shah Shuja. Initially, Dost Muhammad Khan fled to Bukhara, but then returned to surrender to British forces in Kabul before going into exile in India. After a period of calm, however, the British forces began to face serious revolts in different parts of the country.[23] Several thousand British and Indian troops were killed in Kabul, Kandahar and other places. In the bloodiest incident of the war, in January 1842, thousands of British and Indian Sepoy forces that were retreating from Kabul towards the Khyber Pass died as a result of attacks by Afghans warriors. The invasion concluded as one of the worst defeats ever for the British Empire. As William Dalrymple notes, 'At the very height of the British Empire, at a point when the British controlled more of the world economy than they would ever do again, and at a time when traditional forces were everywhere being massacred by industrialised colonial armies, it was a rare moment of complete colonial humiliation'.[24] After the departure of the British forces, Shah Shuja was assassinated in Kabul.[25] In a reprisal attack, the British deployed new forces that occupied Kabul and ransacked the city. However, viewing the British control of Afghanistan as untenable, the British forces evacuated Kabul and allowed Dost Muhammad Khan to return to power again.[26]

Following the disastrous end of the first Anglo-Afghan War, the British refrained from attempting to control Afghanistan directly, allowing Dost Muhammad Khan to remain in power. However, after 1876, Lord Lytton, the new Governor-General of India, became increasingly concerned about Russian influence on the court of Amir Sher Ali Khan. Sher Ali Khan was the third son of Dost Muhammad Khan and had assumed power after a violent succession conflict with his brothers following the death of his father in 1863. Initially, he sought to stay away from the rivalries between the Russians and the British. In 1878, Sher Ali Khan accepted a Russian delegation to Kabul, but ordered

the Afghan forces to refuse entry to Lytton's delegation headed by General
Sir Neville Chamberlain. In response, Lytton ordered the second invasion of
Afghanistan in November 1878, triggering what became known as the second
Anglo-Afghan War. As in the first Anglo-Afghan War, the British and Indian
troops quickly seized control of the country. Sher Ali Khan fled towards Mazar-e
Sharif where he died in the following year.

The British forces installed Yaqub Khan, a son of Sher Ali Khan, as the new
ruler of Kabul, and signed a treaty with him in May 1879. The treaty, which
became known as the Treaty of Gandamak (after a village between Kabul and
Jalalabad where the document was signed), effectively turned Afghanistan into
an indirect protectorate of the British Crown. According to the agreement,
Yaqub Khan ceded the control of foreign affairs of Afghanistan as well the areas
of Korram, Pishin and Sibi (now in Pakistan) to the British and accepted a permanent British mission in Kabul. However, the agreement was short-lived,
as in September 1879, a group of soldiers who had not been paid their wages
and opposed the increased British influence over the country killed the British
envoy, Lieutenant-Colonel Sir Louis Cavagnari, and his escort from the Corps
of Guides.[27] The mutiny spread in many parts of the country and forced Yaqub
Khan to abdicate in October of that year. Initially, the British response was to
despatch a force under Major-General Sir Frederick Roberts to take control
of the country,[28] but given the threat of ongoing revolts this was not a sustainable solution, and by 1880, British officials began to look for a 'dignified'
withdrawal from the country. Sir Lepel Griffin, who was sent to Kabul to find a
solution, described the situation in the following way: 'The country was in the
wildest state of ferment. Our army had met with reverses, and in the month of
December had been shut up in the fortified cantonment of Sherpur by General
Muhammad Jan and a great array of Ghilzai and Kohistani tribesmen and influential chiefs … No one appeared possessed of such authority or following as to
warrant the Government selecting him as Amir with any hope that he would be
able to hold his own when the British Army had left the country'.[29]

As the British searched for another ruler to take the throne, Abdul Rahman
Khan, a cousin of Yaqub Khan, arrived in the north of Afghanistan from Central
Asia. Abdul Rahman had been living in exile in Tashkent after a failed insur-
rection by his father, Mohammad Afzal Khan, against Sher Ali Khan in 1869.
After a series of negotiations with British agents and officials, in July 1880, Abdul
Rahman Khan was proclaimed as the new Amir of Afghanistan. He accepted the
terms of the Treaty of Gandamak by surrendering Afghanistan's foreign policy
to the British and accepting a permanent British mission in Kabul. The agreement with the British placed Abdul Rahman Khan in a very strong position in
relation to his domestic rivals. The British supplied him with vast quantities of
arms and ammunition and a regular financial subsidy. British subsidies began
with a payment of 'twenty lakhs' (two million) Indian rupees immediately after
he took the throne in 1880.[30] In return for the initial payment, the Amir ensured
that British and Indian forces were able to retreat safely to India through the

Khyber Pass. In 1882, the British annual subsidy was 1.2 million Indian rupees, which was further increased to 1.8 million Indian rupees in 1893 when the Amir signed a document accepting the Durand Line, a 2430-kilometre boundary that was drawn by Sir Mortimer Durand to separate Afghanistan from the British domains in the Indian sub-continent. As will be discussed in subsequent chapters, the line has proven to be highly contentious, as it had the effect of dividing the Pushtuns between British India (and now Pakistan) and Afghanistan.

Like his predecessors, the Amir faced many challenges to his rule. During his reign, Abdul Rahman Khan fought numerous wars against rival members of the Muhammadzai dynasty, heads of tribes, and religious establishments. In a semi-autobiographical account, which was published by his secretary Sultan Mahomed Khan in London in 1900, he claimed that his reign saw 40 separate rebellions, four of which he describes as 'civil war'.[31] Among those he fought were key leaders of the Afghan resistance during the second Anglo-Afghan War. In 1881, he fought against Sardar Ayub Khan, a son of Sher Ali Khan, over control of Kandahar. Ayub Khan had gained a heroic status by leading Afghan forces against the British forces in the famous battle of Maiwand in July 1880 in Kandahar. In 1888, he fought against Ishaq Khan, another cousin of the Amir, who was governor of Afghan Turkestan at that time.

The British financial and military assistance provided Abdul Rahman Khan with resources that none of his domestic rivals could match. The Amir used these resources to subdue domestic rival groups, including rival members of the dynasty, the religious establishment (*ulema*) and the landed elites. The subjugation of the ulema to state authority was particularly significant because, historically, the religious establishment exercised great social and political influence. Besides their religious authority as sources of religious knowledge and moral guidance, the ulema also had gained significant economic power, as they controlled vast areas of land in religious endowments (*awqaf*) and other resources. Abdul Rahman moved to bring religious endowments under state control,[32] restricted the economic privileges of the ulema, and required each member of the religious establishment to sit for an examination to prove his credentials. Subsequently, the Amir chose those ulema closest to him to adhere to and promote a particular interpretation of Islam that legitimated his claim to power as divinely ordained. In Kabul, the Amir tasked a group of ulema to prepare and publish a number of books and pamphlets that described obedience to his authority as a religious obligation. These books used religious injunctions to outlaw rebellion against the ruler and elevated the Amir's wars to the status of jihad or war in the way of God.[33]

Abdul Rahman Khan is often credited with building a modern Afghan state with centralised state institutions and clearly delineated boundaries that assumed basic functions such as revenue collection and provision of security.[34] However, the Amir's methods and tactics created deep wounds in the social fabric of the country. He became known as the 'Iron Amir' on account of the extremely heavy-handed approach he took in pursuing his objectives. As Griffin put it in 1888, 'he is always exposed to the risk of assassination from his numerous enemies and rivals, and from men who have a blood feud with him on account of his unjust slaughter of their relations'.[35] The Amir personally oversaw some of the most brutal methods of repression of his opponents and reportedly ordered the execution of about 100,000 people.[36] Furthermore, he combined ferocious tactics of repression with a policy of mobilising one segment of the population against the others. He mobilised non-Pushtuns and rival tribes among the Pushtuns against his own dynastic rivals, and then Pushtuns against other ethnic groups. Furthermore, most of the revolts and uprisings he encountered resulted from his own brutal policies of repression, which were often accompanied by extremely high and arbitrary tax collection. Amir Abdul Rahman's tactics of manipulation of communal divisions as well as his heavy-handedness reached their peak in the war against the Hazara population of the country. In what became known as the Hazara War of 1891–1893, the Amir used sectarian-communal divisions and promises of the spoils of war to mobilise the largest number of warriors of his reign. As he allegedly put it, the Hazara War was 'the last of the four great civil wars that took place during my rule, and I consider that the prestige, the strength and power, as well as the peace and safety of my kingdom, have gained more by this war than perhaps any of the others'.[37]

In short, during the reign of Abdul Rahman Khan, Afghanistan gained many trappings of a modern state such as delineated boundaries and a centralised government that was established through force[38]; furthermore, 'Afghanistan' was formalised as the name of the country in bilateral relations and treaties with British India. Nonetheless, state institutions did not penetrate and govern the society as outlined at the beginning of this chapter. In other words, the subjugation of rival elites and social groups did not necessarily lead to the development of state capabilities to penetrate and govern the society. As Jonathan Lee has argued, the reign of the Amir, 'far from consolidating the Afghan state … was a period of regression, stagnation and devastation, which plunged Afghanistan into a series of economic, political and social crises'.[39] Furthermore, state formation was also derailed by the extreme diplomatic, and significant socioeconomic, isolation of the country. The more obvious aspect of this isolation was diplomatic, after the Amir surrendered his control of foreign policy to British India. This meant that from the very outset of his rule, the development of the state was derailed by lack of interaction with other states that could have led to improvement in its capacities to maintain external relations. Furthermore, the country also entered the world of statehood in the context of social and economic isolation, which was primarily driven by the Amir's own fears of foreign interference. The Amir feared that social contacts with the outside world would allow foreign powers to support his rivals. This extended even to fear of intellectual influences from elsewhere in the Muslim world.[40] As a result of the Amir's deliberate policy of isolation, the country remained outside the social and economic zones that were controlled by the British and Russian imperial powers in the South and Central Asia regions, respectively. After completing the construction of a tunnel through the Khojak Pass in Baluchistan, the British extended their railway line up to Chaman, at the border of Afghanistan's province of Kandahar. Complaining about the British plan to extend the line to Kandahar, Abdul Rahman Khan famously stated 'they were pushing the railway line into my country just like pushing a knife into my vitals'.[41]

The rentier state

When he died in 1901, Abdul Rahman Khan left behind a centralised state, which had achieved an historically high degree of territoriality and sovereignty. He was succeeded by his son and heir-designate, Habibullah Khan, without a succession struggle. This was the first peaceful transition of power since Timur Shah had inherited the throne from Ahmad Shah Durrani in 1772. However, the state faced several challenges. First, it was to a large extent dependent on British aid. Second, the achievement of a greater degree of territoriality and sovereignty did not result in the extensive integration of Afghanistan into the international system of states; Afghanistan's foreign relations remained under external control. Third, Afghanistan's economy remained agrarian, and the society's segmenta- tion persisted. The combination of dependence on British aid and persistence of a traditional economy created structural conditions for the rise of what sub- sequently became known as a 'rentier state'. The concept of rentier state was initially developed by Hossein Mahdavy to describe states that derive substantial external rents.[42] Subsequently, Beblawi defined a rentier state as a state where[43]:

- Rent plays a predominant role
- A substantial part of the rent is derived from external sources
- A small segment of population is involved in the generation of rent
- Government is the 'principal recipient' of the rent

The most typical rentier states developed in the Middle East and North African regions, where after the oil boom of the 1970s, sales of petroleum generated vast and unprecedented revenues for these states. However, non-oil producing states can also become rentier states by achieving similar levels of dependence on rents as a result of bilateral aid or the hosting of foreign military bases. For the purpose of our discussion in this chapter, these may include 'location rents', generated through provision of transportation routes (including overflights by commercial aircraft), 'strategic rents', obtained through grants, loans and military assistance provided by one country to another, and 'political rents', as in donations pro- vided by foreign powers to a country's government institutions.[44] During the Cold War era, many states generated high levels of rents through strategic and political alignments with the Union of Soviet Socialist Republics (USSR) or the United States (US). Rentier states give rise to particular types of state-society relations. These states are more likely to develop authoritarian regimes and resist democratisation, as the ruling elites are likely to rule through distribution of foreign rent rather than mobilisation of domestic revenues. These states also lack incentives to invest in the productive sectors of the economy.[45]

In Afghanistan, although British aid in the form of financial subsidies as well as weapons enabled Abdul Rahman Khan to pursue a coercive state-building strategy, the rents generated were not sufficient to allow him to 'rule by redistribution as in pure rentier states'.[46] Consequently, the Amir tried to increase domestic revenues through increases in taxation. By 1889, he had doubled domestic revenues from 30 to 60 million rupees,[47] and the British financial subsidies accounted for only 3.5 per cent of state revenue in 1889–1891. However, if the monetary value of weapons provided by the British is also included, total British aid came close to 25 per cent of state revenues.[48] The Amir spent much of this revenue on the army and his court. When he died, there were only 60 million rupees left in the state treasury.[49]

Habibullah attempted to abolish some of the repressive policies of his father. He allowed a number of political figures who had been exiled by his father to return to Afghanistan. In 1903, he established Habibia High School, the country's first modern school, where classes were taught by Turkish and Indian teachers. At the same time, some of the families who were allowed to return from exile during this period also imported modern nationalist, anti-colonial ideas. These circles formed the nuclei of the first reformist movements that became known as the first constitutionalist movement of the country. But that said, Habibullah's reforms did not fundamentally alter the relationship of Afghanistan with British India: he continued to receive British subsidies, although he also succeeded in increasing domestic revenues to 80 million rupees annually.[50] Fundamental change came after the assassination of Habibullah Khan during a hunting trip in the east of the country in February 1919. Habibullah's brother Nasrullah proclaimed himself as the next ruler of Afghanistan. However, Habibullah's younger son, Amanullah Khan, challenged his uncle's claim to the throne and even accused him of involvement in the murder of his father. After Amanullah seized control of Kabul, Nasrullah Khan agreed to relinquish his claim to power without any bloodshed.

Once on the throne, Amanullah launched a programme of rapid social, political and economic modernisation that aimed to change the nature of state-society relations. Soon after he took possession of the throne, he declared the complete independence of Afghanistan from British India. The unilateral declaration of independence by Amanullah led to the Third Anglo-Afghan War, which was essentially a series of small-scale clashes between Afghan and British Indian forces along the Durand Line in May–June 1919. However, coming so soon after the First World War, the British were not keen to engage in another prolonged war in Afghanistan, and thus ceded their control over Afghanistan's foreign policy. In a treaty signed in August 1919 in Rawalpindi, the British recognised Afghanistan as a fully independent country.[51] The achievement of complete sovereignty of Afghanistan increased the popularity of Amanullah at home and abroad. He began to open diplomatic relations with many countries around the world. However, the declaration of independence also cost Amanullah the annual British subsidies that had helped sustain the power of his father and grandfather. Domestically, Amanullah pursued a highly ambitious reform agenda, which included promulgation of the country's first constitution in 1923. The constitution guaranteed basic civil and political rights for all citizens of the country. In addition, he passed up to 50 separate laws and regulations[52] that aimed to overhaul state-society relations comprehensively.[53] He also abolished slavery, which freed many Hazaras in Kabul who had still been kept in slavery since the time of Abdul Rahman Khan. He regularised the tax system by abolishing tax farming and internal customs duties, and by requiring payments of tax in cash.[54] As a result, state revenues increased up to 180 million rupees.[55]

However, many of his reforms angered elements of the traditional and religious establishments.[56] Amanullah's wife, Queen Soraya, assumed a public role, accompanying the king in his public appearances at home and during his travels abroad. In 1924, members of the Mangal tribe revolted against the government. Although the government was able to put down the revolt, it pointed to the fragility of Amanullah's position. Thenceforth, Amanullah slowed down his reforms. In 1927, he embarked on a long journey to Europe, visiting countries including Italy, France, Germany, the United Kingdom and the Soviet Union. After he returned, he attempted to increase the pace of reforms. In October 1928, a serious revolt was triggered by cancellation of a government payment to Pushtun tribes of eastern Afghanistan; the government traditionally made the payment to tribes in return for their cooperation in securing the highways.[57] Subsequently, the revolt spread to areas to the north of Kabul. In January 1929, aged only 36, Amanullah was forced to abdicate and go into exile in British India; he died in Switzerland in 1960.

Habibullah Kalakani, a Tajik who led the uprising from the north of Kabul, became the first non-Pushtun ruler of Afghanistan. However, his short reign (January–October 1929) was rather chaotic. He abolished many of Amanullah's reforms, but did not succeed in extending his authority over the rest of the country.[58] In October that year, Nadir Khan, who had served in Amanullah's cabinet as minister of war, mobilised an army of Pushtun tribesmen from eastern provinces against Kalakani; he captured Kabul and Kalakani was executed. Nadir Khan became the first of the so-called Musaheban ('courtier') family that ruled the country until 1978. He was assassinated by a student in Kabul in 1933. His son Zahir Shah was only 19 years old when he ascended the throne; the government was run by Nadir Khan's brothers for the next two decades. Initially, Mohammad Hashim became the prime minister and ruled the country autocratically until 1946. He was succeeded by Shah Mahmoud who liberalised the state, allowing relatively free parliamentary elections to be held in 1948. In 1953, Zahir Shah appointed Muhammad Daoud Khan, his cousin, as prime minister. Daoud reversed some of Shah Mahmoud's reforms and launched another ambitious programme of economic modernisation and centralisation of power in the country.

In his short reign, Nadir Khan set the strategic direction of the state, which would be followed by his successor. Central to the Musaheban approach was a narrow focus on modernisation of urban centres and recognition of the failures of the rapid top-down modernisation of the society. Nadir Khan's 1931 constitution increased the roles of the ulema and landed elites as intermediaries between the state and local communities. Instead of penetrating the society, the government focused on creating 'nation-state enclaves' in a few urban centres.[59] In 1933, the government established the Bank-e Milli (National Bank), the country's first bank. Subsequently, it used the bank to develop a series of state-owned enterprises that were primarily producing for exports. At the same time, the government gradually rolled out public education in urban centres and then in the countryside. Although the approach of governing the countryside through traditional intermediaries helped ensure the stability of Musaheban rule for more than three decades, over time, the focus on urban centres also created a huge divide between urban and rural sections of the country.

Furthermore, while revenues from traditional sources such as taxes on land and livestock stagnated or declined, state monopolies did not generate revenues that could fund large-scale developmental programmes. This became clear as Daoud sought to modernise the economy and centralise power. After the onset of the Cold War in the aftermath of World War II, Afghanistan gained somewhat greater strategic significance for global powers. Daoud sought to exploit this strategic significance to attract foreign aid for large-scale development programmes, which he rolled out in five-year development plans; he 'believed he could with impunity manipulate both the USSR and the United States to his own and his country's advantage'.[60] Initially, he approached the US for aid. However, the US declined to offer him any substantial aid as Daoud refused to recognise the Durand Line as a border with Pakistan, which had become a close US ally after the partition of the Indian sub-continent in August 1947. He supported an irredentist movement for autonomy or complete independence for the Pushtun tribes in Pakistan. Furthermore, Afghanistan also refused to join any formal alliances which were backed by the US. In 1955, Afghanistan participated in the Bandung Conference in Indonesia to become a founding member of the Non-Aligned Movement. At the same time, the country refused to join the US-backed Baghdad Pact in 1955, which eventually led to the formation of the Central Treaty Organization (CENTO) in 1959. While Afghanistan formally remained neutral, it continued to attract aid from one of the two major powers. Rebuffed by the US, Daoud turned to the Soviet Union, which offered him more substantial military and financial aid. The aid enabled him to launch his first five-year plan (1956–1961), which focused on development of major infrastructure such as roads. Unfortunately, Daoud's belligerence towards Pakistan complicated Afghanistan's external relations to an extreme degree, and in 1963, Zahir Shah removed Daoud from the prime ministership and moved to introduce a more representative system of government. The new experiment with constitutional monarchy and representative government brought with it a period of intense contentious politics. In July 1973, however, Daoud, who had been sidelined under the new system, seized power in a coup while Zahir Shah was travelling abroad. Daoud abrogated the 1964 constitution and declared the country a republic, with himself as president.

The Musaheban approach turned Afghanistan into a complete rentier state. Over time, revenues from taxes on land and livestock dropped from 62.5 per cent of domestic revenues in 1926 to 18.1 per cent in 1953, before declining to a mere 1.3 per cent in 1972.[61] Beginning in 1968, Afghanistan also began to sell natural gas to the Soviet Union. The revenues from gas steadily increased from 9.6 per cent of state revenues in 1968 to 15.5 per cent in 1975.[62] By contrast, the share of foreign aid as a percentage of the development budget hovered between 84.8 per cent in 1957 and 60 per cent in 1975.[63] The USSR was by far the largest source of aid and soft loans to Afghanistan. By 1978, Soviet and US aid to Afghanistan had reached $1.265 billion and $471 million, respectively.[64]

Foreign aid significantly increased the autonomy of the state from the society and allowed Daoud to expand and equip the army substantially and further expand public education and the state bureaucracy. Between 1951 and 1972, foreign aid financed construction of 1500 miles[65] of paved roads that connected the main regional centres of the country in a national market. However, dependence of the country on foreign aid had a number of deleterious effects. As a source of revenue, foreign aid proved to be highly unpredictable and did little to improve the capacity of state institutions. In 1971–1972, Afghanistan was struck by one of the worst droughts in its modern history. Wheat production declined significantly, leading to a severe famine that led to the death of up to 50,000 people, especially in poor regions such as the central mountainous regions of Hazarajat. The humanitarian crisis exposed the inability of the state institutions to respond effectively to a crisis of high proportion, and further undermined its legitimacy.[66] Foreign aid also opened the country to foreign influences, disrupting the country's long-standing neutral foreign policies. Its level of dependence on the Soviet Union increased the vulnerability of Afghan elites, and particularly the rapidly expanding, but increasingly dissatisfied educated class, to Soviet ideological influences. The pro-Soviet People's Democratic Party of Afghanistan (PDPA), which was formed in 1965, played an important role in supporting Daoud's 1973 coup, although he moved quite rapidly to marginalise it. The PDPA had infiltrated the ranks of the army, and further expanded its influence in other institutions of the state from 1973 to 1978. Afghan military officers who were sent for training in the Soviet Union were also exposed to ideological training, which increased their tendency to join one of the two factions of the PDPA. Daoud became aware of his over-reliance on the Soviet Union and sought to turn again to the US and its regional ally, Iran, to balance the Soviet influence. The move proved to be futile as the subsequent chain of events radically changed the domestic and regional environments.

The state on life support

On 27 April 1978, the republican regime of Mohammad Daoud was overthrown in a bloody coup that saw Daoud and a large number of his family members killed.[67] This was perhaps the single most decisive event shaping the modern history of Afghanistan. The effect of the coup was to lay the foundation for complex new conflict formations to which Afghanistan almost certainly would not have been exposed had it not been for the events of April 1978 and which continue to shape the lives of ordinary Afghans well into the twenty-first century.[68] The trigger for the coup was the arrest by President Daoud of senior figures of the PDPA following a major demonstration that had taken place at the funeral of a murdered Marxist writer, Mir Akbar Khaibar. These arrests so alarmed party sympathisers within the Afghan Air Force and military that they struck against the regime before it could track them down. Despite much speculation at the time and thereafter, no strong evidence ever emerged to establish Soviet complicity in the coup, although it is clear that relations between Daoud and Soviet General Secretary L.I. Brezhnev had taken a sharp turn for the worse after the two clashed during a visit by Daoud to the USSR in 1977.[69] Nonetheless, the Soviet Union was the first state to recognise the new regime and rapidly moved to shore up its position with assistance.

Some of the key figures in the new regime were relatively well known, having served in the lower house of the Parliament, the *Wolesi Jirga*, between 1965 and 1973. Of particular note in this respect were Babrak Karmal, Hafizullah Amin and Anahita Ratebzad. This did not, however, imply that the key figures in the new regime were notable for their political sophistication or insight; on the contrary, one informed observer described the PDPA as a party of 'teahouse political talk'.[70] Coming at best from the fringes of the political elite, they lacked experience in the exercise of power and did not recognise the value of understanding the limits of one's capacity. The new leader of the so-called 'Saur Revolution' (which took its name from the month in the Zodiac calendar in which the coup had been staged) was Nur Mohammad Taraki, a journalist who had served briefly as an *attaché* at the Afghan Embassy in Washington in the 1950s, but whose lack of dynamism or charisma prompted the new regime to confect a cult of personality for him through the media, mirroring cults that had surfaced elsewhere in communist states to compensate for either weak leadership, or low levels of institutionalisation within party structures, or both.[71]

This reflected in part the problems of legitimacy which the new regime faced. There are a number of bases upon which power can be exercised effectively by rulers. One is coercion, where the powers of rulers are sufficient to strike fear into the hearts of both the general public and the professional administrators who make a system work on a day-to-day basis. Another is exchange, where a tacit bargain exists between rulers and ruled pursuant to which compliance is given in exchange for specific benefits. Both of these typically play some role in the functioning of an autocratic political system, but each is expensive: one needs access to resources to sustain coercive instruments and to provide the benefits that a compliant public receives. A cheaper basis for exercising power is legitimacy or generalised normative support. This goes beyond support for the handling of particular issues and is different from the prudential support that may flow either from a desire to avoid being coerced or from satisfaction with the fruits of exchange. Classically, in the work of the German social scientist Max Weber, legitimate domination was seen to be grounded in factors such as tradition, legal-rational processes, or charisma[72]; and subsequent studies have added other potential bases of legitimacy as well, such as the perception that the performance of a regime merits its being supported. The problem for the new Marxist regime in Afghanistan was that none of these bases of legitimacy was obviously available: rather than relying on traditional credibility, the new rulers were preaching the importance of a break with the past; they had come to power through a coup rather than any kind of constitutional process; and none of the new rulers was especially charismatic.

The temptation for the new regime to rely on coercion as its primary basis for survival was therefore a strong one. Its problem was that its ability to exercise coercion was not unchallenged. In totalitarian regimes, beyond a certain point, a regime may have no need to engage in dramatically overt coercion, since everyone has come to understand that it has the capacity to do so, and that opposition is pointless. Nazi Germany under Hitler, the Soviet Union under Stalin and Iraq under Saddam Hussein provide telling examples. In Afghanistan, the mindset of the new rulers was anything but pluralist. This was captured in a notably sinister remark by Taraki: 'Those who plot against us in the dark will vanish in the dark.'[73] But their regime lacked the kind of entrenched coercive capacities that mark established dictatorships. As a result, the coercive measures they deployed were not enough to stabilise the regime, but were more than enough to provoke a sustained and furious reaction from significant elements of the Afghan population.[74]

The consequence of this reaction was that within a relatively short period of time, the territorial writ of the new regime began to shrink notably. In the immediate aftermath of the coup, large numbers of Afghans took a 'wait-and-see' position, and resistance did not break out at once.[75] But it came soon enough. The principal trigger of resistance proved to be the clumsy attempts of PDPA activists to intrude in the dynamics of rural society, a realm with which they were typically quite unfamiliar, and which a number seem to have regarded with scorn, if not contempt. 'Literacy classes' were configured as tools of political indoctrination, provoking local pushback. 'Land reform' was botched through a complete lack of understanding of the complexities of land ownership and land use in rural Afghanistan, as well as through a neglect of the need to address issues of water and seed supply in parallel with alterations to land tenure. And attempts to empower women not only made women reluctant front-liners in a battle many were not keen to join, but created the impression that the new rulers were 'un-Islamic', a particularly dangerous reputation to acquire in conservative parts of rural Afghanistan. As a result, revolts began to break out in different parts of the country, and the brutal responses of the regime simply added fuel to the fire. In a widely reported massacre, regime forces slaughtered all of the male residents of the village of Kerala in Kunar on 20 April 1979,[76] but this was just one of many episodes of violence at the hands of the regime that had the effect of adding to its problems rather than solving them.[77] The implications for state capacity were dire: Kabul was being cut off from the 'trenches' of the state, and its control of the 'dispersed field offices' of the state was being increasingly compromised as well.

By far the most dramatic manifestation of opposition to the regime came with the Herat revolt of March 1979. Herat is one of the great cities of the Persophone world, which by virtue of its cultural richness has a significance stretching beyond the mere political and geostrategic. On 15 March 1979, it blew up. As Gammell put it, 'the dam of frustration, rage and anger finally broke, unleashing a torrent of chaos. Herat's district and city, aided by a mutinous army, rose up in a chaotic and violent unison which placed Herat on the front line of hostilities against the Afghan government in Kabul and the Soviet Union'.[78] As Gammell's account makes clear, the revolt was more an example of anomic violence than of a carefully planned act of resistance, but it created enormous apprehension in Kabul about where events were heading. In a decidedly panicky 18 March telephone call to the chairman of the Soviet Council of Ministers, Aleksei N. Kosygin, Taraki urgently requested military assistance, including the supply of Soviet troops disguised as Afghans.[79] The Soviet leadership clearly saw the dangers inherent in any such entanglement and brushed off Taraki's request with advice on the need for the regime to modify its brutal approach to the population and promote party unity. This advice, however, came much too late. The divisions within the PDPA were already becoming acute, and it was beyond the capacity of the Soviet leadership to manage these stresses. They persisted well beyond the suppression of the Herat uprising in late March 1979 and contributed directly to the Soviet invasion of Afghanistan at the end of the year.

In communist systems, there has almost always been an apprehension about allowing diverse opinions to flourish. This became plain in Bolshevik Russia in March 1921 when in response to the uprising of the Kronstadt sailors, the 10th Congress of the Russian Communist Party (Bolshevik) adopted a resolution entitled 'On party unity' which imposed a ban on 'factions'. This in effect meant that victors in intra-party struggles could delegitimate the losers by labelling them as members of a 'faction'. The central problem of the PDPA was that it had *always* been faction-ridden because it was itself the product of a somewhat unhappy marriage between two Marxist groups, the *Khalq* ('Masses') and *Parcham* ('Banner') that had initially formed the PDPA in 1965, only to split apart until 1977, when under Soviet urging they reunited.[80] Relations between the Khalqis and Parchamis were toxic from the moment of the April 1978 coup. One notorious Khalqi, the commandant of Pul-e Charkhi prison near Kabul, reportedly stated that 'a million Afghans are all that should remain alive. We need a million Khalqis. The others we don't need, we will get rid of them'.[81] Relations were especially tense between Babrak Karmal (of Parcham) and Hafizullah Amin (of Khalq), and Amin contrived a diplomatic exile for Karmal as ambassador to Czechoslovakia, a state from which he wisely disappeared as pressure on Parchamis mounted under the rule of the Khalq. With hindsight it became clear that he had secured the protection of the Soviet Union.

The tensions that plagued Afghanistan's political elite in 1979 were not just between the Khalq and Parcham. Equally destabilising was the breakdown in relations between Taraki and Amin. This culminated in a series of messy events in September–October 1979 which saw Taraki first displaced by Amin, and then murdered.[82] This was almost certainly the trigger for the Soviet invasion of Afghanistan: Brezhnev was affronted by the killing of Taraki, who had been his guest in Moscow only a month before. But beyond the smouldering tensions in the Afghan elite lay the deeper problems of the burgeoning gulf between rulers and ruled in Afghanistan and the accelerating breakdown of the state as revolts occurred in different parts of the country. As Rubin put it, these events 'could have occurred only in a country with a state that lacked a strong degree of internal coherence … The attempt to use the state apparatus of the old regime to enforce a small faction's program was the final blow: the first and most important loss of legitimacy was within the state itself'.[83] It was exceedingly doubtful whether a Soviet intervention had anything to offer as a solution to any of these problems, but by 12 December 1979, when the decision to invade Afghanistan was finally taken, the momentum for action had reached the point where cautionary arguments to this effect were no longer being taken into account. Amin, who had retreated to the Tajbeg Palace in southern Kabul, was killed in a Soviet military operation on 27 December 1979, and a prerecorded message from Karmal was broadcast to announce Amin's overthrow.

The Soviet invasion, rather than solving the regime's problems, had the effect of aggravating them severely, creating a quagmire which led to enormous grief for the people of Afghanistan and also for thousands of families in the Soviet Union that lost sons in the Afghan war. The invasion had two immediate effects. One effect was to elevate what had thitherto been a sequence of revolts to the status of a fully fledged resistance movement. This resistance, commonly known as the *Mujahideen* movement, was an eclectic mixture of commanders and communities within Afghanistan, and a range of political parties, some operating from Pakistan, that came in various shapes and sizes – Sunni and Shiite, Islamist and traditionalist.[84] The other effect was to engage the attention of the wider world, which had been largely indifferent to developments in Afghanistan after the communist coup.[85] To the US administration under President Carter, the invasion of Afghanistan represented a repudiation of the understandings that had underpinned the *détente* between the Soviet Union and the United States through much of the 1970s.[86] Fearing a newly expansionist USSR, the United States moved to offer support to the Afghan resistance forces which were able to operate from refugee camps in Pakistan, to which millions of Afghan refugees had fled after the invasion. To explore the specific details of the Soviet-Afghan war,[87] and its ebb and flow,[88] would require a separate book: suffice it to say that the years of war that followed the Soviet invasion were catastrophic for ordinary Afghans, many of whom suffered almost all the privations associated with a long war. The Soviets were able to exercise control over cities and large towns, but the bulk of the countryside was lost to the resistance, and as Soviet general secretary Mikhail Gorbachev put it at the 27th Congress of the Communist Party of the Soviet Union in 1986, Afghanistan had become a 'bleeding wound'.[89] The explanation for this was actually very simple: at the November 1986 Politburo meeting that took the decision in principle to withdraw from Afghanistan, the Soviet Chief of the General Staff, Marshal Sergei Akhromeyev, stated bluntly that 'we have lost the battle for the Afghan people'.[90]

One approach that the Soviets took in Afghanistan was to shuffle the local political leadership. Babrak Karmal had been installed as head of the regime following the Soviet invasion, and the Soviets had high hopes that they would be able rapidly to withdraw their troops and hand the running of the country back to Babrak. They found themselves, however, on the horns of a dilemma: in the face of mounting opposition, Babrak's survival depended upon the continuing presence of Soviet forces; but that very dependence blighted his prospects of winning popular legitimacy on the scale necessary for him to be able to survive as an independent actor. This prompted the new Soviet leadership under Mikhail Gorbachev, who had become general secretary of the Soviet Communist Party in March 1985, to seek a more dynamic Afghan client. Moscow ultimately settled on a longstanding Parchami activist, Dr Najibullah, who had headed the regime's secret police (KhAD) from 1980 to 1985. Najibullah indeed had more energy than Karmal, but as a Soviet observer put it, his secret police background 'inherently disqualified him as the architect of national reconciliation'.[91] Afghanistan thus found itself burdened with a 'state' that had significant problems of legitimacy, and was financially dependent on the external support supplied by the USSR.

With no obvious prospects for 'success' in Afghanistan, the Soviet leadership opted to cut its losses and withdraw its troops.[92] Gorbachev had not been directly involved in the decision to invade Afghanistan in December 1979, and this gave him a certain freedom of action with respect to the issue which his predecessors had not enjoyed. In addition, he was able fairly quickly to make his mark on the Soviet political elite by appointing officials more sympathetic to his outlook to positions of significance. Furthermore, the war in Afghanistan was far from popular within the USSR, and he had little to fear from bringing it to an end. The formal mechanism for doing so was the Geneva Accords of April 1988, which provided a cover for Soviet withdrawal, but fell well short of offering a comprehensive solution to Afghanistan's problems. The Afghan resistance parties were not signatories to the Accords; the Accords left unaddressed the issue of future power relations within Afghanistan itself; and in effect, they remitted the Afghanistan issue to the battlefield.[93]

The withdrawal of Soviet forces from Afghanistan did not lead to a cessation of Soviet *aid* to Afghanistan.[94] On the contrary, a very substantial flow of resources from the USSR to Afghanistan permitted the regime of Dr Najibullah to survive from February 1989 until April 1992. Najibullah was able to direct these resources to power holders in various parts of the country in order to secure their prudential support. But this did not mean that his regime enjoyed legitimacy: it was on a life-support system, and one that would cease to function if the resource flow happens to be interrupted. This was what happened in 1991. A failed coup attempt in Moscow against Gorbachev led to a bilateral agreement between the United States and the Soviet Union for the discontinuation by both sides from 1 January 1992 of assistance that they had provided to parties in the Afghan conflict. This was troubling for the *Mujahideen*, but fatal for Najibullah. Faced with revolts, he committed to standing down in favour of an interim government being promoted by the United Nations. His commitment, however, came far too late and the regime collapsed on 15–16 April 1992, with Najibullah dramatically seeking asylum in UN premises in Kabul.[95] As an insightful observer put it, 'When state institutions unravel, and armed factions emerge as the main form of collective action, interim governments offer no quick solution to the problem of political order. No government can compensate for the dissolution of the state'.[96] The dissolution of the state was the principal legacy with which Najibullah's successors had to cope, and its shadow haunts Afghanistan to this day.

The breakdown of the state

In order to understand the ramifications of the breakdown of the state, it is useful to revisit some of the defining features of the state that were mentioned at the beginning of this chapter. Critically, the collapse of the Najibullah regime led to an immediate loss of any capacity to penetrate society, regulate social relationships, extract resources, and appropriate or use resources in determined ways. In Kabul, key ministries and agencies literally ceased to function. Staff abandoned their desks, and many fled the city, fearing what the future would hold for them. The Minister for State Security took his own life, and senior officials looking to save their own skins opened lines of communication to different elements of the *Mujahideen*, often along ethnic lines, with ethnic Pushtuns approaching the likes of *Hezb-e Islami* ('Party of Islam') leader Gulbuddin Hekmatyar, while Tajiks were more likely to approach the charismatic commander Ahmad Shah Massoud, whose forces were positioned just to the north of Kabul. Most seriously of all, the Afghan army fractured catastrophically, with some elements pledging loyalty to the resistance, while others sought to position themselves as autonomous power centres loyal to their own military commanders.[97] The consequence was that the Afghan resistance did not inherit a functioning state, capable of discharging state responsibilities. This, in turn, meant that the new rulers were very-poorly placed to meet any positive expectations associated with the change of regime, since from the outset they lacked the instruments necessary to do so.

A further complicating factor was that a number of parties within the Afghan resistance were committed to the ideal of building a strong state and saw control of 'the state', such as it was, as a necessary first step in this direction. The most threatening party in this respect was the radical Islamist *Hezb-e Islami* of Hekmatyar, which had long made the building of an 'Islamic state' the centrepiece of its political agenda. Hekmatyar was a controversial figure to put it mildly. His approach to politics was widely seen as totalitarian, his party as Leninist and his loyalty primarily to himself and his long-standing patrons in the Inter-Services Intelligence Directorate (ISI) of Pakistan's Armed Forces.[98] His main rival, affiliated with the more moderate *Jamiat-e Islami* ('Islamic Society'), was Massoud, towards whom he made no secret of his antagonism: on 22 April 1992, his spokesman was quoted as saying 'Hekmatyar can't agree to anything that includes Ahmed Shah Massoud'.[99] For parties such as the *Hezb-e Islami*, it did not matter that the state had collapsed; what was important was either to position the *Hezb* to secure control of a future state or to deny anyone else the ability to secure such control. This basic approach was to shape the immediate trajectory of Afghanistan's politics in the aftermath of the collapse of the communist regime, and dictated the adoption of a logic of spoiling[100] which was to have disastrous consequences for the people of Afghanistan, and for the residents of Kabul in particular. Its effect was to compromise any endeavours to reconstitute the instrumentalities of the state.

Kabul found itself under siege because of its *symbolic* significance. When the instrumentalities of the state have disintegrated, ambitious political actors are likely to focus their attention on securing control of such symbols of state power as remain (or on denying anyone else such control). By far the most important such symbol is the capital city of a country; less important, although not trivial, are diplomatic missions the country may maintain abroad and seats in international organisations such as the United Nations. Capital cities are normally important targets because they house the commanding heights and central offices of the state; for this reason, seizing a capital typically implies the obliteration of a government exercising state control. Thus, the fall of Berlin in 1945 marked the effective end of the Third Reich.[101] But that said, capital cities retain their symbolic significance even if the instrumentalities of the state have already dissolved; indeed, in these circumstances, they may be more significant targets than ever. This was Afghanistan's experience in 1992. While Kabul had occasionally come under rocket fire during the life of the communist regime, it was only from 1992 onwards that it became the central focus of struggle. This was to leave large tracts of the capital as damaged as Berlin was in 1945 and to scar the reputations of those resistance groups most responsible for the damage that occurred.

This is not to say that the collapse of the communist regime led to a Hobbesian 'war of all against all'. On the contrary, the bulk of the Sunni parties within the Afghan resistance made an effort to strike an elite settlement with a view to avoiding just such strife. As early as February 1989, coinciding with the completion of the Soviet withdrawal from Afghanistan, a range of Afghan political parties had met in Rawalpindi in Pakistan in a Council (*shura*) aiming to establish an Afghan interim government. It was not a notable success: Shiite groups, shortly to form the *Hezb-e Wahdat* ('Party of Unity') under the leadership of Abdul Ali Mazari, ultimately did not take part, feeling that they were not offered a sufficient role; and even Pakistan did not accord the Interim Government diplomatic recognition, although the interim government did secure control of Afghanistan's seat in the Organisation of the Islamic Conference. The exercise did, however, provide something of a template for what was attempted when the communist regime collapsed. In April 1992, the so-called 'Peshawar Accord' provided that Sebghatullah Mojadiddi, leader of a small resistance party, would serve as president for two months, then to be succeeded for a period of four months by Burhanuddin Rabbani of the *Jamiat-e Islami*, after which a 'Council of Supreme Popular Settlement' was to be held to form an interim government. The *Hezb-e Islami* was to be offered the prime ministership, but Hekmatyar spurned the offer and denounced the new arrangements as 'communist'. In August 1992, Hekmatyar's forces launched a rocket attack on Kabul that killed over 1000 people, and Rabbani labelled him a 'dangerous terrorist who should be expelled from Afghanistan'.[102] Subsequent accords, struck in Islamabad in March 1993 and in Jalalabad in May 1993 proved no more successful in underpinning political order.[103] Ultimately, none of these agreements offered any solution to the problem of the disintegration of the state.

Instead, what transpired was a brutal battle for control of Kabul, the symbolic spoils of the state. When the communist regime collapsed, a range of different forces moved into different parts of Kabul, and as political relations deteriorated between the various groups, clashes broke out, with alliances between different groups frequently shifting. On top of this, the city was subject to rocketing by *Hezb-e Islami* forces located to the south. The existence of these different levels of violence gave rise to the impression in the wider world that Kabul had fallen victim to a kind of mindless irrationality, but as the French scholar Gilles Dorronsoro wrote in 1995, 'everything that has happened since 1992 has been the result of a rigorous political logic. The Afghan civil war is not "primitive" or "tribal," but strongly political'.[104] The human consequences were nonetheless atrocious. A gruesome massacre of Hazaras occurred in the western Kabul district of Afshar on 11 February 1993.[105] The main source of casualties, however, was rocketing and shelling by *Hezb-e Islami* forces: estimates of the number killed between April 1992 and March 1995 (when Massoud's forces brought all of Kabul under their control) range from a conservative figure of 9800 to a larger total of 25,000 provided by Amnesty International.[106] This bombardment not only destroyed large tracts of the city, but lead to massive internal displacement and disruption of the daily lives of ordinary people.

Outside Kabul, a different dynamic was at play. As the state fell apart, diverse actors from within the *Mujahideen* and beyond staked claims to power in different localities. The degree of control which they were able to exercise also varied from place to place. Thus, in Kandahar, a Pushtun religious figure with connections to the *Jamiat*, Mullah Naqib, emerged as a claimant to power with support from Rabbani in Kabul; but his claims were under continuous challenge, not least from the provincial governor, Gul Agha Sherzai, whose late father, Haji Abdul Latif, had been a famous local resistance leader. Not surprisingly, a great deal of disorder afflicted the province as other claimants with particular geographical or tribal bases also sought to assert their own dominance. By contrast, in Jalalabad a broadly collective leadership emerged through a *shura* led by Haji Abdul Qadir, who was a member of the prominent Arsala family (and who, as vice-president of Afghanistan, was to be assassinated in Kabul on 6 July 2002). In the central Hazarajat region, different factions within the Shiite *Hezb-e Wahdat* competed for influence, with Rabbani supporting a faction associated with Mohammad Akbari. A marker of the complexity of Shiite politics was the diverse backgrounds of some of the competitors: Abdul Ali Mazari was an Hazara; Akbari was a Qizilbash; and Asef Mohseni, leader of the *Harakat-e Islami*, was actually a Pushtun.

Other parts of the country witnessed the emergence of individuals who came to be called 'warlords'. The term 'warlord' was first used in Republican China to refer to regional power holders whose very existence constituted a challenge to the authority of the state.[107] Since then, in the context of state disruption, a great deal of discussion has focused on the phenomenon of warlordism. One approach is to see the warlord as an individual who practises predation, extraction and redistribution of a particular kind. From this perspective, a warlord uses coercive capacity in predatory opposition to both state and society, extracting resources from vulnerable suppliers and redistributing them to the warlord's coercive instrumentalities in order to ensure their ongoing support. This matches Kimberly Marten's definition of warlords as 'individuals who control small pieces of territory using a combination of force and patronage'.[108] Some warlords historically may have fitted this model, but it misses key elements of the experience in countries such as Afghanistan. Perhaps the most important is that some 'warlords' have enjoyed particular kinds of legitimacy – hence, Antonio Giustozzi's definition of a warlord as a 'legitimate, charismatic and patrimonial military leader with autonomous control over a military force capable of achieving/maintaining a monopoly of large scale violence over a sizeable territory'.[109] A warlord in this sense may have a loyal constituency of followers, most likely on the basis that the warlord is seen as a defender of the interests of a particular threatened or challenged ethnic group. Thus, Abdul Rashid Dostum, who emerged not as part of the Afghan resistance, but as leader of the 'Jawzjani' Uzbek militia under Najibullah,[110] was able to secure his position after 1992 on the strength of a loyal Uzbek following; and Ahmad Shah Massoud had a cohort of equally loyal supporters to the north of Kabul. Recent scholarship has also highlighted the dangers of offering oversimplified accounts of how warlords interact with the state: rather than positing a simple polarity of antagonism, this research emphasises the ability of warlords to adjust their roles and reinvent themselves as environments change.[111]

One figure who proved especially durable was Ismail Khan in Herat. A former army officer, he had participated in the March 1979 uprising and was a significant *Mujahideen* figure in western Afghanistan during the 1980s. When the communist regime collapsed, he was well-positioned to take control of Herat, which he proceeded to run in a patrimonial fashion. He was greatly aided by an ability to secure revenues from customs posts between Afghanistan and Iran, but disadvantaged by his taste for centralising power in the hands of himself and a small clique of followers. Gammell has described Herat at this time as 'a poorly functioning mini-state of limited competence'.[112] Herat enjoyed a notable vibrancy at this time, especially when compared to Kabul, but when it came under attack from forces of the new 'Taliban' movement on 4–5 September 1995, its defences collapsed almost immediately, ushering in a very grim time indeed for the city's residents.

The emergence of the Taliban cannot be understood without reference to the geopolitical environment within which Afghanistan sits. The crucial factor at play was Afghanistan's tortured relationship with Pakistan. This had a long history. As noted earlier, in 1893, the British official Sir Mortimer Durand drew a boundary between British India and Afghanistan, known as the Durand Line, which had the effect of dividing the Pushtun ethnic group between the two territories. Pushtun nationalists within Afghanistan came to resent this bitterly, and when the partition of the Indian sub-continent came into prospect in 1947, Afghanistan mounted a claim for 'self-determination' on the part of those Pushtuns living along the Northwest frontier of India. Nothing came of the demand, but the consequence was that for the next 30 years, Muslim-majority Afghanistan had cordial relations with Hindu-majority India, but for the most part extremely tense relations with Muslim-majority Pakistan, not least because a range of Afghan governments continued to press for self-determination for 'Pushtunistan',[113] often using highly inflammatory language.[114] Especially in the context of the loss of East Pakistan in 1971 through the emergence of Bangladesh, Pakistan's elite developed a fear of Indian influence in Afghanistan, and after the Soviet invasion of 1979, it sought to develop clients within the Afghan resistance that could be used in the future to ensure a compliant Afghan regime. Its preferred client was the *Hezb-e Islami* of Hekmatyar,[115] which as a strongly Islamist party seemed less likely than some others to seek to revive a purely territorial dispute. As a tool for Pakistani influence, however, the *Hezb* proved to be a weak reed after 1992: it simply lacked the popular support or territorial control in Afghanistan to function effectively as more than a destructive spoiler. It was in this context that Pakistan adjusted its approach, and the emergence of the Taliban was the consequence.

The *talib*, or religious student, has long been a relatively familiar figure in Afghanistan, and in the early 1980s, so-called 'Taliban fronts' surfaced in the southern and eastern areas of Afghanistan, often in association with a particular *Mujahideen* party, namely, the *Harakat-e Inqilab-e Islami* led by Mawlawi Mohammad Nabi Mohammadi. These, however, were distinct from the Taliban *movement* that first appeared in 1994. This particular force was instrumentalised by retired Major-General Naseerullah Babar, interior minister in Benazir Bhutto's government in Pakistan, in response to the disappointing performance of Hekmatyar's *Hezb-e Islami*.[116] Drawing on students from *madrasas* (Islamic colleges) in Pakistan, many of whom had come originally from orphanages in refugee camps, the Taliban movement was pathogenic rather than traditional, although some scholars have detected echoes of the value systems of southern Pushtun villages in Taliban discourse.[117] The leader of the Taliban, Mullah Omar, used the classic Islamic title *Amir al-Momineen* ('Lord of the Believers'), and like his followers (and many Afghan religious figures) was influenced by the so-called 'Deobandi' school of Islamic thought that had emerged in British India in the nineteenth century[118] – although many modern Deobandis would have been hard-pressed to recognise much that was familiar in the views that Taliban figures came to articulate. Well-equipped by Pakistan and supported operation-ally by the ISI, the Taliban succeeded in taking over Kandahar in 1994, Herat in 1995 and finally Kabul in September 1996.

In stark contrast to the Islamist parties that aspired to build a strong state, the Taliban had almost no interest at all in state building. Given their puritani-cal disposition, they did set out to regulate behaviour through the agency of a religious police, known as *Amr bil-Maroof wa Nahi An il-Munkir* (the department for the 'Promotion of Virtue and the Suppression of Vice'), but they had no broader agenda for effective institutional development or resource mobilisation. As a recent study has put it, the Taliban's 'Islamic Emirate of Afghanistan' (IEA) 'entirely failed in producing regular governance and a state system. It fell short in all aspects of stateness. The IEA lacked both internal and external legitimacy, had poor authority, and was incapable of producing basic services'.[119] Two separate observations about the situation at the end of the Taliban regime's tenure paint a clear picture of how far short they had fallen in developing meaningful bureau-cratic policy-making structures or revenue-raising capacity. As far as leadership was concerned, the following patterns prevailed[120]:

> Shura meetings are no longer held, and the Kabul ministers are rarely consulted about key decisions. Mullah Umar has become much more iso-lated. The core group around him includes some Qandahari ulama and judges of the Supreme Court of Qandahar (who are all above 70 years old, have never travelled outside Qandahar, and are extremist and simplistic in their views); a few powerful, hard-line individuals from the Taliban structure such as Mullah Nuruddin Turabi, Minister of Justice and head of the Religious Police, Chief of Army Staff Mullah Mohammed Hasan, and Commander Dadullah; individual Afghans working in Umar's office who were educated in Pakistani madrasas and who have a strongly expansionist and jihadist view of the Taliban's role in the Muslim world; Usama Bin Ladin and other Arabs who advise Umar on foreign policy (some Afghans from Qandahar even claim that Bin Ladin is consulted on domestic issues such as the Buddhas); and Pakistani ISI officers.

Where finance was concerned, the environment in the finance ministry was even more chaotic[121]:

> At the start of 2002 there were no computers in the ministry – the deputy minister in charge of the budget department provided hand-held calculators to line ministry staff to use when preparing their handwritten budget submissions. The treasury system operated a manual ledger system, so no meaningful reconciliation was ever undertaken... Anecdotal evidence suggests that the vast majority of the budget was actually not programmed in any conventional sense; rather, it was kept in discretionary funds that were allocated by the finance ministry or the president's office. This provided considerable scope for corruption and, in July 2002, operations of the finance ministry were reportedly under the control of three significant criminal gangs. Senior positions with access to major revenue sources were said to be bought and sold.

The implications of such a dire situation were stark. The successors to the Taliban had to commence state-building endeavours from Ground Zero.

The neopatrimonial state

The anti-modernist policies of the Taliban had left them with very few friends. Only Saudi Arabia, Pakistan and the United Arab Emirates were prepared to accord diplomatic recognition to the Taliban; most other states wanted nothing to do with them. They became, as a result, somewhat undiscriminating in their choice of 'friends', and this led in part to their dangerous liaison with Al-Qaeda, which ultimately was to prove fatal to their regime.[122] Al-Qaeda attacks on US embassies in Kenya and Tanzania in August 1998 alerted Washington to the threat that had taken shape on Afghan territory, and both US and UN sanctions were applied to the Taliban as a result. Nonetheless, it took the September 11, 2001 Al-Qaeda attacks on the World Trade Center and the Pentagon to drive the United States to take decisive action. This came in the form of a military strike against Al-Qaeda and the Taliban, 'Operation Enduring Freedom', which began on 7 October 2001 and within barely a month precipitated a cascade that culminated in the fall of Kabul to anti-Taliban forces on 13 November. The overthrow of the Taliban, however, created a new challenge for the administration of US President George W. Bush. Bush and his associates had plainly stated before the September 11 attacks that they did not see 'nation building' as an appropriate endeavour for the US to pursue internationally. Yet something had to be done to address the substantial power vacuum that existed in much of Afghanistan. It was in this context that the United States turned to the United Nations for assistance.

In November 2001, the Special Representative of the United Nations Secretary-General for Afghanistan was an eminent, experienced and weighty figure within the UN system, Ambassador Lakhdar Brahimi of Algeria, who in 2000 had chaired the panel that produced the so-called 'Brahimi Report' on UN peace operations.[123] While the Rabbani government, under the title 'Islamic State of Afghanistan', formally occupied Afghanistan's seat in the UN General Assembly, and while the forces that had entered Kabul in place of the Taliban were broadly supportive of Rabbani's regime, there was a widespread recognition that a stable Afghanistan would require a more broadly based government than one simply shaped around Kabul's new rulers. To address this issue, Brahimi chaired a meeting of non-Taliban Afghan political actors that was held with the support of the German government in the city of Bonn from 27 November to 5 December 2001.[124] With the benefit of hindsight, some critics were to argue that the Taliban should have been included in the Bonn conference, but at the time it was held, the Taliban movement was in a state of collapse,[125] and its leaders were fleeing to sanctuaries in Pakistan; furthermore, key parties represented in Bonn might well have boycotted the process had the Taliban been invited to attend. The outcome of the meeting was an 'Agreement on Provisional Arrangements in Afghanistan Pending the Re-establishment of Permanent Government Institutions'. This provided for the establishment of an 'Interim Administration', which was subsequently to be elevated to the status of a 'Transitional Administration' through the holding of an 'Emergency Loya Jirga' ('Great Assembly'), with a 'Constitutional Loya Jirga' subsequently to be held to adopt a new constitution for Afghanistan. A consensus candidate, Hamed Karzai, was chosen to chair the Interim Administration.

The great strength of the conference was that it recognised that more was needed than just a loose elite settlement between a small number of leaders. Its main weakness was that a number of critical decisions about Afghanistan's future state were taken almost inadvertently, without sufficient appreciation of the likely ramifications and of the complexities associated with state building. In particular, issues relating to the future scope and strength of the Afghan state were not sufficiently understood. 'Scope' refers to the *choice* of activities for a state to pursue, whereas 'strength' refers to the *capacities* of a state to pursue them.[126] The Bonn Agreement critically provided that the Interim Administration should be 'composed of the Chairman, five Vice Chairmen and 24 other members. Each member, except the Chairman, may head a department of the Interim Administration'. The reason that approval was granted to have up to 29 departments in the Interim Administration was not that Afghanistan *needed* 29 departments; it was rather that departments were seen as 'positional goods', control of which would be a reward for those groups that had taken part in the Bonn conference.[127] In this way, a particular model of 'central offices' of the state was put in place with very little reflection on longer-term ramifications.

Three major problems flowed from the way in which the Bonn Agreement provided for the establishment of a large number of departments without sufficient rationale for their existence. The first was that the move to put in place a state heavily focused on central (and centralised) agencies came at the expense of imaginative reflection on what alternative ways of organising state power might be found. Organisation of the state into government departments has been a common approach since the Northcote-Trevelyan Report of 1854 in the United Kingdom set out principles of governmental organisation that were subsequently elaborated in Max Weber's theory of bureaucracy. Since then, however, there has been a growing appreciation of a point made by Harry Eckstein: that 'a government will tend to be stable if its authority pattern is congruent with the other authority patterns of the society of which it is a part'.[128] An implication is that it is important to develop an understanding of these other authority patterns at the outset of an institutional design process, in order to ensure that the authority patterns associated with the particular governmental structures proposed will enjoy this kind of congruence. This was not a prominent feature of the Bonn discussions. The second problem was that the allocation of offices to different political groups had the effect of locking into place the broad structure of the central state, even if it proved to be dysfunctional. In a careful discussion of institutional design, Robert E. Goodin identified *revisability* (together with robustness, sensitivity to motivational complexity, and variability) as a desirable feature of an institution.[129] Control of departments of government, however, can be an important source of power, and parties that have secured such control have a strong incentive to resist any attempts to take departments away from them or to simplify the structure of the state in a way that makes their departments redundant. It is unsurprising that there has been no root-and-branch restructuring of the Afghan state since 2001. The third problem was that the doling out of departments under the Bonn Agreement in effect established organisational fiefdoms for different political groups, within which loyalists could be promoted, and other actors rewarded with a view to consolidating their loyalty. The effect was to set the scene for bitter rivalries between different agencies, when what Afghanistan needed was interagency cooperation in order to address the manifold challenges of reconstruction with which the country was confronted after 2001.

Some of the world's most stable countries have achieved that happy status through a slow and steady process of state *formation*, where, through an evolutionary process, new institutions developed and proved their worth as devices for providing security for ordinary people and opportunities for political participation and economic progress. Political systems that evolve in this way can rarely be understood simply by reference to formal structures. As the French writer Alexis de Tocqueville famously pointed out, what he called *les manières*, or particular learned ways of doing things, can be tremendously important in ensuring that systems work effectively. On occasion, such ways of doing things become 'conventions',[130] from which it is in no actors' interests to depart, but even when this is not the case, informality – that is, 'a form of interaction amongst partners enjoying relative freedom in interpretation of their roles' requirements'[131] – can be a vital lubricant for the efficient operation of a system. But that said, learned ways of doing things can also be corrupting and corrosive. A system may be afflicted by norms of solidarity that protect elites from accountability or facilitate generalised exploitation of the weak and vulnerable. This is an acute danger for embryonic states, and one which any serious process of managed state *building* should set out to avoid. But given the challenges of designing, funding and legitimating a new state, this may not prove all that easy.

It has recently been argued that 'a constitution must be written by those who will live under it and not by some outside team of "experts," and must also be approved by the people who will live under it and not by some philosopher-king or cadre of vanguard thinkers'.[132] Afghanistan's new constitution was finalised by a Constitutional Loya Jirga of Afghan delegates held in December 2003–January 2004, but one of the lessons from the experience was that the drafting of a constitution can prove to be a divisive rather than a unifying exercise. The constitution as adopted provided for a highly centralised state with an executive president. This was popular with Pushtuns, who constituted the largest single ethnic group in Afghanistan, but was less popular amongst other groups that feared that the presidential character of the system would allow only one winner to emerge, who was unlikely to come from their ranks. The constitution made no provision for an office of prime minister, giving rise to the danger of the presidency's becoming severely overloaded. Nor was the process entirely free of outside influence. The United States, in particular, was keen to have a presidential system in which a single dynamic individual could function as principal interlocutor with Washington; this was doubtless one of the reasons why the US envoy Zalmay Khalilzad had played a 'behind-the-scenes' role during the Emergency Loya Jirga from 11–19 June 2002 to squash any prospect that the former king of Afghanistan, the elderly Zahir Shah, might be invited back to be head of state.[133] But perhaps the crucial downside of the presidential system was that it created a single office at the apex that could easily be seen by actors as valuable mainly as a source of patronage. This problem was compounded by one other factor. Hamed Karzai had grown up politically in what was essentially a state-free environment, working in exile in Peshawar with a small *Mujahideen* party, that of Sebghatullah Mojadiddi. For figures in such an environment, politics was not seen as involving policy development and implementation, but rather networking, alliance-building and patron-client relations. It was not surprising that Karzai brought this approach to politics with him to Kabul in late 2001, and it is unlikely that any alternative candidate at the time would have been very different in his approach.

We mentioned earlier the debilitated state of the finance ministry at the time the Taliban were overthrown at the end of 2001. In a pathbreaking study of public finance in Afghanistan, Nematullah Bizhan not only noted that the new Afghan government 'inherited an empty Treasury in December 2001'[134]; he also highlighted that 'Afghan state building significantly depended on external military and financial support – this dependence was greater than during any other period since 1747 – and the "war on terror" dominated the nature of foreign donors' engagement'.[135] This was to remain the case for years after the Taliban's displacement, and even on the eve of the third decade of the twenty-first century, the Afghan state is far from fiscally stable. This dependence has had manifold ramifications for the development of the state in Afghanistan since 2001. If a key state function is to appropriate or use resources in determined ways, then dependence on external sources of revenue may seriously compromise the discharge of this function. This is for two reasons. First, external donors may attach conditions to the ways in which funds are to be used ('conditionality'). When this is the case, it is highly debatable whether the state can credibly claim to be using resources available to it in ways that *it* has determined. Second, donor funds may be injected in ways that bypass the local state altogether. As Bizhan put it, 'Donors saw the off-budget aid as a mechanism to substitute for the Afghan government limited capacity and to avoid the risk of waste due to corruption in the Afghan public sector. The government thus neither had fiscal control over … nor considered itself accountable for off-budget expenditure'.[136]

Such a situation is likely to have significant implications for policy coherence, but even more seriously, it can compromise the quest for political legitimacy for a new set of state structures. The Bonn Agreement was alert to the issue of legitimacy, and looked to the return of the former king, the Emergency and Constitutional Loya Jirgas, and the drafting of a new constitution to be followed by elections as means of weaving together sufficient strands of legitimacy to sustain the new state. But several factors undercut this endeavour. One was the manifest fiscal dependence of the new state on external sources. Another was that the mechanisms of legitimation in the Bonn Agreement owed more to foreign conceptions of how legitimacy might be generated than to local conceptions, something which is an endemic problem associated with international state building enterprises.[137] A third was that legitimate *local* actors in different parts of Afghanistan too often found themselves marginalised, especially after the US, in preparation for its invasion of Iraq in March 2003, blocked attempts to expand beyond Kabul the 'International Security Assistance Force' (ISAF) for which the Bonn Agreement had provided. President Karzai, faced with a serious problem of spoilers at the local level, had little option but to try to accommodate potential troublemakers, but was forced to do so at the expense of effective engagement with more legitimate, but less troublesome actors.

This mélange of factors set the scene for the development in post-2001 Afghanistan of what can be called a *neopatrimonial* state, albeit of a regulated rather than predatory form.[138] This is a hybrid system in which personalistic rule, grounded in patron–client relations, is entwined with formal bureaucratic structures which enjoy some degree of autonomy.[139] One notable characterisation of neopatrimonialism is as follows[140]:

> In neopatrimonial regimes, the chief executive retains authority through personal patronage, rather than through ideology or law. As with classic patrimonialism, the right to rule is ascribed to a person rather than an office. In contemporary neopatrimonialism, relationships of loyalty and dependence pervade a formal political and administrative system and leaders occupy bureaucratic office less to perform public service than to acquire personal wealth and status. The distinction between private and

> public interests is purposely blurred. The essence of neopatrimonialism is the award by public officials of personal favors, both within the state (notably public sector jobs) and in society (for instance, licenses, contracts, and projects). In return for material rewards, clients mobilize political support and refer all decisions upward as a mark of deference to patrons.

This neatly captures the entanglement of formal structures and patronage, but captures only one of a number of possible forms of relationship between those at the apex of a system and those occupying lower positions. As Sarah Chayes put it after years of examining the post-2001 Afghan state close up, 'Karzai was not, as conventional wisdom had it, doling out patronage. He wasn't distributing money downward to buy off potential political rivals. If anything – with exceptions especially before elections – the reverse was true. Subordinate officials were paying off Karzai or his apparatus. What the top of the system provided in return was, first, unfettered permission to extract resources for personal gain, and second, protection from repercussions'.[141]

Why does it matter if a state is neopatrimonial in character? One answer is that a state of this kind cannot be understood simply in terms of formal structures or even informal norms that take shape around them. There can be a large gulf between *de jure* and *de facto* states.[142] Indeed, it is almost impossible to make sense of a given neopatrimonial system without an understanding of the *particular networks* that have developed between key actors. Sharan and Bose have argued that 'political networks are a distinct *hybrid hierarchical structure whose members share power and resources through informal and constantly renegotiated deals and pacts*'.[143] Mapping such networks is central to making sense of the politics of a neopatrimonial state, which is why in the next chapter we give contemporary political networks in Afghanistan some attention. Another answer, however, is practical: a neopatrimonial state tends to offer a high level of impunity to people who have the right connections, and at a certain point this can rebound to compromise the legitimacy of the state in the eyes of those who lacks such connections. Furthermore, in a neopatrimonial state, aid may flow to those with the right connections rather than to those with the greatest needs, with similar legitimacy consequences.[144] In other words, the form and character of the new state can matter very much in determining whether or not it contributes to the stabilisation of a previously disrupted state.

It would be easy to interpret the development of neopatrimonialism in Afghanistan as an indictment of Hamed Karzai and his circle, and there is no doubt that his approach to politics encouraged a neopatrimonial drift. But in fairness to Karzai, it is important also to note that Afghanistan was *not*, after 2001 a 'post-conflict' space. On the contrary, within a relatively short period of time, violent attacks by a rejuvenated Taliban with sanctuaries in Pakistan[145] began to take their toll on both instrumentalities of the state, especially the Afghan National Police, and the civilian population. Political actors under fire are likely to revert to survival strategies which they find familiar and think will work.

Karzai and his ministers were faced with the arduous challenge of 'conflictual peacebuilding'.[146] It is a challenge that the Afghan state continues to face on a daily basis, and one that has shaped Afghanistan's contemporary politics in diverse ways. It is to this that we now turn.

Notes

1 See Beatrice Forbes Manz, *The Rise and Rule of Tamerlane* (Cambridge: Cambridge University Press, 1989).
2 See Joseph MacKay, 'International Politics in Eighteenth- and Nineteenth-Century Central Asia: Beyond Anarchy in International-Relations Theory', *Central Asian Survey*, vol. 32, no. 2, 2013, pp. 210–224.
3 See Arjun Chowdhury, *The Myth of International Order: Why Weak States Persist and Alternatives to the State Fade Away* (New York: Oxford University Press, 2018).
4 See James Crawford, *The Creation of States in International Law* (Oxford: Oxford University Press, 2007).
5 Joel S. Migdal, *Strong Societies and Weak States: State-Society Relations and State Capabilities in the Third World* (Princeton: Princeton University Press, 1988) p. 4.
6 Joel S. Migdal, 'The State in Society: An Approach to Struggles for Domination', in Joel S. Migdal, Atul Kohli, and Vivienne Shue (eds.), *State Power and Social Forces: Domination and Transformation in the Third World* (Cambridge: Cambridge University Press, 1994) pp. 7–34 at p. 16.
7 See, for example, Gianfranco Poggi, *The Development of the Modern State: A Sociological Introduction* (London: Hutchinson, 1978); Martin van Creveld, *The Rise and Decline of the State* (Cambridge: Cambridge University Press, 1999); Graeme Gill, *The Nature and Development of the Modern State* (New York: Palgrave Macmillan, 2016).
8 See Charles Tilly, *Coercion, Capital and European States, AD 990–1992* (Oxford: Blackwell, 1992) pp. 67–95; also Mancur Olson, *Power and Prosperity: Outgrowing Communist and Capitalist Dictatorships* (New York: Basic Books, 2000) p. 11; Douglass C. North, John Joseph Wallis and Barry R. Weingast, *Violence and Social Orders: A Conceptual Framework for Interpreting Recorded Human History* (Cambridge: Cambridge University Press, 2013).
9 See Bernhard Dorn, *History of the Afghans Translated from the Persian of Neamat Ullah* (London: Oriental Translation Committee, 1829) pp. 5–25; Baruch Kogan and Harry Rozenberg, 'The Afghan Pashtuns and the Missing Israelite Exiles', *The Jerusalem Post*, 20 February 2018.
10 See Anthony D. Smith, *The Ethnic Origins of Nations* (Oxford: Basil Blackwell, 1986) pp. 24–25.
11 See Mujib Rahman Rahimi, *State Formation in Afghanistan: A Theoretical and Political History* (London: I.B. Tauris, 2017).
12 See J.L. Lee, *The 'Ancient Supremacy': Bukhara, Afghanistan and the Battle for Balkh, 1731–1901* (Leiden: E.J. Brill, 1996); Martin J. Bayly, *Taming the Imperial Imagination: Colonial Knowledge, International Relations, and the Anglo-Afghan Encounter, 1808–1878* (Cambridge: Cambridge University Press, 2016); Jonathan L. Lee, *Afghanistan: A History from 1260 to the Present* (London: Reaktion Books, 2018); Nile Green, 'Introduction: A History of Afghan Historiography', in Nile Green (ed.), *Afghan History Through Afghan Eyes* (London: Hurst & Co., 2015) pp. 1–51.
13 See Nasir A. Andisha, 'Neutrality and its Place in Afghanistan's Foreign Policy', in Srinjoy Bose, Nishank Motwani and William Maley (eds.), *Afghanistan – Challenges and Prospects* (London: Routledge, 2018) pp. 241–259 at p. 245.
14 Ghulam Muhammad Ghubar, *Khorasan* (Kabul: History Association, 1947).
15 Arnold Fletcher, *Afghanistan: Highway of Conquest* (Ithaca: Cornell University Press, 1965).

16 S. Frederick Starr, *Lost Enlightenment: Central Asia's Golden Age from the Arab Conquest to Tamerlane* (Princeton: Princeton University Press, 2013) p. 29.

17 See Michael Barry, *Figurative Art in Medieval Islam and the Riddle of Bizhâd of Herât (1465–1535)* (Paris: Éditions Flammarion, 2004).

18 Zahiruddin Muhammad Babur, *The Baburnama* (London: The Folio Society, 2013) p. 152.

19 Yuri Gankovsky, 'The Durrani Empire: Taxes and Tax System, State Income and Expenditures', in *Afghanistan: Past and Present* (Moscow: USSR Academy of Sciences, 1981) pp. 76–98.

20 For more on the life and legacy of Ahmad Shah see Lee, *Afghanistan: A History from 1260 to the Present*, pp. 116–142; Ganda Singh, *Ahmad Shah Durrani: Father of Modern Afghanistan* (Bombay: Asia Publishing House, 1977); Mahmud al-Husaini Jami, *Tarikh-e Ahmad Shahi* (Tehran and Kabul: Irfan Publishers, 2007).

21 For a discussion of the role of polygamy in the stability of Afghan thrones, see Amin Saikal, *Modern Afghanistan: A History of Struggle and Survival* (London: I. B. Tauris & Co., 2012).

22 For an excellent elaboration of these complexities, see B.D. Hopkins, *The Making of Modern Afghanistan* (Basingstoke: Palgrave Macmillan, 2008).

23 On this period, see Noah Arjomand, *The Folly of Double Government: Lessons from the First Anglo-Afghan War for the 21st Century* (Kabul: Discussion Paper 2/2015, Afghanistan Analysts Network, June 2015).

24 William Dalrymple, *Return of a King: The Battle for Afghanistan* (London: Bloomsbury Publishing, 2013) p. 388.

25 To this day in Afghanistan, to refer to a political figure as a 'Shah Shuja' is virtually the equivalent of calling someone a 'Quisling', a noun taken from the surname of the notorious Norwegian collaborator with Nazi Germany during the Second World War: see Hans Fredrik Dahl, *Quisling: A Study in Treachery* (Cambridge: Cambridge University Press, 1999).

26 For detailed analysis of the reign of Dost Muhammad Khan, see Christine Noelle, *State and Tribe in Nineteenth-Century Afghanistan: The Reign of Amir Dost Muhammad Khan (1826–1863)* (London: Curzon Press, 1998); for accounts of this period from the perspectives of British and Indian officials see Mohan Lal, *Life of the Amir Dost Mohammed Khan of Kabul* (Cambridge: Cambridge University Press, 2012) Vols. I–II; Charles Masson, *Narratives of Various Journeys in Balochistan, Afghanistan and the Panjab* (London: Bentley, 1842) Vol. II.

27 This episode inspired a popular poem entitled 'The Guides at Cabul, 1879': Henry Newbolt, *Collected Poems 1897–1907* (London: Thomas Nelson & Sons, 1907) pp. 108–113.

28 See Rob Johnson, 'General Roberts, the Occupation of Kabul, and the Problems of Transition, 1879–1880', *War in History*, vol. 20, no. 3, 2013, pp. 300–322. For Roberts's account of his activities, see Field-Marshal Lord Roberts of Kandahar, *Forty-One Years in India* (London: Richard Bentley & Son, 1897) Vol. II, pp. 181–375.

29 Sir Lepel Griffin, 'A Page of Afghan History', *Asiatic Quarterly Review*, vol. 6, July–October 1888, pp. 241–269 at p. 247.

30 Ibid., p. 264.

31 Sultan Mahomed Khan (ed.), *The Life of Abdur Rahman: Amir of Afghanistan* (London: John Murray, 1900) Vol. I, pp. 233–292.

32 See Robert D. McChesney, *Waqf in Central Asia: Four Hundred Years in the History of a Muslim Shrine, 1480–1889* (Princeton: Princeton University Press, 1991).

33 Ashraf Ghani, 'Islam and State-Building in a Tribal Society: Afghanistan 1880–1901,' *Modern Asian Studies*, vol. 12, no. 2, 1978, pp. 269–284. See also David B. Edwards, *Heroes of the Age: Moral Fault Lines on the Afghan Frontier* (Berkeley & Los Angeles: University of California Press, 1996) pp. 78–125.

34 See Hasan Kakar, *Government and Society in Afghanistan: The reign of Amir Abd al-Rahman Khan* (Austin: University of Texas Press, 1979).

35 Griffin, 'A Page of Afghan History', p. 269.

36 Frank A. Martin, *Under the Absolute Amir* (New York & London: Harper & Brothers, 1907); Jonathan Lee argues that Abdul Rahman Khan's violent tendencies can be attributed at least in part to his physical and mental health conditions, which progressively deteriorated until his death. See Jonathan Lee, 'Abd al-Rahman Khan and the "maraz ul-muluk"', *Journal of the Royal Asiatic Society*, 3rd Series, vol. 1, no. 2, 1991, pp. 209–242; See also Sayed Askar Mousavi, *The Hazaras of Afghanistan: An Historical, Cultural, Economic and Political Study* (London: Curzon Press, 1998) pp. 111–138; Niamatullah Ibrahimi, *The Hazaras and the Afghan State: Rebellion, Exclusion, and the Struggle for Recognition* (London: Hurst & Co., 2017) pp. 53–86.

37 Khan, *The Life of Abdur Rahman*, Vol. I, p. 276.

38 See Kakar, *Government and Society in Afghanistan*; also Vartan Gregorian, *The Emergence of Modern Afghanistan: Politics of Reform and Modernization 1880–1946* (Stanford: Stanford University Press, 1969) pp. 129–162.

39 Lee, 'Abd al-Rahman Khan and the "maraz ul-muluk"', p. 241.

40 See Christine Noelle, 'The Anti-Wahhabi Reaction in Nineteenth-Century Afghanistan', *The Muslim World*, vol. 85, no. 1–2, January–April 1995, pp. 23–48.

41 Khan, *The Life of Abdur Rahman*, Vol. II, p. 159.

42 Hossein Mahdavy, 'The Pattern and Problems of Economic Development in Rentier States: The Case of Iran', in M.A. Cook (ed.), *Studies in the Economic History of the Middle East: From the rise of Islam to the present day* (London: Oxford University Press, 1970) pp. 428–467.

43 Hazem Beblawi, 'The Rentier State in the Arab World', in Hazem Beblawi and Giacomo Luciani (ed.), *The Rentier State* (London: Croom Helm, 1987) pp. 49–62 at pp. 51–52.

44 Richter and Steiner distinguish six different types of rents, which also includes raw material rents, foreign remittances and tourism rents. See Thomas Richter and Christian Steiner, 'Politics, Economics and Tourism Development in Egypt: Insights into the Sectoral Transformations of a Neo-patrimonial Rentier State,' *Third World Quarterly*, vol. 29, no. 5, June 2008, pp. 939–959 at p. 943.

45 Michael L. Ross, 'Does Oil Hinder Democracy?', *World Politics*, vol. 53, no. 3, April 2001, pp. 325–361.

46 Barnett R. Rubin, *The Fragmentation of Afghanistan: State Formation and Collapse in the International System* (New Haven: Yale University Press, 2002) p. 48.

47 Mir Ghulam Muhammad Ghubar, *Afghanistan dar masir-e Tarikh* (Kabul: Maiwand Publishers, 2014) p. 647.

48 Nematullah Bizhan, *Aid Paradoxes in Afghanistan: Building and Undermining the State* (London: Routledge, 2018), p. 51.

49 Ghubar, *Afghanistan dar masir-e Tarikh*, p. 648.

50 Ghubar, *Afghanistan dar masir-e Tarikh*, p. 710. For accounts that capture some of the atmospherics of this period, see Rhea Talley Stewart, *Fire in Afghanistan 1914–1929: Faith, Hope and the British Empire* (New York: Doubleday, 1973); May Schinasi, *Afghanistan at the Beginning of the Twentieth Century: Nationalism and Journalism. A Study of Seráj Ul-Akhbâr (1911–1918)* (Naples: Istituto Universitario Orientale, 1979).

51 For background, see Ludwig W. Adamec, *Afghanistan, 1900–1923: A Diplomatic History* (Berkeley & Los Angeles: University of California Press, 1967); W.M. Hale, 'Afghanistan, Britain and Russia, 1905–21' (Canberra: Unpublished PhD Thesis, The Australian National University, 1966).

52 Mir Muhammad Siddiq Farhang, *Afghanistan dar panj qarn-e akhir* (Peshawar: Ehsanullah Mayar, 1988) p. 367.

53 Leon B. Poullada, *Reform and Rebellion in Afghanistan, 1919–1929: King Amanullah's Failure to Modernize a Tribal Soceity* (Ithaca: Cornell University Press 1973) pp. 99–103.

54 Ghubar, *Afghanistan dar masir-e Tarikh*, pp. 790–791; see also Farhang, *Afghanistan dar panj qarn-e akhir*, pp. 373–375.

55 Ghubar, *Afghanistan dar masir-e tarikh*, p. 792.

56 See Senzil K. Nawid, *Religious Response to Social Change in Afghanistan 1919–1929: King Aman-Allah and the Afghan Ulama* (Costa Mesa: Mazda Publishers, 1999).

57 M. Nazif Shahrani, 'King Aman-Allah of Afghanistan's Failed Nation-Building Project and its Aftermath (review article)', *Iranian Studies*, vol. 38, no. 4, December 2005, pp. 661–675.

58 See Farhang, *Afghanistan dar panj qarn-e akhir*, pp. 385–403

59 Barnett R. Rubin, 'Lineages of the State in Afghanistan', *Asian Survey*, vol. 28, no. 11, November 1988, pp. 1188–1209 at p. 1200.

60 Leon B. Poullada, 'Afghanistan and the United States: The Crucial Years,' *Middle East Journal*, vol. 35, no. 2, Spring 1981, pp. 178–190 at p. 183.

61 Rubin, 'Lineages of the State in Afghanistan', p. 1202.

62 Ibid.

63 Ibid.

64 M.S. Noorzoy, 'Long-Term Economic Relations between Afghanistan and the Soviet Union: An Interpretive Study,' *International Journal of Middle East Studies*, vol. 17, no. 2, May 1985, pp. 151–173 at p. 160; see also Bizhan, *Aid Paradoxes in Afghanistan*, p. 60.

65 Rubin, *The Fragmentation of Afghanistan*, p. 78.

66 See Thomas Ruttig, *How It All Began: Pre-1979 Origins of Afghanistan's Conflict* (Kabul: Afghanistan Analysts Network, 2013) pp. 11–13.

67 William Maley, *The Afghanistan Wars* (New York: Palgrave Macmillan, 2009) pp. 22–24.

68 See Antonio Giustozzi with Niamatullah Ibrahimi, *Thirty Years of Conflict: Drivers of Anti-Government Mobilisation in Afghanistan 1978–2011* (Kabul: Afghanistan Research and Evaluation Unit, January 2012).

69 Abdul Samad Ghaus, *The Fall of Afghanistan: An Insider's Account* (McLean: Pergamon-Brassey's, 1988) p. 179. There is some evidence that the Soviets may have had some notice that the coup was about to happen. See Christopher Andrew and Vasili Mitrokhin, *The World Was Going Our Way: The KGB and the Battle for the Third World* (New York: Basic Books, 2005), p. 386; Ali Ahmad Jalali, *A Military History of Afghanistan: From the Great Game to the Global War on Terror* (Lawrence: University Press of Kansas, 2017) p. 354.

70 Henry S. Bradsher, 'Communism in Afghanistan', in Hafeez Malik (ed.), *Soviet-American Relations with Pakistan, Iran and Afghanistan* (London: Macmillan, 1987) pp. 333–354 at p. 339

71 See Graeme Gill, 'Personality Cult, Political Culture and Party Structure', *Studies in Comparative Communism*, vol. 17, no. 2, Summer 1984, pp. 111–121.

72 Max Weber, *Economy and Society: An Outline of Interpretive Sociology* (Berkeley & Los Angeles: University of California Press, 1978) Vol. I, p. 215.

73 'Our Revolution is Secure', *Asiaweek*, 17 November 1978, pp. 40–41 at p. 40.

74 See William Maley, 'Social Dynamics and the Disutility of Terror: Afghanistan, 1978–1989', in P. Timothy Bushnell, Vladimir Shlapentokh, Christopher K. Vanderpool and Jeyaratnam Sundram (eds.), *State Organized Terror: The Case of Violent Internal Repression* (Boulder: Westview Press, 1991) pp. 113–131.

75 See M. Hassan Kakar, *Afghanistan: The Soviet Invasion and the Afghan Response, 1979–1982* (Berkeley and Los Angeles: University of California Press, 1995) p. 125.

76 See Edward Girardet, *Afghanistan: The Soviet War* (London: Croom Helm, 1985) pp. 107–110; *Casting Shadows: War Crimes and Crimes Against Humanity: 1978–2001* (Kabul: The Afghanistan Justice Project, 2005) pp. 19–20.

77 Michael Barry, 'Répressions et guerre soviétiques', *Les Temps Modernes*, July–August 1980, pp. 171–234.
78 C.P.W. Gammell, *The Pearl of Khorasan: A History of Herat* (London: Hurst & Co., 2016) p. 289.
79 For the full transcript, see Aleksandr Liakhovskii, *Tragediia i doblest' Afgana* (Iaroslavl': NORD, 2004) pp. 112–116.
80 See Anthony Arnold, *Afghanistan's Two-Party Communism: Parcham and Khalq* (Stanford: Hoover Institution Press, 1983) pp. 52–56; Henry S. Bradsher, *Afghan Communism and Soviet Intervention* (Karachi: Oxford University Press, 1999) pp. 20–23.
81 Barry, 'Répressions et guerre soviétiques', p. 183.
82 For a detailed discussion of these events, see Rodric Braithwaite, *Afgantsy: The Russians in Afghanistan 1979–89* (London: Profile Books, 2011) pp. 58–73.
83 Rubin, *The Fragmentation of Afghanistan*, pp. 120, 121.
84 On the complexities of the Afghan resistance, see Olivier Roy, *Islam and Resistance in Afghanistan* (Cambridge: Cambridge University Press, 1990); Rizwan Hussain, *Pakistan and the Emergence of Islamic Militancy in Afghanistan* (Aldershot: Ashgate, 2005); Abdulkader Sinno, *Organizations at War in Afghanistan and Beyond* (Ithaca: Cornell University Press, 2008).
85 See Thomas T. Hammond, *Red Flag Over Afghanistan: The Communist Coup, the Soviet Invasion, and the Consequences* (Boulder: Westview Press, 1984).
86 See Raymond L. Garthoff, *Détente and Confrontation: American-Soviet Relations from Nixon to Reagan* (Washington, DC: The Brookings Institution, 1994).
87 See Maley, *The Afghanistan Wars*, pp. 32–139; and Robert Johnson, *The Afghan Way of War: How and Why They Fight* (New York: Oxford University Press, 2011) pp. 205–248.
88 For details, see Larry P. Goodson, 'Periodicity and Intensity in the Afghan War', *Central Asian Survey*, vol. 17, no. 3, 1998, pp. 471–488.
89 *Materialy XXVII s"ezda Kommunisticheskoi partii Sovetskogo Soiuza* (Moscow: Izdatel'stvo politicheskoi literatury, 1986) p. 69.
90 A.S. Grossman, 'Sekretnye dokumenty iz osobykh papok: Afganistan', *Voprosy istorii*, no. 3, 1993, pp. 3–33 at p. 25.
91 Kim M. Tsagolov and Selig S. Harrison, 'Afganskaia voina: Vzgliad iz segodniashnego dnia', *Vostok*, no. 3, 1991, pp. 42–57 at p. 53.
92 See Artemy M. Kalinovsky, *A Long Goodbye: The Soviet Withdrawal from Afghanistan* (Cambridge: Harvard University Press, 2011).
93 See William Maley, 'The Geneva Accords of April 1988', in Amin Saikal and William Maley (eds.), *The Soviet Withdrawal from Afghanistan* (Cambridge: Cambridge University Press, 1989) pp. 12–28.
94 See Artemy M. Kalinovsky, 'The Failure to Resolve the Afghan Conflict, 1989–1992', in Artemy M. Kalinovsky and Sergey Radchenko (eds.), *The End of the Cold War and the Third World: New Perspectives on Regional Conflict* (London: Routledge, 2011) pp. 136–154.
95 See Phillip Corwin, *Doomed in Afghanistan: A UN Officer's Memoir of the Fall of Kabul and Najibullah's Failed Escape, 1992* (New Brunswick: Rutgers University Press, 2003).
96 Barnett R. Rubin, 'The Failure of an Internationally Sponsored Interim Government in Afghanistan', in Yossi Shain and Juan J. Linz (eds.), *Between States: Interim Governments and Democratic Transitions* (Cambridge: Cambridge University Press, 1995) pp. 211–236 at p. 236.
97 See Antonio Giustozzi, *The Army of Afghanistan: A Political History of a Fragile Institution* (London: Hurst & Co., 2016).
98 On the ISI, see Hein G. Kiessling, *Faith, Unity, Discipline: The ISI of Pakistan* (London: Hurst & Co., 2016); Owen L. Sirrs, *Pakistan's Inter-Services Intelligence Directorate: Covert Action and Internal Operations* (New York: Routledge, 2017).

99 *International Herald Tribune*, 22 April 1992.
100 See Stephen John Stedman, 'Spoiler Problems in Peace Processes', *International Security*, vol. 22, no. 2, Fall 1997, pp. 5–53; Kelly M. Greenhill and Solomon Major, 'The Perils of Profiling: Civil War Spoilers and the Collapse of Intrastate Peace Accords', *International Security*, vol. 31, no. 3, Winter 2006–07, pp. 7–40.
101 See Ian Kershaw, *The End: Hitler's Germany, 1944–45* (London: Allen Lane, 2011).
102 BBC *Summary of World Broadcasts* FE/1461/B/1, 17 August 1992.
103 For more detail on these accords, see William Maley, 'The Future of Islamic Afghanistan', *Security Dialogue*, vol. 24, no. 4, December 1993, pp. 383–396.
104 Gilles Dorronsoro, 'Afghanistan's Civil War', *Current History*, vol. 94, no. 588, January 1995, pp. 37–40 at p. 37. See also Fotini Christia, *Alliance Formation in Civil Wars* (Cambridge: Cambridge University Press, 2012) pp. 57–100.
105 See Ibrahimi, *The Hazaras and the Afghan State*, p. 191.
106 For the lower figure, see Étienne Gille, 'Les combats à Kaboul depuis 1992', *Les Nouvelles d'Afghanistan*, no. 72, 1996, p. 4. For the higher figure, see *Afghanistan: International Responsibility for Human Rights Disaster* (London: Amnesty International, ASA 11/09/95, 1995) p. 33.
107 See Lucien W. Pye, *Warlord Politics: Conflict and Coalition in the Modernization of Republican China* (New York: Praeger, 1971); Hsi-Sheng Ch'i, *Warlord Politics in China 1916–1928* (Stanford: Stanford University Press, 1976).
108 Kimberly Marten, *Warlords: Strong-arm Brokers in Weak States* (Ithaca: Cornell University Press, 2012) p. 3.
109 Antonio Giustozzi, *Empires of Mud: War and Warlords in Afghanistan* (London: Hurst & Co., 2008) p. 5.
110 Gilles Dorronsoro, *Revolution Unending: Afghanistan, 1979 to the Present* (New York: Columbia University Press, 2005) p. 205.
111 See Dipali Mukhopadhyay, *Warlords as Bureaucrats: The Afghan Experience* (Washington, DC: Carnegie Endowment for International Peace, August 2009); Romain Malejacq, 'Warlords, Intervention, and State Consolidation: A Typology of Political Orders in Weak and Failed States', *Security Studies*, vol. 25, no. 1, 2016, pp. 85–110; Romain Malejacq, 'From Rebel to Quasi-State: Governance, Diplomacy and Legitimacy in the Midst of Afghanistan's Wars (1979–2001)', *Small Wars and Insurgencies*, vol. 28, no. 4–5, 2017, pp. 867–886; Romain Malejacq, *Warlord Survival: The Delusion of Statebuilding in Afghanistan* (Ithaca: Cornell University Press, 2020).
112 Gammell, *The Pearl of Khorasan*, p. 325.
113 See Rajat Ganguly, *Kin State Intervention in Ethnic Conflicts: Lessons from South Asia*, (New Delhi: SAGE Publications, 1998) pp. 162–192; Elisabeth Leake, *The Defiant Border: The Afghan-Pakistan Borderlands in the Era of Decolonization, 1936–1965* (Cambridge: Cambridge University Press, 2017) pp. 104–148; Elizabeth Leake, 'Afghan Internationalism and the Question of Afghanistan's Political Legitimacy', *Afghanistan*, vol. 1, no. 1, April 2018, pp. 68–94.
114 See Ahmad Shayeq Qassem, *Afghanistan's Political Stability: A Dream Unrealised* (Aldershot: Ashgate, 2009) pp. 47–50.
115 See Mohammad Yousaf and Mark Adkin, *The Bear Trap: Afghanistan's Untold Story* (London: Leo Cooper, 1992).
116 On the background and emergence of the Taliban, see Anthony Davis, 'How the Taliban Became a Military Force', in William Maley (ed.), *Fundamentalism Reborn?: Afghanistan and the Taliban* (London: Hurst & Co., 1998) pp. 43–71; Neamatollah Nojumi, *The Rise of the Taliban: Mass Mobilization, Civil War, and the Future of the Region* (New York: Palgrave, 2002) pp. 117–124; Michael Griffin, *Reaping the Whirlwind: Afghanistan, Al Qa'ida and the Holy War* (London: Pluto Press, 2004) pp. 30–47; Steve Coll, *Ghost Wars: The Secret History of the CIA, Afghanistan and Bin Laden, from the Soviet Invasion to September 10, 2001* (London: Penguin, 2005)

pp. 280–300; Robert D. Crews and Amin Tarzi (eds.), *The Taliban and the Crisis of Afghanistan* (Cambridge: Harvard University Press, 2008); Ahmed Rashid, *Taliban: Militant Islam, Oil and Fundamentalism in Central Asia* (New Haven: Yale University Press, 2010) pp. 17–30; Alex Strick van Linschoten and Felix Kuehn, *An Enemy We Created: The Myth of the Taliban/Al-Qaeda Merger in Afghanistan, 1970–2010* (London: Hurst & Co., 2012); Roy Gutman, *How We Missed the Story: Osama Bin Laden, the Taliban, and the Hijacking of Afghanistan* (Washington, DC: United States Institute of Peace Press, 2013) pp. 63–82.

117 See Anand Gopal, 'The Combined and Uneven Development of Afghan Nationalism', *Studies in Ethnicity and Nationalism*, vol. 16, no. 3, December 2016, pp. 478–492 at pp. 481–482; Anand Gopal and Alex Strick van Linschoten, *Ideology in the Afghan Taliban* (Kabul: Afghanistan Analysts Network, June 2017).

118 See Barbara D. Metcalf, *Islamic Revival in British India: Deoband, 1860–1900* (Princeton: Princeton University Press, 1982).

119 S. Yaqub Ibrahimi, 'The Taliban's Islamic Emirate of Afghanistan (1996–2001): "War-Making and State-Making" as an Insurgency Strategy', *Small Wars and Insurgencies*, vol. 28, no. 6, 2017, pp. 947–972 at p. 948.

120 Barnett R. Rubin, Ashraf Ghani, William Maley, Ahmed Rashid, and Olivier Roy, *Afghanistan: Reconstruction and Peacebuilding in a Regional Framework* (Bern: KOFF Peacebuilding Reports 1/2001, Swiss Peace Foundation, 2001) p. 12.

121 Michael Carnahan, 'Next Steps in Reforming the Ministry of Finance', in Michael Carnahan, Nick Manning, Richard Bontjer and Stéphane Guimbert (eds.), *Reforming Fiscal and Economic Management in Afghanistan* (Washington, DC: The World Bank, 2004) pp. 123–149 at p. 123.

122 On this relationship, see Anne Stenersen, *Al-Qaida in Afghanistan* (Cambridge: Cambridge University Press, 2017) pp. 69–95.

123 *Report of the Panel on United Nations Peace Operations* (New York: United Nations, A/55/305 – S/2000/809, 21 August 2000).

124 For more detailed discussion, see Maley, *The Afghanistan Wars*, pp. 224–228.

125 See Linschoten and Kuehn, *An Enemy We Created*, pp. 219–260.

126 See Francis Fukuyama, *State-Building: Governance and World Order in the 21st Century* (Ithaca: Cornell University Press, 2004).

127 See James F. Dobbins, *After the Taliban: Nation-Building in Afghanistan* (Washington, DC: Potomac Books, 2008) p. 96.

128 Harry Eckstein, *Regarding Politics: Essays on Political Theory, Stability and Change* (Berkeley & Los Angeles: University of California Press, 1992) p. 188.

129 Robert E. Goodin, 'Institutions and their design', in Robert E. Goodin (ed.), *The Theory of Institutional Design* (Cambridge: Cambridge University Press, 1996) pp. 1–53 at pp. 39–43.

130 See David Lewis, *Convention: A Philosophical Study* (Cambridge: Harvard University Press, 1969) p. 78.

131 Barbara A. Misztal, *Informality: Social Theory and Contemporary Practice* (London: Routledge, 2000) p. 46.

132 Donald S. Lutz, *Principles of Constitutional Design* (Cambridge: Cambridge University Press, 2006) p. 186.

133 See William Maley, *Rescuing Afghanistan* (London: Hurst & Co., 2006) p. 35.

134 Nematullah Bizhan, *Aid Paradoxes in Afghanistan: Building and Undermining the State* (London: Routledge, 2018) p. 104.

135 Ibid., p. 77.

136 Ibid., p. 91.

137 See in general David A. Lake, *The Statebuilder's Dilemma: On the Limits of Foreign Intervention* (Ithaca: Cornell University Press, 2016). In the Afghan context, see Florian P. Kühn, 'Risk and Externalisation in Afghanistan: Why Statebuilding Upends State-formation', in Berit Bliesemann de Guevara (ed.), *Statebuilding and*

State-formation: The Political Sociology of Intervention (London: Routledge, 2012) pp. 23–39; and Srinjoy Bose, 'Death by a Thousand Cuts or Dance of the Seven Veils?: Legitimacy and Generation of Authority in Afghanistan's Statebuilding Enterprise, 2001–2014' (Canberra: Unpublished PhD thesis, The Australian National University, 2015).

138 On this distinction, see Daniel C. Bach, 'Patrimonialism and Neopatrimonialism: Comparative Trajectories and Readings', *Commonwealth and Comparative Politics*, vol. 49, no. 3, July 2011, pp. 275–294.

139 For more detailed discussion, see William Maley, *Transition in Afghanistan: Hope, Despair and the Limits of Statebuilding* (London: Routledge, 2018) pp. 37–40; Weeda Mehran, 'Neopatrimonialism in Afghanistan: Former Warlords, New Democratic Bureaucrats?', *Journal of Peacebuilding and Development*, vol. 13, no. 2, 2018, pp. 91–105 at pp. 94–95.

140 Michael Bratton and Nicolas Van de Walle, 'Neopatrimonial Regimes and Political Transitions in Africa', *World Politics*, vol. 46, no. 4, July 1994, pp. 453–489 at p. 458.

141 Sarah Chayes, *Thieves of State: Why Corruption Threatens Global Security* (New York: W.W. Norton, 2015), pp. 59–60. See also Andreas Wilde and Katja Mielke, 'Order, Stability, and Change in Afghanistan: From Top-down to Bottom-up State-making', *Central Asian Survey*, vol. 32, no. 3, September 2013, pp. 353–370.

142 Anne Evans, Nick Manning, Yasin Osmani, Anne Tully and Andrew Wilder, *A Guide to Government in Afghanistan* (Kabul: The World Bank and Afghanistan Research and Evaluation Unit, March 2004) pp. 14–21.

143 Timor Sharan and Srinjoy Bose, 'Political Networks and the 2014 Afghan Presidential Election: Power Restructuring, Ethnicity and State Stability', *Conflict, Security and Development*, vol. 16, no. 6, November 2016, pp. 613–633 at p. 615.

144 See William Maley, 'Institutional Design, Neopatrimonialism, and the Politics of Aid in Afghanistan', *Asian Survey*, vol. 58, no. 6, November-December 2018, pp. 995–1015.

145 See Seth G. Jones, *The Insurgent Sanctuary in Pakistan* (Washington, DC: Center for Strategic and International Studies, September 2018).

146 See Astri Suhrke and Arne Strand, 'The Logic of Conflictual Peacebuilding', in Sultan Barakat (ed.), *After the Conflict: Reconstruction and Development in the Aftermath of War* (London: I.B. Tauris, 2005) pp. 141–154.

3

POLITICS

Afghan politics is marked by just as much complexity as Afghan society. In many countries, politics is seen as an elite activity concerned with the running of the state. This may be a useful focus for analysis in highly developed and stable systems, but in a country such as Afghanistan, politics in a broader sense tends to infuse everyday life for practical reasons. Whilst ordinary Afghans may not necessarily have a detailed textual understanding of the Afghan Constitution, they tend to have an acute awareness of power relations, since these can affect their lives and prospects on a daily basis. These relations of power are central to politics in a country such as Afghanistan. In this chapter, we explore five particular types of politics – institutional politics, network politics, warlord politics, contentious politics, and identity politics – before turning to the issue of how insurgency has shaped politics in Afghanistan.

Institutional politics

As noted in the previous chapter, Afghanistan in 2004 acquired a new constitution (*Qanun-e asasi*).[1] Whilst decisions at the Bonn conference on the structure of the Interim Administration had done much to shape the character of the new state, the question of exactly what kind of political (as opposed to administrative) institutions the country should have came up for discussion predominantly at the Constitutional Loya Jirga. Afghanistan does not simply have a written constitution; it has a *codified* constitution, that is, a single document which purports to map the contours of the principal institutions of the state. That said, the key word here is 'purports', for 'institutions' in a deeper sense are not limited to structures mentioned in some formal text. As Ostrom has put it, 'institutions are the prescriptions that humans use to organise all forms of repetitive and structured interactions including those within families, neighbourhoods, markets, firms, sports leagues, churches, private associations, and governments at all scales'.[2] Rules are central to institutions. Social institutions, according to Nicholas Rowe, 'are constituted by agents following *rules of action* and believing others to follow *rules of action*'.[3] Institutions in this sense are not necessarily the product of either decree or agreement; they can evolve and become self-sustaining equilibria.[4] Furthermore, political systems can be 'institutionalised' or 'consolidated' to varying degrees,[5] depending upon the extent to which institutions provide the fundamental contours of political life; and some formal institutions may be more highly developed, institutionalised and consolidated than others. Afghanistan's experience illustrates this rather starkly.

At the core of Afghanistan's constitutional framework is a formally strong executive presidency. This reflected a sense that Afghanistan was in need of a 'strong leader', although recent scholarship has cast doubt on whether having a leader dominate colleagues and the policy process is actually desirable.[6] The office of president (*Rais-e Jamhur*) was occupied from 2004 to 2014 by Hamed Karzai (following his service as Chair of the Interim and Transitional Administrations between 2001 and 2004) and from 2014 by Dr Ashraf Ghani. Under Article 61 of the Constitution, the president is permitted to serve two consecutive five year terms, after which, he or she must relinquish the office. Employing an electoral system modelled on that used in France, if no candidate in an initial round of voting secures an absolute majority (that is, over 50 per cent) of votes cast in the first round, a 'run-off' election is supposed to be held between the two candidates who polled the most strongly. In the first election, on 9 October 2004, President Karzai secured 55.4 per cent, and no run-off was required. In 2009, great controversy surrounded the first round of voting on 20 August, with credible analysis pointing to extensive fraud, much of it benefiting President Karzai[7]; and while Karzai in the face of international pressure agreed to a run-off which he had initially resisted, his main challenger, former Foreign Minister Dr Abdullah, withdrew from the process, given the likelihood of extensive fraud in the run-off as well. In 2014, when Karzai was ineligible to stand, Dr Abdullah held a substantial lead over Dr Ashraf Ghani after the first round of voting on 5 April, but fraud again intervened, albeit this time in the run-off on 14 June,[8] and with a looming political crisis, a power-sharing agreement, of sorts, was put in place to establish a 'National Unity Government'.

The history of such arrangements in the wider world has rarely been a happy one. Very rarely, during acute national crises of sufficient scale to render partisan politics virtually irrelevant, they may work: the classic example was in Britain from 1940 to 1945.[9] But for the most part, they tend to paper over tensions rather than resolve them; indeed, they often stand in the way of addressing the very problems that seem to give rise to the need for a national unity government in the first place. This was what happened in Afghanistan. Dr Ghani was sworn in as president while Dr Abdullah was designated 'Chief Executive Officer', but this did not mean that they became intimate partners in administration, and still less that their associates were able to develop trustful relationships of a kind that would lubricate the operation of government. On the contrary, whilst both Ghani and Abdullah had talented supporters, those supporters found it quite difficult to work effectively with each other, and it was not long before insinuations or allegations of ethnic bias began to circulate, with opponents of Ghani accusing him of favouring Pushtuns at the expense of Tajiks and Hazaras. Furthermore, the commitment to electoral reform, central to the original agreement to establish the national unity government, led nowhere; and given that the office of 'Chief Executive Officer' had no constitutional status, it was not surprising that Ghani was soon accused of refusing to share real power.

In practice, the office of president has not provided the cohesive and decisive leadership for which its architects had hoped. It has reflected the unfortunate reality that an elected president may often have *some* of the talents required to make a success of the job, but rarely all of them. Karzai sought to govern in an inclusive fashion, but was not a dynamic innovator in the realm of policy, and by favouring friends and cronies did much to put in place the neopatrimonial system that Dr Ghani inherited.[10] Ghani, by contrast, was immensely energetic and had devoted years to thinking about the challenges of state building,[11] but, while greatly respected by younger Afghans of technocratic bent, was not by disposition an inclusive coalition-builder. But that said, each bore the curse of having to deal with a major partner, the United States (US), which itself suffered from dysfunctional policy processes embodying a great deal of destructive competition between different agencies about how developments in Afghanistan should be approached[12]; and Ghani in addition had to cope with a US commitment that was shrinking dramatically. In such circumstances, even an Afghan president with a quite remarkable array of talents might well have struggled to achieve his objectives.

Institutional politics in Afghanistan is not purely executive; it also has a legislative dimension. Under Article 82 of the Constitution, the 'National Assembly' (*Shura-i Milli*) is a two-chamber parliament comprising a popularly elected, 250 member lower house, the House of the People (*Wolesi Jirga*), and a partly appointed, partly indirectly elected, 102 member upper house, the House of Elders (*Meshrano Jirga*, sometimes called the Senate). The term 'Wolesi Jirga' mirrored the terminology used to identify the lower house in Afghanistan's 1964 Constitution, but the resemblance between that and the new *Wolesi Jirga* has proved to be more than just one of language. In the earlier period, the failure of the king to sign a political parties bill meant that parties were either clandestine or weak during the period of the 1964 Constitution's operation. Members of the *Wolesi Jirga* functioned more as intermediaries or brokers than as custodians in some sense of the 'public interest'.[13] In the post-2001 period, *Wolesi Jirga* elections were held on 18 September 2005, 18 September 2010, and 20 October 2018. The electoral system used for all three of these polls is one known as the 'Single Non-Transferable Vote', or SNTV.[14] Votes are tallied on a provincial basis, and seats are allocated simply according to the total number of votes cast for individual candidates. The perversity of the system is the following: if, in a province with ten seats to fill, a popular and moderate candidate secures

90 per cent of the *vote*, that candidate still wins just one seat, with 90 per cent of the *seats* going to other candidates, who might all be extremists. Under such a system, it may be legal for parties to operate, but it is likely to be extraordinarily difficult for them to flourish. That has proved to be the case since 2001, with the *Wolesi Jirga* proving to be unstable and unpredictable as blocs develop and dissolve. Furthermore, membership turnover has typically been extensive, as one would expect with an SNTV system. One notable element within the chamber has been the large number of women members, thanks not just to the existence of 68 reserved seats, but also to the competence and popularity of some female legislators. The women members, however, have not functioned as a bloc and often have been at odds with each other when contentious legislation has been put forward.[15] While there are some very competent individuals within the *Wolesi Jirga*, its reputation has suffered from the grandstanding of at least some members and from persistent rumours of favours being offered in exchange for votes.

It is notoriously the case that the bureaucratic institutions of the state can provide venues for political competition,[16] and Afghanistan is no exception, although considerable variation in focus and performance can be detected between different ministries and agencies,[17] and some agencies, such as the Afghanistan Independent Human Rights Commission chaired by Dr Sima Samar, developed excellent reputations. The allocation of departments within the Interim Administration to different political factions set the scene for intense politicisation of public administration, and compromised effective policy-making and service delivery. In the classic Weberian model of bureaucracy, bureaucrats are selected on the basis of professional competence, typically determined by a competitive examination. This was not how key positions were initially filled in the new Afghan state. Whilst the roots of the problem went back to the Bonn Agreement, President Karzai did little to address it. He was relatively uninterested in the complexities of public policy and was not under much pressure to give them much attention. On the contrary, international actors if anything added to the problem. All too readily, they sought the cooperation of 'favourites' within bureaucratic agencies – typically recent returnees fluent in Western languages and capable of packaging their ideas in language that resonated with what donors wanted to hear. In the process, some very able Afghans were overlooked as potential administrative partners. A further problem was the emergence of what came to be called the 'second civil service', made up of 'NGOs, consultants, advisors and employees of UN and other international agencies, including expatriate consultants and Afghans attracted by relatively high salaries'.[18] In contrast to Karzai, President Ghani had a detailed understanding of administrative issues[19] and moved to revive the moribund Independent Administrative Reform and Civil Service Commission by appointing a dynamic young technocrat, Nader Nadery, to head it. Nonetheless, the obstacles to effective administration in Afghanistan remain considerable.[20]

The highly centralised character of the Afghan state is an obstacle in itself. Afghanistan is divided into 34 provinces, but these are administrative units rather than distinct legal jurisdictions of the kind that one finds in a federal system, where 'general and regional governments are each, within a sphere, co-ordinate and independent'.[21] Within the provinces are 407 administrative districts under an administrator known as a *woleswal*.[22] This form of administration has a long history in Afghanistan, but hardly a sterling reputation,[23] and President Karzai paid it relatively little attention.[24] Highly centralised states often lack local or tacit knowledge of the kind that can allow prompt, effective responses to problems as they arise in specific localities. Yet interestingly, it is at the local level that the phenomenon of *governance* is most often to be found. As a noted scholar has put it,

> governance is a system of rule that works only if it is accepted by the majority (or, at least, by the most powerful of those it affects), whereas governments can function even in the face of widespread opposition to their policies. In this sense, governance is always effective in performing the functions necessary to systemic persistence, else it is not conceived to exist.[25]

Informal institutions can emerge to assist in the solution of collective action problems,[26] and a major recent study by Jennifer Brick Murtazashvili has pointed to the emergence of such institutions in Afghanistan. In particular, she argues persuasively that

> prolonged civil conflict may not lead to utter social destruction, but instead to a strengthening of self-governance. Although in many instances the self-governing mechanisms that emerge may be far from optimal coping mechanisms in the eyes of liberal peacebuilders, they remain legitimate in the eyes of the individuals who have constituted them.[27]

This is one of the reasons why some serious scholars have argued for the reinvigoration of formalised community self-governance in Afghanistan.[28]

In many countries, especially those keen to burnish their democratic credentials, a credible independent judiciary is an essential institution of state. In disrupted states, substantial sums have in recent times been spent with the objective of 'building the rule of law'. In Afghanistan, however, far less has been achieved than one might have wished. For a legal system to be credible in the eyes of ordinary people, the judiciary must be organised in a systematic rather than *ad hoc* fashion, access to the law has to be affordable, judgments must be produced in a timely but professional fashion, and above all, the courts must be impartial, granting no favours to a party simply because it appears to be the more powerful in the courtroom or in the wider society. This, unfortunately, is not how the legal system has come to function in Afghanistan, and as a recent report from The Asia Foundation put it, the

> formal judicial system is known for its corruption, high cost, and lengthy process, whereas informal justice mechanisms are expeditious and often less expensive, so many Afghans choose to use these informal systems. This is not always a matter of choice, however: many women are forced to use these informal systems when they try to report violent crimes to formal authorities, which too often leaves perpetrators unpunished and women still in danger.[29]

The rule of law in Afghanistan remains very weak,[30] and to the extent that the judiciary has undertaken the task of judicial review, it has largely done so in a politicised and inconsistent fashion.[31]

One area of particular significance since 2001 has been the establishment of an Afghan National Army (ANA), which in January 2019 comprised 190,423 personnel.[32] For nearly a decade before the overthrow of the Taliban regime, Afghanistan had no national army worthy of the name, and re-establishing one was an urgent and immediate task. It was also a complex task, since the re-establishment of a military involves not just the recruitment of soldiers, but the establishment of a management and logistics capability with a matching middle management stratum, and the inculcation of a culture of loyalty to the civilian authorities to avoid the seizures of power by the military of the kind which have become common, for example, in neighbouring Pakistan. The United States took the lead in supporting the re-establishment of the ANA, and it continued, despite the withdrawal by the end of 2014 of the bulk of US combat troops, to assist in the ANA's training in partnership with a number of allied states. For all the challenges that it faces, the ANA survived this withdrawal, and ANA soldiers are very much the 'face' of the Afghan state in providing security for Kabul and other major cities. The issue of exactly which Afghan actors and forces would exercise effective control over the ANA and its resources has of course always been a highly political one. Unsurprisingly, the former *Mujahideen* who saw themselves as standing steadfastly against the Taliban before 2001 regarded effective control of the ANA as something which they had earned, and this resulted in the position of Minister of Defence being granted to Mohammad Qasim Fahim, a Tajik and former close associate of the assassinated leader Ahmad Shah Massoud. In 2004, however, Fahim was sidelined in favour of Abdul Rahim Wardak, a Pushtun connected in the 1980s with a small royalist *Mujahideen* party, who served from 2004 to 2012. Both appointments prompted mutterings about ethnic agendas being played out in the ANA, and rivalry between different cliques in the Defence Ministry was a serious problem,[33] but the deeper problems of the ANA were and are high attrition rates and 'ghost soldiers', a weak sense of mission, poor morale, a disconnect between the soldiers and the foreign trainers, and above all a model for the army that is of questionable sustainability.[34] Nonetheless, the ANA has remained subordinated to civilian authority. Afghanistan is not a praetorian state.[35]

The balance of the Afghan National Defense and Security Forces comprises the Afghan National Police (ANP), which in January 2019 numbered 116,384 personnel.[36] The aim of community policing is not the defeat of an enemy, but the protection of law and order, and the professional skills that are required for effective policing are very different from those which soldiers require.[37] Few observers have had a good word to say about the ANP, which has often acted in predatory or abusive ways,[38] and the damning conclusions of an Afghan observer are worth noting[39]:

> Since it became a state in the 18th century, Afghanistan has never had an effective national police force…When the United States and NATO created the International Security Assistance Force (ISAF) in 2001, a variety of police training efforts began, but the new policing institutions were all shaped by the assumptions and values of the countries providing the trainers: European police trainers had good goals but few resources to implement them; the American effort relied primarily on contractors who advocated a culture of militarization rather than civilian policing. Deepseated Afghan cultural habits of political patronage continued to undermine the policing institutions brought in from outside the country. As a result of these competing cultures, the Afghan National Police is a hodgepodge of various entities and organizations, none of which are very effective.

But that said, three additional points should be borne in mind. First, the casualty rate within the ANP is extremely high, and even senior officers are vulnerable: the Kandahar ANP chief, General Abdul Raziq, was assassinated in Kandahar on 18 October 2018.[40] Reform is hard to promote when one is under fire. Second, and somewhat surprisingly, popular assessments of the ANP appear more positive than one might have expected, with 84 per cent of respondents in the 2018 Asia Foundation survey of Afghan opinion agreeing either strongly or somewhat that the ANP 'is honest and fair with the Afghan people' and 83 per cent agreeing that the ANP 'helps improve security in Afghanistan'.[41] It is possible that this represents simply a lack of candour on the part of most respondents, but it may also reflect a certain respect for people taking on a very dangerous job. Third, the very weakness of the ANP prevents it from being an effective tool of coercion against the citizenry. In contrast to a number of states in its neighbourhood, Afghanistan is not a police state.[42]

Network politics

In the period after the 2001 US-led military intervention and subsequent statebuilding enterprise, the nexus of formal and informal politics led to what has been described by Sharan as 'network politics', a condition 'where the state and political networks have become co-constitutive in state-building'.[43] The concept of network politics denotes an organisational form of politics as well as the capture and infiltration of state institutions by informal political networks. As a mode of political organisation, network politics is characterised by 'distinct open-hierarchical structures whose members are interdependent on each other's power and resources for political outcomes in an informally structured and continuously renegotiated arrangement.'[44] The networks, however, are not entirely flat, as particular individuals who amass high levels of material and social resources can exercise high levels of influence as key nodes in the network. Because these networks are based on informal power relations, opportunism and bargaining by their members, they can undermine the formal politics of the state as a rule-based game. Afghanistan's network politics emerged and evolved as a result of the confluence of a number of factors. Two factors deserve particular attention.

First, years of war and acute uncertainty that prevailed from the late 1970s created conditions which favoured flexible and open political affiliations over firm and enduring commitment to particular organisations. In this sense, informal politics, based on personal relations of trust and reciprocity, can be seen as the outcome of years of learning and adjustment by Afghan political elites in a situation of war and instability. As opposed to political parties, networks offer greater opportunities for changing allegiances, allowing members to shift alliances and loyalties as the political and social conditions change.

Network politics as a form of informal politics that occurs outside formal institutions is not an entirely new phenomenon. As we discussed in Chapter 2 of this book, the Afghan state historically confronted major challenges in penetrating society and regulating the social and political affairs of the country. The inability to integrate social and political actors in the formal institutions of the state meant that important areas of social and political life of the country were shaped by actors that were only loosely connected to national state institutions. At times, such as during the Musaheban rule from 1933 to 1973, local actors worked as intermediaries between the state and their local communities. The April 1978 coup by the People's Democratic Party of Afghanistan (PDPA) marked a violent disruption of the fragile state-society relations that had developed under the Musaheban rule. The years of war against the PDPA regime and the Soviet occupation from 1979 to 1989 gave rise to a multitude of political and military groups that thrived in environments where state authority was weak or non-existent. Over time, most of the countryside fell outside government control. Similarly, a generation of Afghans grew up as refugees in Iran and Pakistan where they had minimal interaction with state institutions. There were seven major Sunni *Mujahideen* organisations, which were based in Pakistan. Another eight Shia organisations were based in Iran. Inside Afghanistan, a number of military commanders emerged who had various degrees of affiliation with the *Mujahideen* leaders in Pakistan and Iran. Many of these commanders established their own networks of alliances and relationships that were dictated by their local political and security environments.[45]

The *Mujahideen* organisations, which were known as *tanzeem*, displayed a high level of diversity in their organisational forms and strategies. The *Hezb-e Islami* of Gulbuddin Hekmatyar adopted a Leninist organisational style, marked by centralised leadership and mechanisms of command and control. Many others were less hierarchical and relied on networks of commanders that had different degrees of autonomy from their party leaderships.[46] Despite their variations, these organisations developed in state-free environments and were often driven by competitive efforts to attract financial and military assistance from Islamic and Western countries, which were distributed through Pakistan's Inter-Services Intelligence Directorate. Over time, the state-free environment in which the *Mujahideen* parties operated gave rise to a distinctive form of 'Peshawar politics', notable for the complete absence of policy development and implementation as elements of political life. This was in no sense surprising, but it did mean that a generation of Afghan political figures who were to become prominent after 2001 grew up in an environment in which their very conception of politics was based on alliance building, networking and patron-client relationships. It was therefore little wonder that after 2001, networking persisted with a vengeance in the new Afghanistan.

Second, network politics was also encouraged by the institutional structure of the post-2001 Afghan state. As outlined above, the 2001 Bonn Agreement and the 2004 constitution created a highly centralised presidential system. The constitution provided for direct elections of both the president and members of the bicameral National Assembly. However, the post-2001 elections were held without genuinely national and programmatic political parties. In 2003, President Karzai promulgated a law on political parties, which led to a mushrooming of political parties in subsequent years. The law established minimum conditions for registration of a political party, setting the membership bar as low as just 700. This allowed ambitious individuals with sizeable social networks to meet the criteria for registration of a political party. Many of these parties were formed by small circles of former leftist, secular and liberal groups who had been sidelined from politics since the end of the 1980s. These included groups that had their roots in various factions of the PDPA; others originated from a Maoist movement that was active in Kabul and other major urban centres during the 1960s and 1970s, but was mostly marginalised in the war between the PDPA and the *Mujahideen* during the 1980s.[47] Despite their different historical origins and trajectories, these parties attempted to offer a liberal-democratic platform by taking stances in favour of democratisation and against religious fundamentalism.[48]

The increase in the number of political parties was also due to fragmentation and splintering of major former *Mujahideen* organisations. Established during the years of war and instability, these parties tended to be dominated by leaders who controlled the party's resources and political networks in highly personalised manners. Consequently, a genuine transformation of these parties would also entail establishment of some form of internal democratic mechanisms that could change leaders or hold them accountable to their members. In the first few years after the overthrow of the Taliban regime, a younger generation of political cadres in these *Mujahideen tanzeem* demanded internal political reforms. These reform efforts achieved only partial successes. Some parties held congresses and established some level of organisational structure. However, these reforms typically stalled when they threatened the leader's control over the party's resources and cadres. Unable to bring about any reforms, many of these younger cadres registered their own political parties. For example, members of *Jamiat-e Islami* led by Burhanuddin Rabbani established new parties or launched coalitions with members of other groups.[49] Similarly, *Hezb-e Wahdat* fragmented into at least four separate major parties.[50] Other parties, most notably *Junbesh Milli Islami* led by Abdul Rashid Dostum, resisted both reforms and the trend towards internal fragmentation.[51] The proliferation of such a large number of parties pointed to poor institutional regulation as well as fragmentation of the political groups in the country.

By 2009, there were 110 political parties formally registered with the Ministry of Justice in Kabul. This raised significant concerns about the growing fragmentation of the political elite in Afghanistan. In response, the Afghan parliament amended the law to alter the requirements for registration of political parties: the minimum membership required was increased from 700 to 10,000. Furthermore, parties were also required to demonstrate that they recruited members from different regions and provinces of the country. The re-registration process undertaken in accordance with the new law reduced the number of parties to 63 in 2015, but achieved little in the way of institutionalising and consolidating parties as national and inclusive organisations.[52]

The development of political parties during this period was also constrained by the adoption of SNTV and a widespread attitude among political elites that associated political parties with the discord and violent histories of the leftist and Islamist parties after 1978.[53] SNTV, in particular, did not provide many incentives for individual politicians to attach themselves to any political party. The parliament elected through the SNTV was dominated by independent members who mostly did not have any programmatic commitment to a political party. Over time, although the detrimental effects of the SNTV became obvious, the president and members of the parliament found an interest in maintaining the system rather than adopting a different system that could encourage long-term development of political parties.[54] In an important respect, the distrust towards political parties was reminiscent of a similar attitude towards political parties in the 1960s, when the reluctance of Zahir Shah to promulgate a law on political parties resulted in a similar democratic experiment without formal political parties.[55] The major difference between the two periods was that after 2001, political parties were legally recognised, but were effectively denied any major roles in the political process.

However, the parties varied significantly in their influence and capacity to play any roles in politics. Many of the small 'liberal-democratic' parties that were left out of the post-Bonn distribution of power also lacked the material resources to compete with the major groups. From the very beginning, two major groups dominated the state and politics: the former *Mujahideen*, and the Afghan diaspora who returned from the West. Beginning from the Interim Administration that was formed at the Bonn conference in 2001, these groups dominated state institutions and thereby gained access to patronage resources, which further entrenched their power. Following the collapse of the Taliban regime in 2001, the former *Mujahideen* groups also took control of state institutions at the provincial level. Subsequently, President Karzai confirmed the positions of these local power brokers as provincial and district governors and police chiefs, providing their hold on power and resources with a cover of state legitimacy. For obvious reasons, groups and individuals that took control of resource-rich provinces such as Balkh, Herat, Kandahar and Nangarhar also formed particularly strong political networks. These local and regional oligarchs became the nodes of a network by virtue of their ability to mobilise and distribute resources.

Warlord politics

Many of the political networks that emerged in the period after 2001 were dominated by individuals who were pejoratively described as 'warlords'. As noted in the previous chapter, the term is a complex and contentious one, for as MacKinlay argues, it is an 'ugly, pejorative expression, evoking brutality, racketeering and the suffering of civil communities'.[56] The term is often used to describe commanders of non-state armed groups functioning as violent and predatory actors. By extension, because warlords emerge during periods of wars and state weakness, these actors are also often assumed to resist and oppose extension of state authority in their areas. However, while many such actors are highly predatory and rely on their brutality to maintain power, an emphasis on the predatory, violent and anti-state behaviour of warlords alone often fails to capture the social and political complexity of warlordism as a phenomenon. Furthermore, warlords do not necessarily stand in opposition to state authority. Many such actors draw upon their coercive power to claim significant roles as political players, and some may even have a long-term interest in building state institutions.[57]

MacGinty[58] argues that warlordism, as a system, consists of three core elements: state weakness, resources and legitimacy. By definition, warlords emerge in situations where states are disrupted, and lose their legitimacy and capacity to enforce their authority and to perform basic functions such as maintaining a monopoly over the use of force. In these circumstances, warlords and armed groups emerge in areas where state authority is weak or non-existent. Successful warlords also need to mobilise sufficient resources to maintain their private militias. They often rely on exploitation of natural resources such as minerals or timber, 'tax' the local communities, or obtain funds from external powers such as neighbouring states. Finally, warlords cannot sustain their influence without acquiring some level of legitimacy in the eyes of at least some sections of the local communities. At the very least, warlords can gain support through their personal charisma as military leaders or can maintain the loyalty of their subordinates by demonstrating an ability to provide patronage and distribute resources. Others position themselves as defenders of their local clan, tribe and even ethnic communities.

In Afghanistan, individuals that became known as warlords grew to prominence following the Soviet occupation of Afghanistan during the 1980s. The gradual weakening of the state after the April 1978 coup by the PDPA created a vacuum that was gradually filled by a wide range of armed groups. Many such individuals achieved their prominence in the course of armed resistance against the Soviet occupation of the country. These military commanders had various levels of allegiance to the leaders of the *Mujahideen* organisations who were based in Pakistan or Iran. In contrast to the leaders of the *Mujahideen* organisations who were based in Pakistan or Iran, the military leaders were often based in Afghanistan and as a result developed stronger support bases among their subordinates or local communities. Among the most significant of these military commanders were Ahmad Shah Massoud in Panjsher and Ismail Khan in Herat. Some of these commanders created local structures that aimed to assume basic functions of the state in the areas of security, conflict resolution and even provision of some basic social services.

There was another group of so-called warlords that emerged as a result of policies of the Soviet-backed PDPA regime to create state-backed militias directed against the *Mujahideen* organisations.[59] These militias, which were variously formed by the Ministry of Defence, Interior or the national intelligence agency, became particularly influential after the departure of the Soviet troops from Afghanistan in 1989. The most significant and well-known of these militias was led by Abdul Rashid Dostum. Dostum's militia, which numbered several thousand combatants, was eventually incorporated into the formal military forces as the 53rd division. Another similarly significant unit was formed in Baghlan under the leadership of Sayed Jafar Naderi and was upgraded to a division level (division 80) in 1988. Division 80, which was dominated by members of the Ismaili community, was tasked with securing the highway between Kabul and northern provinces that runs through the Salang Tunnel and Baghlan province. Similarly, militia units were established elsewhere in Afghanistan, but the success of these units also depended on local social and political conditions. For example, in the southern provinces of Helmand and Kandahar, despite government efforts, local tribal segmentation meant that local militias did not achieve any level of strength that would be comparable to that of the militias in the north.[60]

In the period after the 2001 overthrow of the Taliban regime by the US-led military intervention, the leaders of armed groups presented a major challenge for the state-building enterprise in the country. As military leaders, warlords were accused of perpetrating human rights violations against civilian populations and of posing significant challenges to the expansion and consolidation of state power across the country. Throughout the years of war, human rights groups documented a range of mass atrocities perpetrated by militia groups against civilians.[61]

In 2001, at the core of the conundrum was the question of whether to integrate these individuals into the structures of the state, or sideline them. These actors held both civilian and military roles as provincial governors as well as commanders of large militias. A number of these actors engaged in fierce conflicts to consolidate their influence locally. For example, between 2002 and 2003, Abdul Rashid Dostum, the leader of *Junbesh*, and Atta Mohammad Noor, a local leader of *Jamiat-e Islami*, fought a series of wars over control of the strategic province of Balkh. Each of the two sides commanded large armies of several thousand members that were equipped with tanks and heavy artillery. The conflict between the two groups ended with the appointment of Noor as governor of Balkh in 2004 and consolidation of the influence of Dostum over Jawzjan and Faryab provinces. Similarly, in the southeast region, Padshah Khan Zadran, a participant in the Bonn conference, sought to exert his control over the provinces of Paktia and Khost. Initially, he was appointed as provincial governor of Paktia, but was prevented from entering the city by a local rival, Haji Saifullah. In April 2002, he launched a revenge rocket attack on the city of Gardez, killing dozens of people. Subsequently, in the neighbouring province of Khost, he challenged the authority of Hakim Taniwal, a distinguished academic who was appointed by Karzai as the province's governor.[62] In the southern province of Kandahar, Gul Agha Sherzai, a local militia leader, established similar control. In the western province of Herat, Ismail Khan, the former *Mujahideen* leader affiliated with *Jamiat-e Islami*, re-established his political and military influence. Initially, he was simultaneously governor of the province and commander of an army of several thousand forces, which he funded through the province's customs revenues. Ismail Khan fought a series of violent conflicts with Amanullah Khan, a local commander, in the district of Shindand.[63]

The central government faced significant hurdles in responding to the challenges posed by the local armed groups. In 2001, the central government did not have a national army or police force of its own that was capable of containing these powerful actors. The Ministry of Defence in Kabul was nominally in control of what was known as the Afghan Military Force, a large number of disjointed, mostly militia, forces that were nominally organised in formal military units, but were directly commanded by local and regional actors. Local strongmen such as Ismail Khan in Herat, Noor in Balkh and Gul Agha Sherzai in Kandahar, who commanded such contingents also took control of customs revenues from these strategic trading provinces. Consequently, these actors had a combination of political roles (which resulted from their status as governors) and military roles as commanders of significant armed groups. In the absence of coercive capacity, the government under Karzai resorted to a combination of pressure and bargaining to weaken the grip of these actors on sub-national administration. In 2003, the United Nations (UN) launched a programme of Disarmament, Demobilisation and Reintegration (DDR) that aimed to disarm these local groups by helping their armed men to resume normal civilian lives. Simultaneously, the central government and international community engaged in negotiations and pressures on local actors to remove them from their positions of power. As a result, some of the key actors were removed from their positions, but only to be appointed in other similar positions or replaced by candidates of their own choice. In August 2003, Karzai replaced Sherzai in Kandahar with Yosuf Pashtun, a Pashtun technocrat who had previously worked under Sherzai. Subsequently, Sherzai was appointed as governor of the eastern province of Nangarhar, where he held office from 2005 until 2013. In September 2004, Ismail Khan was appointed as Minister of Energy and Water in Kabul. While the central government succeeded in removing major figures such as Sherzai and Ismail Khan from their local power bases, the local networks of these actors were not necessarily weakened. Nonetheless, by removing these actors from their power bases, the central government did increase its control over critical revenue sources. Yet these efforts to marginalise strongmen were not always successful. In contrast to Ismail Khan and Sherzai, Noor negotiated an arrangement with Karzai which allowed him to remain as governor of Balkh until January 2018, when he was replaced by President Ghani after several months of protracted political crisis.[64]

Over time, the combination of DDR and the reshuffling of strongmen from one province to another achieved some degree of success in weakening and dismantling the networks of militias that these actors commanded in their provinces. The DDR process was striking for many of its flaws,[65] but despite its weaknesses, it had an important effect in collecting heavy weaponry and tanks from these local actors. At the same time, as we discussed above, the Afghan National Army and the Afghan National Police also grew in number and strength. Nonetheless, the main leaders and commanders of the former armed groups retained their social and political influence. At the national level, the former *Mujahideen* crafted a narrative based on their role in the armed resistance against the Soviet occupation of Afghanistan during the 1980s and subsequently against the Taliban from 1996 to 2001 to legitimate their claims to power. The technocratic elites who returned to Afghanistan, often after spending many years in the West, used their technocratic expertise and their skills to negotiate with Western donors to claim power. In the context of power rivalries between these groups, the term 'warlord' was also used as a weapon to delegitimise rival groups.

The extension of state authority to the provinces thitherto dominated by local warlords was also undercut by contradictions that resulted from competing agendas of the Afghan elites in Kabul and the US and North Atlantic Treaty Organization (NATO) military forces. On the one hand, an agenda of institutional reform and accountability for human rights violations emphasised meritocratic appointments of public officials through clear and transparent procedures. On the other, the central government, and the US and NATO forces in the country, viewed some local strongmen and their local networks as resources that could be used in the 'War against Terror' and in counterinsurgency campaigns.[66] In provinces affected by Taliban insurgency, local strongmen and their militias were seen as bulwarks against Taliban insurgency, particularly after 2006, when the Taliban significantly expanded their activities in several provinces. These contradictions had clear effects on government policies. While some power brokers increased their power and influence through close alliances with the US and other foreign forces, others felt marginalised. Consequently, the central government was accused of selectively using the term 'warlord' as a weapon against its political opponents.

Somewhat ironically, these contradictions in the policies and priorities of the Afghan government, and the US and NATO, assisted the rise of a new generation of warlords. Beginning from the early days of the US-led military intervention in October 2001, the US enlisted many local militia commanders in the fight against the Taliban and Al-Qaeda in various parts of the country. Many of these individuals received significant support from the US military and intelligence agencies that enabled them to reinstitute their local networks. Subsequently, although the influence as military actors of known strongmen such as Ismail Khan was weakened, the international forces helped the rise of a new generation of warlords in the contexts of counterinsurgency operations against Taliban insurgents. For example, in the province of Kandahar, although Sherzai gradually lost his influence, a new generation of militia leaders rose to prominence as a result of their close relationships with the US and other military forces in the provinces. The most notable of these was General Abdul Raziq, mentioned earlier, who began his career as commander of a unit of border police in the Spin Boldak area of Kandahar under Sherzai. In 2011, he was appointed as provincial police chief of Kandahar.[67] Similarly, Matiullah Khan, a local militia commander in the province of Uruzgan, grew to prominence as police chief of the province, largely thanks to his close connections with the Australian military forces that were stationed in the province.[68] Both Abdul Raziq and Matiullah Khan became incredibly powerful individuals with high levels of influence on local police and informal militias. In March 2015, Matiullah Khan was killed by an assassin in Kabul.[69] Similarly, Abdul Raziq was killed by a Taliban infiltrator after a meeting with US General Austin S. Miller in October 2018.

Contentious politics

Contentious politics is a routine part of public life in democracies. Consequently, it must not be seen as a total aberration from the normal functioning of institutional politics. Nonetheless, people engage in contentious politics when they do not see any prospect of furthering their goals through formal institutions. McAdam, Tarrow and Tilly define contentious politics as 'episodic, public, collective interaction among makers of claims and their objects when (a) at least one government is a claimant, an object of claims, or a party to the claims, and (b) the claims would, if realised, affect the interests of at least one of the claimants'.[70] Thus, central to this sub-type of politics is claim-making by groups of individuals that is collective in nature, has the potential to affect the interests of other parties, and involves a government authority. This definition excludes other forms of collective claim-making that may occur through formal institutions such as deliberations and decision-making processes in cabinets or parliaments. The term episodic also excludes regularly organised political processes such as elections. Similarly, the term 'public' excludes politics that take place within well-bounded political institutions and organisations. Contention tends to follow a repertoire, routine forms of action that shape the interaction between authorities and protestors. These may include peaceful tactics such as street protests, petitions to authorities, and sit-ins, as well as violent actions such as armed rebellion and assaults on authorities or repressions of protestors.[71]

In this broad definition, contentious politics may also include violent claim-making such as civil wars, insurgencies and other forms of violent action. Here, we will define it more narrowly, focusing on peaceful forms of contention. In Afghanistan, organised contention with clearly articulated claims can be traced to the early decades of the twentieth century. The formation of the Afghan state led to empowerment of some groups and the marginalisation of others. However, traditionally the most common response to state repression or exclusion was armed rebellion, often led by traditional notables such as tribal and religious elites. However, beginning in the early twentieth century, relatively small groups within a growing urban intelligentsia began to articulate clearer demands for fundamental changes in state policies and programmes. The country's first constitutionalist movement emerged during the reign of Habibullah (1901–1919). As discussed in Chapter 2, Habibullah established the Habibia High School, which became the country's first secondary educational institution, and allowed a number of families who were exiled by his father to return to Afghanistan. In 1906, these groups launched *Seraj ul-Akhbar Afghanistan* (Torch of News of Afghanistan), a biweekly paper, which stopped after the publication of its first issue. In 1909, a group of these reformists submitted a petition to Habibullah Khan to demand a constitutional form of government. The petition was ignored and many of its signatories were arrested and executed in Kabul and Jalalabad. Several others were given long-term gaol sentences.[72] In 1911, a second publication, *Seraj ul-Akhbar Afghaniya,* was launched by Mahmud Tarzi, a member of the Muhammadzai ruling dynasty who had been exiled by Abdul Rahman Khan. While in exile, Tarzi had travelled to Damascus and Istanbul, where he was exposed to modern ideologies of pan-Islamic revivalism and nationalism. In Afghanistan, he played an influential role in what became known as the 'Young Afghans', which, like the 'Young Turks' in the Ottoman Empire at that time, was a nationalist movement that advocated complete independence of Afghanistan from the British. Tarzi's daughter, Soraya, was married to Amanullah Khan, Habibullah's reformist son and future ruler of the country. However, this generation of Afghanistan's initial reformist groups was intent on pursuing top-down modernising reforms, focusing on influencing the royal family and finding allies within the ruling elites. As Chapter 2 showed, these movements were also highly fragile, as they depended on the goodwill and survival of modernist elites.

Subsequently, two periods stand out in the modern history of Afghanistan for their particularly high level of contentious politics: 1964–1973, and 2001 to the present. The 1960s proved to be one of the most contentious and formative decades in the history of Afghan politics. The period from 1964 to 1973, which became known as a *dahe demokrasi* (decade of democracy) in the country's history, was an epoch marked by a high level of passionate and highly ideological politics. In 1964, Zahir Shah promulgated a new constitution that created a constitutional monarchy in which members of the royal family were barred from holding executive offices. However, as discussed above, the new parliamentary democracy was launched without legally recognised political parties.[73] A number of new political and ideological movements nonetheless emerged during this period. In January 1965, a number of leftist members of the intelligentsia formed the People's Democratic Party of Afghanistan, the first pro-Soviet party to emerge in the country. In the same year, a number of other activists coalesced around the Progressive Youth Organisation, a communist group inspired by Mao Zedong, the Chairman of the Chinese Communist Party. In 1969, a number of faculty members of Kabul University formed the *Sazman-e Jawanan-e Musulman* (Organisation of Muslim Youth) to challenge the leftist groups in the country. The new group included many members of the Sharia Faculty of Kabul University who had studied at Al-Azhar University in Egypt and been exposed to the ideology of the Muslim Brotherhood. Among them were Ghulam Muhammad Niazi, who subsequently became the dean of the Sharia Faculty at Kabul University, Burhanuddin Rabbani, Musa Tawana and Minhajuddin Gahiz.[74] Table 3.1 shows the opening of social and political space under the new constitution overlapped with the rapid expansion of the country's public education system.[75]

Throughout the 1960s, these groups engaged in fierce competition, sometimes violently, over the control of schools and university campuses in Kabul. The students of high schools and Kabul University took the central roles in several waves of protests across Kabul. According to Koshkaki,[76] three main episodes of contention played particularly disruptive roles in the life of the new democracy. First, on 25 October 1965, hundreds of protestors clashed with security forces outside the new parliament building in Kabul. The protestors were objecting to a decision by the parliament to convene a closed meeting of the

TABLE 3.1 Student enrolment, 1955–1972

Year	1955	1960	1967	1972
Primary	111,650	213,100	444,240	540,700
Secondary	5730	14,100	54,400	107,600
Vocational	1950	2500	5700	5200
Teacher Ed.	1000	3900	5600	4170
Higher Ed.	760	1700	4320	6600
Total	121,090	235,300	514,260	664,270

parliament to vote on members of the first cabinet of Dr Muhammad Yousuf, the first democratically elected prime minister under the new constitution. During the confrontation, a unit of the security forces opened fire on a group of protestors who had gathered outside the parliament building; as a result, three protestors died. The incident had profound effects on the new government. The king asked Dr Yousuf to resign and nominated Muhammad Hashim Maiwandwal as a new prime minister on 29 October. Second, during 1968–1969, a series of protests were organised by students of Kabul University against laws and regulations governing the universities and the education system. The protests, which lasted for several months, forced the government to revoke the laws and ask the minister of education to resign. Third, in 1972, another series of demonstrations and strikes led to the resignation of the then minister of education and chancellor of Kabul University. These protests were remarkably successfully in forcing the government to change significant policies and to change government officials, including ministers.

Subsequently, the polarisation of politics between the pro-Soviet PDPA and the *Mujahideen* during the 1980s, and the civil war during the 1990s, left little space for peaceful contentious politics. Groups that emerged as peaceful during the 1960s were militarised, and the PDPA, which was a key instigator of protests during the 1960s, took control of the government. The process of militarisation and violent confrontation also led to marginalisation of many others groups and complete takeover of civil society by the warring factions.

Consequently, the relatively liberal and stable social and political environment that was created by the fall of the Taliban regime in 2001 offered an opportunity for reorganisation of peaceful movements. As in the 1960s, a new generation of educated figures was at the centre of this more recent episode of contentious politics. The number of students in schools and universities likewise increased dramatically. For example, the number of school students increased from about 875,605 in 1999[77] to 9.6 million in 2018.[78] Similarly, the number of university students increased from less than 7800 in 2001 to 369,317 in 2018.[79] The post-2001 expansion of the education sector went in tandem with what is called a 'youth bulge', with a high number of young people as a proportion of the overall population of a country. With an estimated 68 per cent of its population under the age of 24, and a rapidly expanding education sector, Afghanistan faces enormous challenges in creating opportunities for employment and social and political participation for its young population.[80] The combination of the growth in the young population and expansion of the education sector attracted many ideological and political groups to the country's schools and universities, which were already highly politicised as a result of years of war and instability.[81] Groups that became active in educational centres included violent groups such as the Taliban and peaceful Islamists as well as liberal and democratic forces.[82]

Nonetheless, in important respects, the post-2001 patterns of contention varied significantly from those of the 1960s. During the 1960s, as the key centre of higher education, Kabul University was at the heart of contentious politics.

The memory of the disruptive roles played by students of Kabul University during the 1960s was so strong that after 2001, the Afghan government actively discouraged politics on the university campus. However, the expansion of secondary and higher education during this period created more diverse opportunities for social and political activism. In 2018, there were a total of 160 universities and institutes of higher education, 122 of which were private.[83] This meant that Kabul University was just one of many centres of learning and of activism as well.

Furthermore, the organisers of this recent wave of protests represented a new generation of social and political elites who were deeply influenced by the globalising changes that the society experienced during this period. This meant that unlike in the 1960s, when leaflets and newspapers were the primary media of ideological debate, for the post-2001 activists, the Internet, especially social media platforms such as Facebook and Twitter, became central media of communication and social mobilisation. Another qualitative shift concerned the role of ideology. In contrast to the 1960s, when the protests were dominated by a deep schism between Islamists and leftists, ideology became less significant after 2001. Although a new generation of Islamists and left-leaning activists also protested against certain policies of the government or the presence of foreign forces, the largest protests were organised in response to failures of the government to provide security and basic social services.

Significantly, the most notable protests occurred after 2014, a year marked by two major developments. First, during 2014, most of the US and NATO forces pulled out of the country. Second, in September of that year, after an intensely contested presidential election failed to produce a clear winner, power was transferred from President Karzai to a 'National Unity Government', in which Dr Ashraf Ghani became the President and Dr Abdullah Abdullah assumed the role of Chief Executive Officer. The drawdown of forces was followed by a rapid deterioration of security conditions as the Afghan National Security Forces were left to defend the country largely on their own. Similarly, the manner in which the National Unity Government emerged out of a deeply contested election had a significant impact on its legitimacy and capacity to respond to deteriorating security and socio-economic conditions. The first major wave of protests was triggered by the killing of a young woman, Farkhunda Malikzada, by a violent mob on 19 March 2015 in the centre of Kabul. The mob was motivated by a rumour that Malikzada had burnt the Quran at the Shahi Du Shamshira, a major shrine at the centre of Kabul. The rumour, which was subsequently proven to be completely baseless, mobilised several hundred people to attack her brutally in the presence of several police officers. A number of protests followed the killing. One of the largest of these rallies on 24 March brought several thousand people outside the Supreme Court in Kabul.[84]

The protests against the killing of Farkhunda became the first of a series of other protests against rising insurgent violence and the inability of the government to protect its citizens. One of the largest such protests took place on

11 November 2015 in Kabul. The protest that became known as the Tabassum Movement was triggered by the abduction and subsequent killing of seven civilian Hazaras in the southern province of Zabul. Among those killed in this incident were Shukria Tabassum, a nine-year-old girl, and her parents. The protestors carried the coffins of the victims as they marched towards the presidential palace to demand that the government provide security against insurgent violence. During the previous months, the insurgents had launched a campaign of abducting civilian Hazaras along highways in the north and the south of the country. Another major protest prompted by deteriorating security conditions was triggered by a series of deadly terrorist attacks in Kabul in June and July 2017. On 31 May 2017, a truck bomb exploded at Zanbaq Square, a busy roundabout just outside the German Embassy in Kabul, killing 150 people and injuring more than 400 others. In response, a new protest movement emerged in Kabul that became known as the Uprising for Change (*Junbesh-e Rashtakhiz-e Taghir*). On 2 June 2017, the protestors clashed with government security forces as they marched towards the Presidential Palace. During the clashes, the security forces opened fire on the protestors, killing six people. Among those killed was Salem Ezedyar, son of Muhammad Alam Ezedyar, a senior political figure of *Jamiat-e Islami* and deputy speaker of the Meshrano Jirga, the upper house of the parliament. One day later, on 3 June, the funeral of Ezedyar was attacked by a suicide bomber, killing at least seven participants. In response, the movement pitched a series of tents at several roundabouts of the city, and increased their demands to include the resignation of key security officials who, they alleged, were responsible for the deteriorating security conditions. On 20 June, the government security forces forcibly removed the last tent, which effectively closed any opportunity for the movement to continue protesting.

The most significant of these protest movements in terms of a following was the *Junbesh-e Roshanai* (Enlightenment Movement), which was formed in January 2016. In comparison to other protests that focused on security conditions, the Enlightenment Movement pushed for greater socio-economic development of the historically marginalised region of Hazarajat. Dominated by Hazara activists, the movement was triggered by a January 2016 cabinet decision to change the route of a major power transmission line from the central province of Bamiyan to the Salang Pass in the north of Kabul. Initially known as TUTAP (after the names of the participating countries – Tajikistan, Uzbekistan, Turkmenistan, Afghanistan and Pakistan), the line was designed to import electricity from the Central Asian republics to Afghanistan and Pakistan. In response, the movement organised a series of protests in Kabul and other cities in Afghanistan. One of its first major rallies on 16 May 2016 in Kabul brought several thousand people to the streets of Kabul. Its second major rally on 23 July 2016 proved to be the bloodiest protest rally in the history of the country. As the protestors planned to set up tents at the Deh Mazang Square of Kabul, two suicide bombers detonated explosive vests among a crowd of its supporters. According to a UN investigation, the attack, which was claimed by the Islamic State, killed 86 of the protestors and injured 413 others.[85] Contentious politics may be the only option for meaningful political participation in the eyes of many Afghans, but it is also an increasingly dangerous activity.

Identity politics: Ethnicity and gender

In our introductory chapter, we emphasised that Afghanistan is a complex country. An appreciation of the complexity of the country is particularly pertinent to understanding how identity categories intersect with politics of the country. As Lebow argues, identities 'are really composites of multiple self-identifications that are labile in character and rise and fall in relative importance'.[86]

To unpack the complexity of identities and the politics of identities in Afghanistan, it is useful to draw on a distinction that Brubaker and Cooper make between identities as 'categories of social and political practice' and categories of 'social and political analysis.[87] The former refers to the everyday use and experiences of identities by ordinary social actors or identity entrepreneurs. In this context, ordinary people may use identity categories to make sense of their social environments and everyday interaction with other actors. Similarly, political entrepreneurs may also deploy identity categories to encourage people to prioritise some forms of identification over others. As categories of analysis, identities are used by social scientists to study the changing nature and significance of group identification with categories such as nation, ethnicity or gender.

As members of a complex society, Afghans can identify with a range of social and political categories, including nation, race, ethnicity, gender, socio-economic status, kinship and places of residence. Gender as an identity category, especially the status of women, can illustrate this complexity. As a category of practice, since the early twentieth century, the status of women has been the subject of profound and often violent contestation. King Amanullah in the 1920s, and to a limited extent the Musaheban elites subsequently, prioritised emancipation of women as a central component of their modernisation programmes. In 1978, the PDPA launched its own programme of female emancipation,[88] although large numbers of women suffered enormous harm as a result of the regime's wider suite of policies.[89] In response to 'progressive' gender policies, conservative groups such as some of the leaders of the rebellion against Amanullah Khan, and most recently the Taliban since the mid-1990s, have invented alternative conceptions of gender relations, which are equally unfamiliar to the day-to-day gender reality of relations among the ordinary men and women of the country.[90] Such juxtaposition of the two rival conceptions of the role of women conceals significant autonomy and agency that women display in the routine life of many local communities. Furthermore, women in Afghanistan may also identify with one or more of other identity categories such as their individual socio-economic status or ethnic and political affiliations.[91]

Most discussions of gender in Afghanistan tend to focus almost exclusively on the position of women, and this is hardly surprising given the barriers to self-expression and self-realisation that Afghan women have historically faced – and continue to face in the twenty-first century. This focus is especially understandable given the apprehension that the fragile, but significant gains made by women since the overthrow of the Taliban could be traded away as part of a 'peace process' in which women are at best marginal participants.[92] Furthermore, there are now highly articulate women in Afghan public life who have used the *Wolesi Jirga*, Afghan media and international platforms to air their concerns. One consequence, however, is that the analysis of gender identity is less wide-ranging than in many other countries, with discussion of issues such as homosexuality and transgender identity virtually taboo. It would be a courageous activist indeed who sought to carry forward the discussion of such issues. There has been some recognition of the phenomenon of the *bacha posh*,[93] in which a girl is raised as a boy: this was the subject of a 2003 Afghan feature film, *Osama*, directed by Siddiq Barmak and starring Marina Golbahari, which won a Golden Globe Award for Best Foreign Language Film. But another phenomenon, that of the *bacha bazi* ('dancing boy'), has proved just how complex and difficult issues of gender identity can be in the political sphere. The grooming of teenage boys to entertain older men brings together a range of challenging issues, including the problem of asymmetries of social power, the very definition of childhood and adulthood in a particular context, and the moral responsibilities of those who learn what is happening.[94] In May 2017, Chapter 5 of the Afghan Criminal Code was gazetted to put in place rigorous prohibitions on what large numbers of Afghans regard as a grossly abusive form of child exploitation.[95] However, as in many situations, the real challenge is enforcement of the law, and some in the US proved reluctant to touch an issue in which some of Washington's local allies were involved,[96] and respect for 'culture' could be used as an excuse for doing nothing.

Beyond issues of gender, Afghanistan's population is highly diverse culturally and linguistically. Students of Afghanistan who have attempted to count ethno-linguistic groups have produced highly disparate numbers. One of the highest such figures is produced by Orywal, who estimated there were about 54 separate ethno-linguistic groups in the country.[97] Dupree identified 21 separate ethno-linguistic groups.[98] Afghanistan's 2004 constitution counts 16 ethnic groups as constituting the 'nation of Afghanistan'. These estimates diverge so significantly because the meaning and nature of ethnic groups and boundaries also vary, depending on one's conceptual approach, and also social and political conditions in which ethnic identities are studied in Afghanistan. In other words, whether an individual identifies with one or a combination of these identity categories depends as much on the specific social and political context as the individual's own choices and preferences. The largest ethnic groups are the Pushtuns, Tajiks, Hazaras and Uzbeks, followed by smaller minorities of Turkman, Baluch, Pashai, Nuristani, Aymaq, Arab, Qirghiz, Qizilbash, Gujur and Brahui. Historically, Pushtuns have been the dominant ethnic group in the country. From the formation of the Durrani Empire in 1747, Pushtun monarchies ruled the country almost uninterruptedly until 1978. The only major exception was the short-lived reign of Habibullah Kalakani in 1929. Tajiks were the second most influential group and dominated some key urban centres as well as the ranks of the bureaucratic agencies of the state. Hazaras, who are also mostly Shia, were the country's most persecuted group and suffered particularly high levels of marginalisation and persecution since the reign of Amir Abdul Rahman Khan.

As categories of everyday practice, however, ethnic identifications can be subjective and contextual. The complex ways in which people in Afghanistan can identify with groups can be captured by the notion of *qawm*. Qawm can be used to describe an ethnic group, tribe, kinship network and even the residents of a particular village and sub-district. The specific meaning of the term can be defined by the context in which it is used. At the local context, it can be used to distinguish residents of a village or tribe, but at the national level, it can draw the boundaries between the major ethnic groups of the country.[99]

Ethnic categories as categories of practice by political elites involve the question of national identity, and contestation for national power and resources. At the national level, since the early twentieth century, Afghan elites have struggled between an ethnic and territorial conception of national identity. Pushtun elites at different times have attempted to construct a national identity based on Pushtun history and identity as an ethno-cultural core of the country's identity. Mahmud Tarzi and the modernist circle that published *Seraj ul-Akhbar* in 1911 sought to define 'both the nature and the ultimate aims of Afghan nationalism and to formulate a theoretical basis in order to direct and justify the projected socio-economic transformation of Afghanistan'.[100] However, as Hyman argued, the development of a national identity remained weak and was challenged by 'rival ideas of the nation held by the country's different ethnic groups'.[101] Subsequently, the Musaheban dynasty invested significant efforts in defining a national identity that was grounded in an exclusive historical narrative based on the historical domination of the Pushtun monarchies and ruling elites. During the 1930s, these efforts were more institutionalised with the foundation of *Anjuman-e Adabi-e Kabul* (Kabul Literary Society) in 1931 and the subsequent formation of *Anjuman-e Tarikh Afghanistan* (Afghanistan Historical Society) in 1942. Backed by state resources, these institutions published periodicals and history books that essentially aimed at rewriting Afghanistan's history.[102] Central to this new historiography was the conception of Afghanistan as a modern reincarnation of the ancient Aryana, thus tracing the origin of the country to at least 3000 BC.[103] Pushtuns and Tajiks were redefined as descendants of the Aryan race. Pushto was promoted as the language of bureaucracy and instruction at the schools and universities. Afghanistan's Farsi, which was the *lingua franca* of the country, was sidelined and renamed Dari to distinguish it from the Farsi spoken in Iran and Tajikistan. As a result, Aryana became a popular national symbol. Soon after its formation, the Afghanistan Historical Society published a monthly magazine called *Aryana*, and a six-volume encyclopaedia under the same name during the 1950s and 1960s. In 1955, the country's first national carrier was named Ariana Airlines. At the same time, the government actively renamed or broke up regions, including important historical sites, which contradicted the nationalist historical narratives or highlighted the history of other ethnic groups.[104]

During the 1960s, this state-backed construction of national history and identity encountered both support and a backlash among the new political movements that emerged during this period. While many of these movements were dominated by a schism between Islamists and leftists, a number of groups in this period had clear ethno-nationalist agendas. One of these parties was the Afghan Social Democratic Party, popularly known as *Afghan Millat* after a magazine the party published. Founded in 1966 by Ghulam Muhammad Farhad, the party promoted the idea of a greater Afghanistan, which entailed irredentist claims on the Pushtun territories inside Pakistan. Another influential group, but one that challenged Pushtun political hegemony, was *Mahfil Entezar* (Awaiting Circle), which was popularly known as *Setam-e Milli* or national oppression. The group was founded in 1967 by Tahir Badakhshi, a Tajik intellectual from the province of Badakhshan. Badakhshi was one of the founding members of the PDPA, but broke away from the party, arguing that rather than class inequalities, Afghanistan's major problem was the national oppression of non-Pushtuns by the ruling Pushtun elites.[105] Smaller groups with clear ethno-linguistic tendencies emerged among the Hazaras, although none of them achieved any organisational or political success that was comparable to *Mahfil Entezar* or *Afghan Millat*.

During the years of war against the Soviet occupation of Afghanistan, these ethno-nationalist groups were marginalised by *Mujahideen tanzeem*, as Islam became the overarching framework of social mobilisation against a foreign invasion. As a source of unifying ideology, Islam helped the *Mujahideen* recruit across religious, ethnic and regional identities.[106] However, the *Mujahideen* were also divided internally with several organisations competing for international support and recognition as well as control of territories in Afghanistan. A number of these *tanzeem* were dominated by political or military leaders who had stronger followings in their native regions or provinces than the rest of the country. Such local ties, which often also overlapped with ethno-linguistic identities, helped these groups establish domination in some regions of the country. In the long term, these local and regional support bases also drove these organisations into identity politics, which surfaced more strongly during the civil strife following the collapse of the government of President Najibullah in April 1992.

Following the fall of the Taliban regime, it was broadly recognised that the new government should be representative of the country's diverse ethno-cultural and political groups. This recognition was the result of the failures of ethnically and politically exclusive regimes such as the Taliban in Afghanistan as well as explosions of ethnic conflicts in other parts of the world such as the Balkans during the 1990s.[107] Nonetheless, the new state-building enterprise revived similar questions to those that confronted Afghan modernists such as Amanullah Khan and Mahmud Tarzi. One such question concerned defining the national identity. As we have outlined above, Afghanistan lacks a clear ethno-cultural majority.

Although historically Pushtuns have dominated the politics of the country and are the largest ethnic group, they do not constitute an absolute majority of more than 50 per cent of the population of the country. As a result, Pushtuns are often recognised as the first among a number of major ethno-linguistic groups.[108] Afghans and Pushtuns were historically synonymous and 'Afghanistan' literally means the land of Afghans. The 1964 constitution extended the term 'Afghan' to refer to all citizens of Afghanistan. The 2004 constitution struck a compromise between declaring all citizens of the country as 'Afghan' whilst also mentioning other ethnic groups as constituting the nation. However, the recognition of the need for inclusive and broad-based politics did not lead to the establishment of a formal consociational system, which guarantees certain roles and powers for representatives of social groups in key institutions of the state.[109] Neither the Bonn Agreement in 2001 nor the 2004 constitution created any formal mechanisms that could address and assess such group-based claims. In fact, the 2004 constitution (Article 35) discouraged identity-based claims by explicitly banning formation of political parties on the basis of 'ethnicity, language, religion and region'. This was partly because a key criticism of consociational arrangements is that they can elevate one social cleavage over others and turn it into a permanent social and political divide.[110]

In the absence of clear constitutional provisions and institutionalised political parties, ethnic representation was left to informal bargaining and compromises among the country's ruling elites. Although the level of influence of different groups varied over time, an informal ethno-political hierarchy among the major political networks was at the centre of much of the distribution of power in state institutions. The hierarchy was most clearly reflected in the office of the president. Hamed Karzai, a Durrani Pushtun from Kandahar who was chosen as Chairman of the Interim Administration, became the first popularly elected president of the country in 2004. In 2009, Karzai was elected for another 5-year term. Initially, Muhammad Qasim Fahim, a Tajik from the province of Panjsher, served as the first vice-president in the Transitional Administration of Afghanistan. In 2004, Ahmad Zia Massoud, a brother of the late Ahmad Shah Massoud, who was also from the province of Panjsher, became the first vice-president. In 2009, Fahim joined Karzai's team as the first vice-president until he died in 2014. Karim Khalili, a Hazara and leader of *Hezb-e Wahdat Islami Afghanistan*, served as the second vice-president to Karzai until 2014.

The composition of the presidential tickets led by Karzai and other leading candidates reflected a coalition-building strategy that combined ethnic representation with elite bargaining over state power and patronage resources. This meant that most credible teams would include members from one of the four major ethnic groups. The result of the first national elections seemed to confirm the hierarchy between the Pushtun, Tajik, Hazara and Uzbek political networks. In 2004, Karzai won 55.4 per cent of the vote. The next leading candidate was Younus Qanuni, a Tajik from the province of Panjsher, who secured 16.3 per cent of the national votes. Mohammad Mohaqiq, a Hazara, came third with 11.7 per cent and Abdul Rashid Dostum, an Uzbek, came fourth with 10 per cent of the votes. For many of the candidates that did not have any reasonable chance of winning the presidency, elections became a platform through which they could demonstrate the strength of their ethnic or regional power bases for subsequent bargaining over power and resources. The second presidential elections in 2009, which were tarnished by extensive allegations of fraud and irregularities, demonstrated a further shift towards ethnic voting. Karzai failed to secure a victory in the first round against Abdullah Abdullah, the second top runner, who was also from the province of Panjsher and led a coalition of political groups dominated by former *Mujahideen*. Ramazan Bashardost, a Hazara politician who had served as minister of planning, came third. As a result, a run-off election was planned on 7 November of that year, but one week prior, Abdullah withdrew from the elections, citing continued distrust in the electoral process. Subsequently, the Afghanistan Independent Election Commission declared Karzai the winner of the election.

In 2014, the presidential election was just as heavily tainted with electoral fraud and irregularities, and ethicised political mobilisation. Ashraf Ghani, a former World Bank official and minister of finance under Karzai (2002–2004) who had secured about 2 per cent of the votes in 2009, emerged as a leading candidate, facing Abdullah Abdullah. Ghani's electoral ticket did not include a Tajik. He chose Abdul Rashid Dostum and Sarwar Danish as the first and second vice-presidents, respectively. On 5 April 2014, Abdullah and Ghani won 45 and 31 per cent of the votes, respectively. The second round of voting on 14 June, which provisionally put Ghani ahead of Abdullah with 56 per cent of the vote, was completely overshadowed by credible reports of widespread fraud and mismanagement involving high-level officials of the Independent Election Commission. Furthermore, the votes cast in support of the two teams demonstrated clearer ethnic patterns. While Ghani received most of his votes from Pushtun and Uzbek majority provinces, Abdullah gained the vast majority of votes from Tajik and Hazara majority areas.[111] Several weeks of auditing of the result failed to produce a clear winner. The ensuing political crisis was resolved through a political agreement in September that was brokered by US Secretary of State John Kerry and led to the National Unity Government mentioned earlier.

As the 2014 presidential elections demonstrated, ethnic power relations and ethnicised perceptions of electoral outcomes became an important factor in coalition-building strategies of the political elites. Electoral coalitions were built with a view to maximising votes by including ethnic and regional leaders who could appeal to 'vote banks'. Not surprisingly, as the experience of General Dostum under Ghani showed, such calculations led to serious policy and political differences in running the government. Furthermore, the leading candidates often infused their national policies and programmes with specific appeals targeting ethnic communities.[112] This also meant that in their competing attempts to gain support, electoral teams made promises which they were unable to fulfil once in the government. The National Unity Government of Ghani and

Abdullah since 2014 also showed that grand bargains in the form of multi-ethnic electoral teams do not necessarily result in inclusive government policies and services at other levels of state institutions. For example, as the outburst of the Enlightenment Movement showed, the inclusion of Sarwar Danish as a vice-president did not mitigate widespread perceptions of marginalisation among Hazaras from the politics and administration of the country.

While tensions of identity politics over electoral outcomes were more easily resolved through elite bargaining and compromises, in other areas, ethnic politics have produced symbolic, but more intractable tensions. One such key area that involves more radical ethno-nationalists concerns the symbolic representation of the *ethnie* and language at the national level. For several years, a dispute over whether simply to describe citizens of the country as 'Afghan' or add the ethnic identity of every citizen to the national identity card derailed a donor-funded project for rolling out a national electronic identity card (*e-taskera*).[113] Similarly, a dispute over whether to call a university *Daneshgah* (as in Dari) or *Pohantun* (its Pushto equivalent) has stirred heated debates among law makers and several protests over signs in universities. Pushtun nationalists claim that *Pohantun* and academic and military ranks, which were historically in Pushto, are national terminologies and hence must be used in both national languages of the country. Farsi speakers have demanded that their rights to use their own language in formal educational settings be equally recognised.[114]

The frequency of these disputes over political and symbolic representation indicates an increased role of ethnic identity as a category of practice among many political elites of the country.[115] However, as a category of analysis, one must be careful about sweeping generalisations about the influence of ethnicity on Afghan politics. Broad ethnic categories conceal significant intra-ethnic competition that continues to shape the meaning and nature of ethnic boundaries. Furthermore, a culture of pragmatism among political elites as well as the varied, overlapping networks of identity categories is likely to mitigate full ethnicisation of politics in the country in the foreseeable future.[116] A further push towards ethnicisation is also likely to be resisted by a younger generation of Afghans that has been exposed to globalising changes to a greater extent than any previous generations of Afghans.

Politics and insurgency

One of the curiosities of Afghan politics is that all the while that politicians plan and plot their stratagems, the ongoing problem of insurgency casts a long and dark shadow over the lives of large numbers of Afghans. For those caught up in the violence of insurgency, the political issues that often dominate elite discussion can make Kabul appear something of a bubble, detached from the challenges that baulk prominently in daily lives. A 2018 official US report, recording what was most probably a highly optimistic assessment, noted statistics from the US military suggesting that in July 2018, 34 per cent of the population was under

Afghan government 'control', 31 per cent under Afghan government 'influence', 24 per cent 'contested', 9 per cent under insurgent 'influence' and 2 per cent under insurgent 'control'.[117] It went on, however, to state that 'a district categorised as under government control or influence may continue to experience attacks or other forms of insecurity' (Table 3.2).[118] The insurgency has also been very costly in human terms, as UN data on civilian deaths from 2007 to 2018 make clear.[119]

The insurgency has taken an even heavier toll on the security forces. While data on casualties amongst the security forces are no longer regularly released by the Afghan government, historical statistics point to very substantial losses. A 2018 study from Brown University concluded that 58,596 national military and police had died between October 2001 and October 2018,[120] and in a November 2018 speech, President Ghani stated that since 2015, 28,529 members of the security forces had died.[121] At the World Economic Forum in January 2019, he offered an even higher figure of 45,000 since he had taken office.[122]

The insurgency is a complex phenomenon. Insurgencies have often been associated with the idea of peasant rebellion,[123] but this is not the case in Afghanistan. What has been called 'tribal warfare' in Afghanistan is distinctively seasonal: as the late Louis Dupree put it, one 'can't farm and fight'.[124] By contrast, the insurgency claims victims in Afghanistan the year round, and in their tactics and organisation, the insurgents are very different from disgruntled peasants. When Kunduz in the north of Afghanistan fell to the Taliban from 28 September–13 October 2015, the attackers were 'professional full-time fighters, put through rigorous training by experienced instructors in the camps in Pakistan, with uniforms, vehicles, heavy weapons, encrypted radios, and a formal command structure'.[125] And as the Taliban tightened their grip around the city of Ghazni in 2018, they made use of night vision equipment and sniper rifles to which the ANA troops on the ground did not have access.[126] Similar sophistication accompanied their attack on the city on 10 August 2018 and a subsequent 5-day occupation. This does not, however, mean that the armed opposition forces constitute an integrated hierarchy. After being scattered in 2001, the Taliban re-grouped with ISI support in Pakistan, and from around 2003 resumed attacks in Afghanistan.[127] They are nevertheless best understood as a 'network of networks',[128] albeit with some more important than others, and the so-called 'Haqqani network' one of the most destructive components.[129] Furthermore, since the death of Mullah Omar in April 2013, the movement has experienced leadership issues, including the suspicious death of Omar's successor in a US drone strike in May 2016.[130] Much to do with power relations and decision-making amongst the Taliban remains decidedly murky. The Taliban are not, however, the only brutal group on the ground. Vicious attacks, especially directed against Hazara Shia,[131] have also been mounted in Afghanistan by the so-called 'Islamic State in Khorasan',[132] or 'Daesh' (al-Dawlah al-Islamiyyah), which has made extensive use of suicide attacks of a kind that were unknown in Afghanistan before the assassination of Ahmad Shah Massoud on 9 September 2001.[133]

TABLE 3.2 Recorded number of civilian deaths by parties to the conflict

	07	08	09	10	11	12	13	14	15	16	17	18	Total
AGEs:	700	1160	1533	2041	2255	2238	2471	2677	2324	2138	2303	2243	24,083
PGFs:	629	828	588	430	528	324	354	610	628	905	745	1185	7754
Other:	194	130	291	323	350	107	144	414	613	467	390	376	3799
Total:	1523	2118	2412	2794	3133	2669	2969	3701	3565	3510	3438	3804	35,636

AGEs = Anti-government elements; PGFs = Pro-government forces.

There is little evidence that the armed insurgents enjoy high levels of genuine popularity, although this has varied over space and time, and in areas where they appear the strongest force, they may be successful in extracting prudential compliance from citizens. The Asia Foundation in 2018 addressed this issue in its annual survey of Afghan opinion. Quizzed about the Taliban, 82 per cent of respondents stated that they had 'no sympathy at all' for the Taliban; only 5 per cent expressed 'a lot of sympathy' while a further 11 per cent voiced 'a little sympathy'. Furthermore, of those who voiced sympathy, more than two-thirds did so not out of any apparent affinity with the Taliban's political agenda, but simply because they saw them as Afghans (47 per cent) or Muslims (20 per cent); only 3 per cent expressed sympathy because 'they fight against foreign forces'. Daesh proved to be even less popular: fully 96 per cent of respondents stated that they had 'no sympathy at all' for Daesh.[134] It is not mass popularity, but external funding and sanctuaries in Pakistan which make it difficult for the Afghan government and its allies to carry the fight effectively to their enemies.[135] The significance of sanctuaries of this sort in sustaining insurgency in certain cases is well documented and has been widely recognised by both politicians and analysts. President Musharraf of Pakistan admitted as much when he stated during a visit to Kabul that 'There is no doubt Afghan militants are supported from Pakistani soil. The problem that you have in your region is because support is provided from our side'.[136] Likewise, Theo Farrell and Michael Semple conclude that the Taliban leadership 'is acutely aware that its military campaign is dependent upon retaining access to Pakistani territory'.[137] This is an important issue to which we will return in Chapter 5.

That said, it is a serious mistake to interpret all conflict in Afghanistan as simply a local manifestation of the national conflict between the state and insurgents. The ground reality is considerably more complicated. In many parts of Afghanistan, one encounters patterns of rivalry and competition with pedigrees much longer than the life of either the current Afghan state or its opponents.[138] In some cases, these reflect the potency of norms of revenge[139]; in other cases, they reflect the salience of different lineages or networks to which local political actors may be attached in various ways. Resource scarcity can also be a major source of conflict at the local level, and practitioners of local politics may be constantly in search of new resources on which to draw in order to boost their standing at the expense of their competitors. It is not hard to see how actors such as the Taliban could exploit this complexity in pursuit of their own objectives, playing different local actors off against each other, and leaving the international supporters of the Afghan state thoroughly perplexed by the operational environment. In Pushtun-dominated provinces, it could even be quite unclear exactly in what guise people were speaking. No case illustrates this better than the experience in Helmand, to which British forces were deployed. Multiple actors were in competition with each other; disentangling the complexities of what was going on proved to be a huge challenge; and all too often, the international actors did not fully understand the ramifications of what they themselves were doing and of the choices they were making.[140]

Whilst sanctuaries in Pakistan provide a critical operational enabler for the Taliban, poor performance by the Afghan government has too often created a situation in which those with no affection for the Taliban nonetheless feel little inclination to side with the Afghan government against them. As an experienced US observer put it in 2013, 'President Karzai's weak government remains the Taliban's best talking point…The police are a hindrance, the bureaucrats are inefficient and corrupt, and the ministries are ineffective'.[141] As a latecomer to mass education, Afghanistan has offered a particularly accommodating environment for the flourishing of corruption,[142] and Asia Foundation survey data show that it is seen as a major problem. Some 81.5 per cent of respondents in the 2018 survey saw corruption as a major problem 'for the country', and 70.6 per cent saw it as a problem 'in their daily life'. Interestingly, in the province of Panjsher, 97.6 per cent saw corruption as a major problem in Afghanistan, but only 25.6 per cent saw it as a major problem in their daily lives,[143] which shows the limitations of perception as opposed to more concrete criteria in measuring the scale of some phenomenon. Nonetheless, from a political point of view, perception may be what matters.[144] Of course, not *all* Afghan officials by any means are corrupt; but what matters politically is that *some* are, on a grand scale, and very often the neopatrimonial system has operated to protect them from being held accountable for their behaviour. This is exactly the kind of system that can begin to encounter real problems of legitimacy that insurgents can then exploit.

It is not simply failings on the part of the Afghan state that have provided opportunities for insurgents. There is some tantalising evidence that well-intentioned aid can also have perverse effects. For example, after the United States blocked the expansion beyond Kabul of the International Security Assistance Force, states committed to assisting the Afghan government scrambled for alternative ways of doing so, and one approach which became very popular was the establishment of so-called Provincial Reconstruction Teams, or PRTs. There was no single PRT model, and a great deal of diversity marked the various PRTs in different parts of the country.[145] One common disposition on the part of contributing states, however, was to see aid injected into the contested areas where PRTs were typically to be found, as a 'force multiplier' to consolidate the security which the military sides of PRTs were designed to foster. In practice, things did not work out quite like that. A 2016 study concluded that aid reduced insurgent violence when injected into areas already controlled by the government, but had the opposite effect when injected into contested districts.[146] Externally injected resources can constitute a stake over which local groups struggle for control or influence; but more seriously, the prospect of effective development through aid can inspire insurgents to undertake more substantial attacks to ensure that no such development results.

Insurgency thus both exploits and adds to the vulnerability of actors and forces that the state cannot adequately protect, and this vulnerability in turn becomes a source of instability in diverse ways. Some relate to the vulnerability of the administrative offices of the state itself. Few areas of the state are more vulnerable than those that Migdal has called the dispersed field offices and the trenches. By definition, these parts of the state are distributed across the country, many of them relatively isolated from sources of protection or support. Yet their status as components of the state can make them attractive targets for an enemy keen to symbolise the incapacity of the upper echelons of the state to protect its distributed elements. And even if such components do not come under direct attack, they are extremely susceptible to pressure or intimidation by insurgents. The 2015 attack on Kunduz and the 2018 attack on Ghazni provide depressing examples of this vulnerability: officials of the state all too often were either absent or of limited value when prompt and decisive leadership against the insurgents was required.[147]

The ANA and ANP have also proved to be highly vulnerable, as the death toll from 2015 cited by President Ghani make clear. Several factors account for this. One was simply the changed operating environment from 2014, at which point the ANA in particular had to carry a much heavier burden of combat responsibility than when substantial numbers of foreign military personnel, and especially Special Forces from the US and some of its key allies, were deployed in the field. Furthermore, for an enemy interested in highlighting for symbolic purposes the incapacity of the Afghan state to protect its citizens, Afghanistan is a target-rich environment; the Afghan security forces simply cannot be everywhere where they might be required, as Taliban attacks on the Hazara-dominated districts of Malestan and Jaghori in November 2018 made painfully clear.[148] Two other factors, however, have also contributed to the vulnerability of the security forces, and they relate to state policies that impact on morale and cohesion. On the one hand, cohesion cannot be created by decree. It tends to arise when armed forces combine an intense overarching sense of mission with face-to-face solidarity at the level of combat units. This was a very notable attribute of elements of the *Mujahideen* during the 1980s, but is much less obvious with the ANA. On the other hand, when the high organs of the state express an interest in pursuing a negotiated settlement of ill-defined dimensions with the enemy, it does little for morale at the frontline level: why would an ANA soldier or an ANP officer want to die in battle today if a deal might be cut with the enemy tomorrow?

It is also important to note that the vulnerability of ordinary Afghans does not relate just to the threat of death or injury; it also relates to the very real danger of forced displacement, either internally or beyond Afghanistan's boundaries as refugees. Internal displacement is difficult to quantify precisely, since at any given moment some people will be on the move voluntarily rather than as a result of coercion, but there is credible evidence that internal displacement in Afghanistan is very substantial indeed.[149] And 2015, President Ghani's first full year in office, witnessed large movements to Europe of Afghan refugees, more than 200,000 in all.[150] The effect was to expose the Afghan government to considerable pressure from European governments and agencies alarmed by the influx, and its response was notably inglorious. President Ghani publicly stated that he had 'no sympathy'[151] with those fleeing the country, a remark that provoked deep anger from Afghans who lacked access to the elaborate and expensive security that the president enjoyed. As one blistering critique put it:

> Last fall, the Afghan government made a deal with the European Union that ensured the deportation of Afghan refugees. Kabul's government was granted billions of euros in aid money on the condition that it helps repatriate Afghans deported from Europe. Since then, Afghan refugees all over Europe have been thrust into a state of dread. Meanwhile, the Afghan government pretends to be in control of the country's security. According to President Ashraf Ghani, the European Union's money is needed to boost the country's economy. However, most of it might vanish in Afghanistan's corrupt political system, as has happened in the past with international aid.

The author went on to remark pointedly that 'the children of President Ghani live in the United States, while the family of Abdullah Abdullah, the country's chief executive, lives in India'.[152] The fury underlying this critique is palpable, and it serves as a reminder that a failure to empathise with the vulnerable can tarnish a leader's image very quickly.

There is of course a strong moral argument for ensuring that the vulnerable are protected, and variants of this argument have been developed with respect to both domestic political arrangements and international affairs.[153] But ultimately, there is a compelling political argument as well, and it has to do with the standing of the state in the eyes of those whose support it wishes to retain. There may be more diversity and complexity in the modern world of states than the analysis of Max Weber might have led one to expect, but Weber's realisation that citizens look to the state as a source of protection and security remains valid. It is therefore important that the actions of the state signal that it has both the capacity and the disposition to protect people who otherwise are vulnerable to attack. A state that manifestly cannot do so will likely shed support and ultimately legitimacy, for as Thomas Hobbes famously wrote, 'Reputation of power, is Power'.[154] In the politics of Afghanistan, it does not pay to look like a loser.

Notes

1 For the Dari text and a parallel English translation of the Constitution, see Nadjma Yassari (ed.), *The Shari'a in the Constitutions of Afghanistan, Iran and Egypt – Implications for Private Law* (Tübingen: Mohr Siebeck, 2005) pp. 269–329.
2 Elinor Ostrom, *Understanding Institutional Diversity* (Princeton: Princeton University Press, 2005) p. 3.
3 Nicholas Rowe, *Rules and Institutions* (New York: Philip Allan, 1989) p. 22.
4 See Barry R. Weingast, 'The political foundations of democracy and the rule of law', *American Political Science Review*, vol. 91, no. 2, June 1997, pp. 245–263.
5 On institutionalisation, see Samuel P. Huntington, *Political Order in Changing Societies* (New Haven: Yale University Press, 1968). On consolidation, see Andreas Schedler, 'What is democratic consolidation?', *Journal of Democracy*, vol. 9. no. 2, April 1998, pp. 91–107.

6 See Archie Brown, *The Myth of the Strong Leader: Political Leadership in the Modern Age* (London: The Bodley Head, 2014).

7 See Nils B. Weidmann and Michael Callen, 'Violence and election fraud: Evidence from Afghanistan', *British Journal of Political Science*, vol. 43, no. 1, January 2013, pp. 53–75 at p. 74.

8 See William Maley and Michael Maley, 'Appraising electoral fraud: Tensions and complexities', *Conflict, Security and Development*, vol. 16, no. 6, November 2016, pp. 653–671; Thomas H. Johnson, 'The myth of Afghan electoral democracy: The irregularities of the 2014 presidential election', *Small Wars and Insurgencies*, vol. 29, no. 5–6, 2018, pp. 1006–1039.

9 See Roger Hermiston, *All Behind You, Winston: Churchill's Great Coalition 1940–45* (London: Aurum Press, 2016).

10 See Joshua Partlow, *A Kingdom of Their Own: The Family Karzai and the Afghan Disaster* (New York: Alfred A. Knopf, 2016).

11 Ashraf Ghani and Clare Lockhart, *Fixing Failed States: A Framework for Rebuilding a Fractured World* (New York: Oxford University Press, 2008).

12 See Dov S. Zakheim, *A Vulcan's Tale: How the Bush Administration Mismanaged the Reconstruction of Afghanistan* (Washington, DC: Brookings Institution Press, 2011); Conor Keane, *US Nation-Building in Afghanistan* (New York: Routledge, 2016).

13 See Marvin G. Weinbaum, 'Afghanistan: Nonparty parliamentary democracy', *Journal of Developing Areas*, vol. 7, no. 1, October 1972, pp. 57–74; Marvin G. Weinbaum, 'The legislator as intermediary: Integration of the center and periphery in Afghanistan', in Albert F. Eldridge (ed.), *Legislatures in Plural Societies: The Search for Cohesion in National Development* (Durham: Duke University Press, 1977) pp. 95–121.

14 For more detailed discussion of SNTV, see Andrew Reynolds and John Carey, *Fixing Afghanistan's Electoral System: Arguments and Options for Reform* (Kabul: Afghanistan Research and Evaluation Unit, July 2012).

15 See Anna Wordsworth, *A Matter of Interests: Gender and the Politics of Presence in Afghanistan's Wolesi Jirga* (Kabul; Afghanistan Research and Evaluation Unit, June 2007); Lauryn Oates, *A Closer Look: The Policy and Lawmaking Behind the Shiite Personal Status Law* (Kabul: Afghanistan Research and Evaluation Unit, September 2009).

16 See T.H. Rigby, 'Bureaucratic politics: An introduction', *Public Administration*, vol. 32, no. 1, March 1973, pp. 1–20.

17 See Sarah Parkinson, *Means to What End? Policymaking and State-Building in Afghanistan* (Kabul: Afghanistan Research and Evaluation Unit, November 2010).

18 *Afghanistan—State Building, Sustaining Growth, and Reducing Poverty* (Washington, DC: The World Bank, 2005) p. 47.

19 See Ashraf Ghani, 'Afghanistan: Administration', in Ehsan Yarshater (ed.), *Encyclopædia Iranica*, Vol. I (London: Routledge & Kegan Paul, 1985) pp. 558–564.

20 For recent discussions, see Ivan Arreguín-Toft, 'The meaning of "state failure": Public service, public servants and the contemporary Afghan state', *International Area Studies Review*, vol. 15, no. 3, September 2012, pp. 263–278; Mirwais Ayobi and Haroun Rahimi, *A Study of Afghanistan's Organization and Structure of Public Administration under the 2004 Constitution* (Kabul: Afghanistan Research and Evaluation Unit, December 2018).

21 K.C. Wheare, *Federal Government* (London: Oxford University Press, 1963) p. 10.

22 For a detailed listing of these provincial and district units, see *Shenasnamah-e mukhtasar-e adarat-e mahali Afghanistan* (Kabul: Islamic Republic of Afghanistan, 2018).

23 See Thomas J. Barfield, 'Weak links on a rusty chain: Structural weaknesses in Afghanistan's provincial government administration', in M. Nazif Shahrani and Robert L. Canfield (eds.), *Revolutions and Rebellions in Afghanistan: Anthropological Perspectives*, (Berkeley: Institute of International Studies, University of California, 1984) pp. 170–184.

24 See Hamish Nixon, *Subnational State-Building in Afghanistan* (Kabul: Afghanistan Research and Evaluation Unit, April 2008).

25 James N. Rosenau, 'Governance, order, and change in world politics', in James N. Rosenau and Ernst-Otto Czempiel (eds.), *Governance without Government: Order and Change in World Politics* (Cambridge: Cambridge University Press, 1992) pp. 1–29 at pp. 4–5.

26 See Elinor Ostrom, *Governing the Commons: The Evolution of Institutions for Collective Action* (Cambridge: Cambridge University Press, 1990).

27 Jennifer Brick Murtazashvili, *Informal Order and the State in Afghanistan* (Cambridge: Cambridge University Press, 2016) p. 250.

28 See M. Nazif Shahrani, 'The future of the state and the structure of community governance in Afghanistan', in William Maley (ed.), *Fundamentalism Reborn? Afghanistan and the Taliban* (London: Hurst & Co., 1998) pp. 212–242; M. Nazif Shahrani, 'The state and community self-governance: Paths to stability and human security in post-2014 Afghanistan', in Srinjoy Bose, Nishank Motwani and William Maley (eds.), *Afghanistan – Challenges and Prospects* (London: Routledge, 2018) pp. 43–62.

29 *A Survey of the Afghan People: Afghanistan in 2018* (Kabul: The Asia Foundation, 2018) p. 120.

30 See Whit Mason (ed.), *The Rule of Law in Afghanistan: Missing in Inaction* (Cambridge: Cambridge University Press, 2011); John Braithwaite and Ali Wardak, 'Crime and war in Afghanistan. Part I: The Hobbesian solution', *British Journal of Criminology*, vol. 53, no. 2, March 2013, pp. 179–196; Ali Wardak and John Braithwaite, 'Crime and war in Afghanistan. Part II: A Jeffersonian alternative?', *British Journal of Criminology*, vol. 53, no. 2, March 2013, pp. 197–214; William Maley, 'State strength and the rule of law', in Srinjoy Bose, Nishank Motwani and William Maley (eds.), *Afghanistan – Challenges and Prospects* (London: Routledge, 2018) pp. 63–77.

31 See Ghizaal Haress, *Judicial Review in Afghanistan: A Flawed Practice* (Kabul: Afghanistan Research and Evaluation Unit, August 2017).

32 *Operation Freedom's Sentinel: Lead Inspector General Report to the United States Congress January 1, 2019 – March 31, 2019* (Washington, DC: Department of Defense, 2019) p. 33.

33 See Antonio Giustozzi, *The Army of Afghanistan: A Political History of a Fragile Institution* (London: Hurst & Co., 2016) pp. 131–147.

34 See Martin Loicano and Craig C. Felker, 'In our own image: Training the Afghan national security forces', in Aaron B. O'Connell (ed.), *Our Latest Longest War: Losing Hearts and Minds in Afghanistan* (Chicago: University of Chicago Press, 2017) pp. 109–130; Antonio Giustozzi with Peter Quentin, *The Afghan National Army: Sustainability Challenges beyond Financial Aspects* (Kabul: Afghanistan Research and Evaluation Unit, February 2014).

35 See Amos Perlmutter, 'The praetorian state and the praetorian army: Toward a taxonomy of civil-military relations in developing polities', *Comparative Politics*, vol. 1, no. 3, April 1969, pp. 382–404.

36 *Operation Freedom's Sentinel: Lead Inspector General Report to the United States Congress*, p. 33.

37 See Alice E. Hills, 'The policing of fragmented states', *Low Intensity Conflict and Law Enforcement*, vol. 5, no. 3, Winter 1996, pp. 334–354.

38 See Andrew Wilder, *Cops or Robbers?: The Struggle to Reform the Afghan National Police* (Kabul: Afghanistan Research and Evaluation Unit, July 2007); Tonita Murray, 'Security sector reform in Afghanistan, 2002–2011: An overview of a flawed process', *International Studies*, vol. 48, no. 1, January 2011, pp. 43–63; Antonio Giustozzi and Mohammed Isaqzadeh, *Policing Afghanistan: The Politics of the Lame Leviathan* (London: Hurst & Co., 2013).

39 Pashtoon Atif, 'The impact of culture on policing in Afghanistan', in Aaron B. O'Connell (ed.), *Our Latest Longest War: Losing Hearts and Minds in Afghanistan* (Chicago: University of Chicago Press, 2017) pp. 131–155 at pp. 132–133.

40 Taimoor Shah and Mujib Mashal, 'Taliban Assassinate Afghan Police Chief Ahead Of Elections', *The New York Times*, 18 October 2018. One of Raziq's predecessors as Chief of Police in Kandahar, Akram Khakrezwal, was also assassinated: see Sarah Chayes, *The Punishment of Virtue: Inside Afghanistan after the Taliban* (New York: Penguin, 2006).

41 *A Survey of the Afghan People: Afghanistan in 2018*, pp. 258–259.

42 See Brian Chapman, *Police State* (Basingstoke: Macmillan, 1971).

43 Timor Sharan, 'The dynamics of informal political networks and statehood in post-2001 Afghanistan: A case study of the 2010–2011 special election court crisis,' *Central Asian Survey*, vol. 32, no. 3, September 2013, pp. 336–352 at p. 336. For further details of Sharan's arguments, see Timor Sharan, 'The dynamics of elite networks and patron-client relations in Afghanistan', *Europe-Asia Studies*, vol. 63, no. 6, August 2011, pp. 1109–1127; Timor Sharan, *Dawlat-e shabakahi: Rabeteh-i qodrat wa sarwat dar Afghanistan pas az sal-e 2001* (Kabul: Vazhah Publications, 2017); Timor Sharan, 'Webs and spiders: Four decades of violence, intervention, and statehood in Afghanistan (1978–2016)', in M. Nazif Shahrani (ed.), *Modern Afghanistan: The Impact of 40 Years of War* (Bloomington: Indiana University Press, 2018) pp. 102–120.

44 Sharan, 'The Dynamics of Informal Political Networks and Statehood in Post-2001 Afghanistan', p. 337.

45 See Gilles Dorronsoro, *Revolution Unending: Afghanistan, 1979 to the Present* (New York: Columbia University Press, 2005) pp. 93–136.

46 See Abdulkader H. Sinno, *Organizations at War in Afghanistan and Beyond* (Ithaca: Cornell University Press, 2008).

47 Niamatullah Ibrahimi, *Ideology without Leadership: The rise and decline of Maoism in Afghanistan* (Kabul: Thematic Report no.03/3012, Afghanistan Analysts Network, August 2012).

48 Anna Larson, *Afghanistan's New Democratic Parties: A Means to Organise Democratisation?* (Kabul: Afghanistan Research and Evaluation Unit, March 2009).

49 The first of these was *Hezb-e Afghanistan Naween*, which backed the candidacy of Younus Qanuni in the 2004 presidential elections. Similarly, *Jabh-e Milli Afghanistan* backed the candidacy of Abdullah Abdullah in the 2009 presidential elections.

50 See Niamatullah Ibrahimi, *The Dissipation of Political Capital Among Afghanistan's Hazaras: 2001–2009* (London: Working Paper no.51, Crisis States Research Centre, London School of Economics and Political Science, June 2009).

51 See Robert Peszkowski, *Reforming Jombesh: An Afghan Party on its Winding Path to Internal Democracy* (Kabul: Afghanistan Analysts Network, August 2012).

52 Srinjoy Bose and Niamatullah Ibrahimi, 'Afghanistan's Political Parties: A Tale of Incomplete Reform and Transformation,' in Srinjoy Bose, Nishank Motwani and William Maley (eds.), *Afghanistan – Challenges and Prospects* (London: Routledge, 2018) pp. 122–139; Anna Larson, *Political Parties in Afghanistan* (Washington, DC: Special Report no.362, United States Institute of Peace, March 2015) p. 3.

53 *Political Parties in Afghanistan* (Kabul/Brussels: International Crisis Group, June 2005) pp. 11–12.

54 Andrew Reynolds and John Carey, *Fixing Afghanistan's Electoral System: Arguments and Options for Reform* (Kabul: Afghanistan Research and Evaluation Unit, July 2012).

55 See Weinbaum, 'Afghanistan: Nonparty Parliamentary Democracy'.

56 John MacKinlay, 'Defining warlords', *International Peacekeeping*, vol. 7 no. 1, November 2007, pp. 48–62 at p. 48.

57 For a review of the literature on warlords and warlordism see Antonio Giustozzi, *The Debate on Warlordism: The Importance of Military Legitimacy* (London: Discussion Paper no. 13, Crisis States Research Centre, London School of Economics and Political Science 2005). For discussion of further specific Afghan cases, see Dipali Mukhopadhyay, *Warlords, Strongman Governors and the State in Afghanistan* (New York: Cambridge University Press, 2014).

58 Roger MacGinty, 'Warlords and the liberal peace: Statebuilding in Afghanistan', *Conflict, Security and Development*, vol. 10, no. 4, August 2010, pp. 577–598 at p. 584.

59 See Gilles Dorronsoro and Chantal Lobato, 'The militias in Afghanistan', *Central Asian Survey*, vol. 8, no. 4, 1989, pp. 95–108.

60 Antonio Giustozzi and Noor Ullah, *'Tribes' and Warlords in Southern Afghanistan, 1980–2005* (London: Crisis States Research Centre, London School of Economics and Political Science, September 2006).

61 See *'Killing you is a very easy thing for us': Human rights abuses in Southeast Afghanistan* (New York: Human Rights Watch, 2003).

62 Barry Bearak, 'Two Afghan Paths: Warlord or Professor', *The New York Times*, 11 May 2002.

63 Abdul Waheed Wafa, '32 Killed in Factional Fighting in Western Afghanistan', *The New York Times*, 23 October 2006.

64 Mujib Mashal, 'The President, the Strongman, and the Next U.S. Headache in Afghanistan', *The New York Times*, 15 January 2018.

65 See Caroline A. Hartzell, *Missed Opportunities: The Impact of DDR on SSR in Afghanistan* (Washington, DC: Special Report no. 270, United States Institute of Peace, April 2011); *Afghanistan: Getting Disarmament Back on Track* (Kabul/Brussels: International Crisis Group, February 2015).

66 Martine van Bijlert, *Between Discipline and Discretion: Policies Surrounding Senior Subnational Appointments* (Kabul: Afghanistan Research and Evaluation Unit, May 2009).

67 Matthieu Aikins, 'Our Man in Kandahar,' *The Atlantic*, November 2011.

68 Paul McGeough, 'Who Killed Australia's Warlord in Afghanistan?', *The Sydney Morning Herald*, 26 June 2015. See also Susanne Schmeidl, *The Man who would be King: The Challenges to Strengthening Governance in Uruzgan* (The Hague: Netherlands Institute of International Relation *Clingendael*, 2010).

69 Azam Ahmed, 'Powerful Afghan Police Chief is Killed in Targeted Suicide Attack', *The New York Times*, 20 March 2015.

70 Doug McAdam, Sidney Tarrow, and Charles Tilly, *Dynamics of Contention* (Cambridge: Cambridge University Press, 2004) p. 5.

71 Charles Tilly, *Regimes and Repertoires* (Chicago: University of Chicago Press, 2006) pp. 30–59.

72 Mir Ghulam Muhammad Ghubar, *Afghanistan dar masir-e tarikh* (Kabul: Maiwand Publishers, 2014) pp. 718–720.

73 Weinbaum, 'Afghanistan: Nonparty Parliamentary Democracy'.

74 For a discussion of Afghanistan's political parties during this period and their subsequent development, see Thomas Ruttig, *Islamists, Leftists – and a Void in the Center: Afghanistan's Political Parties and where they come from (1902–2006)* (Kabul: Konrad Adenauer Stiftung, 2006).

75 Saif R. Samady, *Education and Afghan Society in the Twentieth Century* (Paris: UNESCO, November 2001) p. 29.

76 Sabahuddin Koshkaki, *Dahe qanun-e asasi* (Islamabad: Shura-i saqafati jihad-e Afghanistan, 1986) pp. 121–140.

77 The figure for 1999 includes primary school students only. See Samady, *Education and Afghan Society in the Twentieth Century*, p. 23.

78 *Afghanistan Statistical Yearbook, 2017–18* (Kabul: National Statistics and Information Authority, August 2018), p. 1.

79 Ibid.

80 For a comparative analysis of the main protest movements of this period, see Srinjoy Bose, Nematullah Bizhan and Niamatullah Ibrahimi, *Youth Protest Movements in Afghanistan: Seeking Voice and Agency* (Washington, DC: Peaceworks, United States Institute of Peace, January 2019).

81 Jeaniene Spink, 'Education and politics in Afghanistan: The importance of an education system in peacebuilding and reconstruction', *Journal of Peace Education*, vol. 2, no. 2, 2005, pp. 195–207.

82 See Tejendra Pherali and Arif Sahar, 'Learning in the chaos: A political economy analysis of education in Afghanistan', *Research in Comparative and International Education*, vol. 13, no. 2, 2018, pp. 239–258; Antonio Giustozzi and Ali Mohammad Ali, *Reaching Boiling Point: High School Activism in Afghanistan* (Kabul: Afghanistan Research and Evaluation Unit, October 2015).

83 *Afghanistan Statistical Yearbook, 2017–18*, p. 41.

84 Robert Mackey, 'Afghan Protesters Demand Justice for Woman Killed by Mob', *The New York Times*, 24 March 2015. See also Niamatullah Ibrahimi, 'Rumor and collective action frames: An assessment of how competing conceptions of gender, culture and rule of law shaped responses to rumor and violence in Afghanistan', *Studies in Conflict and Terrorism* (forthcoming, 2019).

85 *Special Report: Attack on a Peaceful Demonstration in Kabul, 23 July 2016* (Kabul: United Nations Assistance Mission in Afghanistan, October 2016); See also Bose, Bizhan and Ibrahimi *Youth Protest Movements in Afghanistan*.

86 Richard N. Lebow, *National Identities and International Relations* (Cambridge: Cambridge University Press, 2016) p. 7

87 Rogers Brubaker and Frederick Cooper, 'Beyond "Identity"', *Theory and Society*, vol. 29, no. 1, February 2000, pp. 1–47; See also Rogers Brubaker, 'Categories of analysis and categories of practice: A note on the study of Muslims in European countries of immigration', *Ethnic and Racial Studies*, vol. 36, no. 1, 2013, pp. 1–8.

88 See Nancy Hatch Dupree, 'Revolutionary rhetoric and Afghan women', in M. Nazif Shahrani and Robert L. Canfield (eds.), *Revolutions and Rebellions in Afghanistan: Anthropological Perspectives* (Berkeley: Institute of International Studies, University of California, 1984) pp. 306–340.

89 See William Maley, 'Women and public policy in Afghanistan: A comment', *World Development*, vol. 24, no. 1, January 1996, pp. 203–206.

90 Niloufar Pourzand, 'The problematic of female education, ethnicity and national identity in Afghanistan (1920–1999)', *Social Analysis: The International Journal of Social and Cultural Practice*, vol. 43, no. 1, March 1999, pp. 73–82.

91 For careful exploration of these issues, see Julie Billaud, *Kabul Carnival: Gender Politics in Postwar Afghanistan* (Philadelphia: University of Pennsylvania Press, 2015); Torunn Wimpelmann, *The Pitfalls of Protection: Gender, Violence, and Power in Afghanistan* (Oakland: University of California Press, 2017).

92 See Elizabeth Cameron and Jorrit Kamminga, *Behind Closed Doors: The Risk of Denying Women a Voice in Determining Afghanistan's Future* (Oxford: Oxfam International, 2014).

93 See Jenny Nordberg, *The Underground Girls of Kabul: In Search of a Hidden Resistance in Afghanistan* (New York: Penguin Random House, 2014).

94 See Cornelia Vikan, 'Responsibility in complex conflicts: An Afghan case', *Journal of Military Ethics*, vol. 16, nos. 3–4, 2017, pp. 239–255.

95 See Sayed Jalal Shajjan, 'The revised Afghanistan criminal code: An end for Bacha Bazi?', *South Asia@LSE*, 24 January 2018.

96 See Joseph Goldstein, 'U.S. Soldiers Told to Ignore Sexual Abuse of Boys by Afghan Allies', *The New York Times*, 20 September 2015; Alex Horton, 'Pentagon Tried to Block Independent Report on Child Sex among Afghan Forces, Senate Office says', *The Washington Post*, 26 November 2017.

97 Erwin Orywal, *Die ethnischen Gruppen Afghanistans: Fallstudien zu Gruppenidentität und Intergruppenbeziehungen* (Wiesbaden: Dr. Ludwig Reichert Verlag, 1986).

98 Louis Dupree, *Afghanistan* (Princeton: Princeton University Press, 1980) pp. 58–64.

99 For a discussion of *qawm*, see Barnett R. Rubin, *The Fragmentation of Afghanistan: State Formation and Collapse in the International System* (New Haven: Yale University Press, 2002) pp. 25–28.

100 Vartan Gregorian, 'Mahmud Tarzi and Saraj-ol-Akhbar: Ideology of nationalism and modernization in Afghanistan', *Middle East Journal*, vol. 21, no. 3, Summer 1967, pp. 345–368, at p. 347.

101 Anthony Hyman, 'Nationalism in Afghanistan', *International Journal of Middle East Studies*, vol. 34, no. 2, May 2002, pp. 299–315 at p. 299.

102 For a review of the historiography of this period see Senzil Nawid, 'Writing national history: Afghan historiography in the twentieth century', in Nile Green (ed.), *Afghan History Through Afghan Eyes* (London: Hurst & Co., 2015) pp. 185–210.

103 For example, see Mohammad Ali, *Aryana or Ancient Afghanistan* (Kabul: Afghanistan Historical Society, 1963).

104 For a discussion of how both Afghan government and various ethnic groups contested sub-national geographical identities see Conrad Schetter, 'Ethnoscapes, national territorialisation and the Afghan war', *Geopolitics*, vol. 10, no. 1, 2005, pp. 50–75.

105 See Antonio Giustozzi, 'Ethnicity and politics in Afghanistan: The role played by Setam-e Melli', in Micheline Centlivres-Demont (ed.), *Afghanistan: Identity, Society and Politics since 1980* (London: I.B. Tauris, 2015) pp. 151–153.

106 See Olivier Roy, *Islam and Resistance in Afghanistan* (Cambridge: Cambridge University Press, 1990).

107 See William Maley, 'The United Nations and ethnic conflict management: Lessons from the disintegration of Yugoslavia', *Nationalities Papers*, vol. 25, no. 3, September 1997, pp. 559–573.

108 See Nassim Jawad, *Afghanistan: A Nation of Minorities* (London: Minority Rights Group, 1992).

109 Consociational democracy as a system of government for divided societies was introduced to academia by Lijphart: see Arend Lijphart, 'Consociational democracy', *World Politics*, vol. 21, no. 2, January 1969, pp. 207–225.

110 For broader assessment of debates on consociational democracy, see Donald L. Horowitz, 'Ethnic power sharing: Three big problems', *Journal of Democracy*, vol. 25, no. 2, April 2014, pp. 5–20; Rudy B. Andeweg, 'Consociational Democracy', *Annual Review of Political Science*, vol. 3, 2000, pp. 509–536.

111 See Niamatullah Ibrahimi, 'Framing ethnicity under conditions of uncertainty: The case of Hazaras during Afghanistan's 2014 presidential elections', *Conflict, Security and Development,* vol. 16, no. 6, November 2016, pp. 635–652.

112 Arif Sahar, 'Ethnicizing masses in post-Bonn Afghanistan: The case of the 2004 and 2009 presidential elections', *Asian Journal of Political Science*, vol. 22, no. 3, August 2014, pp. 289–314; Arif Sahar and Aqila Sahar, 'Press and ethnic polarization in post-2001 Afghanistan: The 2014 presidential election experience', *Central Asian Survey*, vol. 35, no. 1, 2016, pp. 105–120.

113 Hamid Shalizi, 'Who is an Afghan? Row over ID Cards Fuels Ethnic Tension', *Reuters*, 8 February 2018; Azam Ahmed and Habib Zahor, 'Afghan Ethnic Tensions Rise in Media and Politics', *The New York Times*, 18 February 2018.

114 See Lutz Rzehak, *How to Name Universities or: Any Linguistic Problem in Afghanistan?* (Kabul: Afghanistan Analysts Network, 17 May 2012).

115 Conrad Schetter, 'Playing the ethnic card: On the ethnicization of Afghan politics', *Studies in Ethnicity and Nationalism*, vol. 16, no. 3, December 2016, pp. 460–477.

116 Thomas Barfield, 'Afghanistan is not the Balkans: Ethnicity and its political consequences from a Central Eurasian perspective', *Central Eurasian Studies Review*, vol. 4, no. 1, 2005, pp. 1–8.

117 *Operation Freedom's Sentinel: Lead Inspector General Report to the United States Congress*, p. 16.

118 Ibid., p. 17.

119 These data are extracted from *Civilian Casualties during 2007* (Kabul: United Nations Assistance Mission in Afghanistan, 2008) p. 1; *Afghanistan: Annual Report on Protection of Civilians in Armed Conflict, 2008* (Kabul: Human Rights Unit, United Nations Assistance Mission in Afghanistan, January 2009) p. ii; *Afghanistan: Protection of Civilians in Armed Conflict. Annual Report 2017* (Kabul: United Nations Assistance Mission in Afghanistan and United Nations Human Rights Office of the High Commissioner, February 2018) p. 5; *Afghanistan: Protection of Civilians in Armed Conflict. Annual Report 2018* (Kabul: United Nations Assistance Mission in Afghanistan and United Nations Human Rights Office of the High Commissioner, February 2019) pp. 1,4,5.

120 Neta C. Crawford, *Human Cost of the Post-9/11 Wars: Lethality and the Need for Transparency* (Providence: Watson Institute of Public and International Affairs, Brown University, November 2018) p. 1.

121 Rod Nordland and Fahim Abed, 'Afghan Leader Confirms More Than 28,000 Military Deaths Since 2015', *The New York Times*, 17 November 2018.

122 Taimoor Shah and Fahim Abed, 'Airstrikes in Taliban Area Kill 29 Afghans Despite Peace Talks', *The New York Times*, 25 January 2019.

123 See Raj Desai and Harry Eckstein, 'Insurgency: The transformation of peasant rebellion', *World Politics*, vol. 42, no. 4, July 1990, pp. 441–465.

124 Louis Dupree, 'Post-withdrawal Afghanistan: Light at the end of the tunnel', in Amin Saikal and William Maley (eds.), *The Soviet Withdrawal from Afghanistan* (Cambridge: Cambridge University Press, 1989) pp. 29–51 at p. 30.

125 David Kilcullen, *Blood Year: Islamic State and the Failures of the War on Terror* (Melbourne: BlackInc., 2016) p. 177.

126 Ehsan Qaane, *The Insecure Spring of Ghazni: Results of Third-grade Treatment by the Centre?* (Kabul: Afghanistan Analysts Network, 25 July 2018).

127 See Antonio Giustozzi, *Koran, Kalashnikov and Laptop: The Neo-Taliban Insurgency in Afghanistan* (London: Hurst & Co., 2007); Amin Tarzi, 'The Neo-Taliban', in Robert D. Crews and Amin Tarzi (eds.), *The Taliban and the Crisis of Afghanistan* (Cambridge: Harvard University Press, 2008) pp. 274–310; Antonio Giustozzi (ed.), *Decoding the New Taliban: Insights from the Afghan Field* (London: Hurst & Co., 2009).

128 See Thomas Ruttig, 'How Tribal are the Taliban?', in Shahzad Bashir and Robert D. Crews (eds.), *Under the Drones: Modern Lives in the Afghanistan-Pakistan Borderlands* (Cambridge: Harvard University Press, 2012) pp. 102–135.

129 See Vahid Brown and Don Rassler, *Fountainhead of Jihad: The Haqqani Nexus, 1973–2012* (New York: Oxford University Press, 2013).

130 See Carlotta Gall and Ruhullah Khapalwak, 'Taliban Leader Feared Pakistan Before He Was Killed', *The New York Times*, 9 August 2017.

131 Alissa J. Rubin, 'Questions Rebels Use to Tell Sunni from Shiite', *The New York Times*, 24 June 2014.

132 On this force, see Antonio Giustozzi, *The Islamic State in Khorasan: Afghanistan, Pakistan and the New Central Asian Jihad* (London: Hurst & Co., 2018).

133 See David B. Edwards, *Caravan of Martyrs: Sacrifice and Suicide Bombing in Afghanistan* (Oakland: University of California Press, 2017).

134 *A Survey of the Afghan People: Afghanistan in 2018*, pp. 274, 276.

135 See Seth G. Jones, *Waging Insurgent Warfare: Lessons from the Vietcong to the Islamic State* (New York: Oxford University Press, 2017) p. 149. On external funding of the Taliban, see Antonio Giustozzi, *The Taliban at War 2001–2018* (London: Hurst & Co., 2019).

136 See Taimoor Shah and Carlotta Gall, 'Afghan Rebels Find Aid in Pakistan, Musharraf Admits', *The New York Times*, 13 August 2007.

137 Theo Farrell and Michael Semple, 'Making Peace with the Taliban', *Survival*, vol. 57, no. 6, December 2015–January 2016, pp. 79–110 at p. 92.

138 See Conrad Schetter (ed.), *Local Politics in Afghanistan: A Century of Intervention in the Social Order* (London: Hurst & Co., 2013).

139 See Jon Elster, 'Norms of Revenge', *Ethics*, vol. 100, no. 4, July 1990, pp. 862–885.

140 See Mike Martin, *An Intimate War: An Oral History of the Helmand Conflict* (London: Hurst & Co., 2014) pp. 234–240; Theo Farrell, *Unwinnable: Britain's War in Afghanistan 2001–2014* (London: The Bodley Head, 2017).

141 Joseph J. Collins, *Understanding the War in Afghanistan* (New York: Skyhorse Publishing, 2013) p. 92.

142 See Eric M. Uslaner, *The Historical Roots of Corruption: Mass Education, Economic Inequality, and State Capacity* (Cambridge: Cambridge University Press, 2017).

143 *A Survey of the Afghan People: Afghanistan in 2018*, pp. 116, 117.

144 See Robert Jervis, *Perception and Misperception in International Politics* (Princeton: Princeton University Press, 1976).

145 See William Maley and Susanne Schmeidl (eds), *Reconstructing Afghanistan: Civil-Military Experiences in Comparative Perspective* (London: Routledge, 2015).

146 Renard Sexton, 'Aid as a tool against insurgency: Evidence from Contested and controlled territory in Afghanistan', *American Political Science Review*, vol. 110, no. 4, November 2016, pp. 731–749.

147 See Obaid Ali, *The 2015 Insurgency in the North (3): The fall and recapture of Kunduz* (Kabul: Afghanistan Analysts Network, 16 October 2015); Fazal Muzhary, *Unheeded Warnings (1): Looking Back at the Taleban Attack on Ghazni* (Kabul: Afghanistan Analysts Network, 16 December 2018).

148 See Niamatullah Ibrahimi and William Maley, 'Afghanistan: the Hazaras are not safe', *The Interpreter*, 26 November 2018.

149 See Susanne Schmeidl, 'Internal displacement in Afghanistan: The tip of the iceberg', in Srinjoy Bose, Nishank Motwani and William Maley (eds), *Afghanistan – Challenges and Prospects* (London: Routledge, 2018) pp. 169–187.

150 William Maley, *What is a Refugee?* (New York: Oxford University Press, 2016) p. 1. For more background see Chona R. Echavez, Jennefer Lyn L. Bagaporo, Leah Wilfreda RE Pilongo, and Shukria Azadmanesh, *Why do children undertake the unaccompanied journey? Motivations for departure to Europe and other industrialised countries from the perspectives of children, families and residents of sending communities in Afghanistan* (Kabul: Afghanistan Research and Evaluation Unit, December 2014); Antonio Donini, Alessandro Monsutti and Giulia Scalettaris, *Afghans on the Move: Seeking Protection and Refuge in Europe. "In this journey I died several times; In Afghanistan you only die once"* (Geneva: Global Migration Research Paper no. 17, Global Migration Centre, 2016); Hameed Hakimi and Barin S. Haymon, *The Voices behind the Refugee Outflow from Afghanistan* (Barcelona: Barcelona Centre for International Affairs, 2016).

151 Yalda Hakim, 'President Ghani calls for Afghans to Remain in Country', *BBC News*, 31 March 2016.

152 Emran Feroz, 'Forced Home to a War Zone', *The New York Times*, 6 June 2017.

153 See Robert E. Goodin, *Protecting the Vulnerable: A Reanalysis of our Social Responsibilities* (Chicago: University of Chicago Press, 1986); Ian Clark, *The Vulnerable in International Society* (Oxford: Oxford University Press, 2013).

154 Thomas Hobbes, *Leviathan* (Cambridge: Cambridge University Press, 1996) p. 62.

4

THE AFGHAN ECONOMY

Political factors contribute significantly to the stability of the state. So do economic factors. For centuries, scholars have been concerned with how factors of production – land, labour, capital (that is, produced means of production), enterprise and technology – have been exploited to better the lives of some or all the members of communities, not least through specialisation in production processes, and the enhancement of exchange and trade. In the eighteenth century, figures such as Bernard Mandeville and Adam Smith reflected on the ways in which self-interest contributed to economic processes, with Smith famously deploying the metaphor of an 'invisible hand' at work. It is not, he wrote in 1776, 'from the benevolence of the butcher, the brewer or the baker, that we expect our dinner, but from their regard to their own self interest'.[1] 'Economics', a later scholar wrote, 'is the science which studies human behaviour as a relationship between ends and scarce means which have alternative uses'.[2] While this may seem somewhat abstract, it captures the way in which choices about the allocation of resources are of fundamental importance to the character of a society. Economics has become a complex, diverse and in some respects highly technical discipline, with its own complicated sub-fields – macroeconomics, microeconomics, welfare economics, behavioural economics, mathematical economics, econometrics and many others. Furthermore, as in political theory, significant divergence of opinion has marked economic thought – for example, on the issue of the respective roles of states and markets in determining resource allocations, with arguments for more centralised state planning competing with arguments for the use of markets, based on exchangeable private property rights, as a way of making efficient use of information and encouraging innovation.[3] And in a neopatrimonial system, one would need to add networks to markets and state instrumentalities as determinants of resource allocations.[4] Different schools of thought – classical, neoclassical, Keynesian, Austrian – have proliferated over time, although within all of these schools there have historically been important variations in focus and emphasis.

Economic factors contribute significantly to how people see the world around them. In 2018, The Asia Foundation in reporting the results of its annual survey of Afghan opinion recorded that

> Among the 61.3% of Afghans who think the country is moving in the wrong direction, a majority cite economic issues such as unemployment (23.7%), a bad economy (12.1%), and high prices (3.6%). When asked about the biggest problems facing youth, more than three-fourths of respondents (87.4%) cite economic concerns, and this holds true regardless of gender, place of residence, or ethnicity.[5]

In the light of the complexities noted above, a whole book could easily be devoted to economic aspects of Afghanistan's contemporary experience, and it is therefore necessary to be somewhat selective. In this chapter, we focus on five particular areas of significance for contemporary Afghanistan. The first section deals with issues of aid, budgeting and finance. Moving to the so-called 'real economy', the second explores the relations between businessmen, entrepreneurs and the state. The third investigates the complex challenges faced by Afghan agriculture and the rural sector. The fourth, recognising that not all areas of economic activity are legal, discusses the issue of opium cultivation, and the fifth looks at the relationship of the Afghan economy to the wider world.

Aid, budgeting and finance

One myth that one often encounters is that at various stages in the last four decades, the Afghan economy has 'collapsed'. This misses the point that through-out this period, the bulk of the Afghan population has been inside the country, not outside, and has survived not on the strength of foreign aid or state policy, but on the basis of the circular flow of income in an economy that may have been dysfunctional, but nonetheless proved capable of meeting the day-to-day needs of millions of people. One reason for this was that Islamic law provided a social basis for contracts to be honoured, and that therefore trade and exchange per-sisted as economic activities in addition to production.[6] But that said, the Bonn Agreement, simply by setting the scene for the establishment of the ministries of finance, commerce and economics, created expectations of a more activist state than Afghanistan had experienced for over a decade. And the only realistic source in the short-to-medium term for funds to sustain such a state was foreign aid. The burden of aid dependency has haunted Afghanistan ever since. We have already discussed some of the consequences of the development of a rentier state before 1978; in the post-2001 period, the effects of aid dependency were even more dramatic, in effect contributing to a 'sovereignty gap' as donors decided how the monies that they were supplying to the Afghan government should be spent.[7]

Quantifying the exact amount of aid that has gone into Afghanistan since 2001 is difficult, partly for definitional reasons – how should foreign military and Provincial Reconstruction Teams (PRTs) spending be classified? – and partly because of the diverse channels through which funds have flowed. What is indisputable, however, is that many billions of dollars have been transferred. A December 2017 United States analysis concluded that the US had supplied approximately US$111 billion since the overthrow of the Taliban, about 60 per cent of it to train and equip the ANA and ANP.[8] World Bank data (using constant 2015 US dollars) state that net official development assistance and official aid received from 2002 to 2016 totalled $65.094 billion.[9] Afghan government data record that from 2009–2010 to 2016–2017, 'committed' aid totalled US$54.149 billion, while 'disbursed' aid totalled US$35.222 billion, or 65 per cent of what had been committed.[10] The quantum of aid, however, is only one aspect of aid effectiveness. Just as important are issues of coordination, and of effective management of funds supplied. The Afghan government, in cooperation with international partners, assembled an Interim Afghanistan National Development Strategy, outlined at a conference in London in 2006, and a Joint Coordination and Monitoring Board to assist in giving effect to it. Neither, however, succeeded in overcoming a fundamental problem that afflicted aid from the start, namely, that a proliferation of 'off-budget' activities funded from foreign sources served to undermine rather than build the new state. As Bizhan put it, 'Of the US$57 billion in aid disbursed between 2002 and 2010, only $10.5 billion (18%) was provided on-budget. The off-budget aid made societal actors who received direct funding from donors accountable to the donors'.[11] Implicit in this was a *lack* of accountability of societal actors to the Afghan state.

Beyond this lies a further problem, namely, the potential disconnect between announcements of aid – and the expectations that such announcements can create – and the actual delivery of aid monies. This is implicit in the discrepancy between committed and disbursed aid set out in the Afghan government statistics quoted above. There is no easy solution to this problem, because what it reflects is the entanglement of Afghan reconstruction activities with the budgetary processes of donor states. Well-run countries often have complex mechanisms for the determination of aid priorities and objectives,[12] as well as for the authorisation of spending by governments that may have made aid commitments during international conferences. Very often in the Afghan case, this has required the approval by a legislature of a budget into which a commitment to Afghanistan has had to be inserted. When this is the case, there can be a substantial time-lag between the announcement of an aid package and the delivery of funding; and in the meantime, the Afghan government can be confronted with expectations that it rapidly 'deliver the goods'. This may be less of a problem with 'off-budget' spending, simply because it is often far from transparent,[13] but when large 'on-budget' commitments are announced and then nothing much seems to happen, it is all too easy for cynical observers to conclude that funds promised by the wider world have been sluiced away in a great sewer of corruption, a perception which potentially has ramifications for state legitimacy.

One significant achievement in Afghanistan has been the revival of the Finance Ministry, for which much of the credit belongs to Ashraf Ghani, who was appointed as minister in June 2002 and served until December 2004. Finance ministries can serve multiple roles. On the one hand, a finance ministry may be at the heart of macroeconomic management. Ever since J.M. Keynes published *The General Theory of Employment, Interest and Money* in 1936,[14] there has been a recognition that 'fiscal policy' – that is, the determination of levels and rates of government expenditure and revenue raising – can be used in an attempt to influence aggregate demand in an economy and the broader level of economic activity, specifically with a view to preventing slumps in production and employment of the kind that marked the Great Depression from late 1929. On the other hand, an effective finance ministry will have overarching control of both the revenue-raising and the expenditure activities of a government. This requires a high level of capacity in respect of public accounting, funds management, and administration. A major development in this respect in Afghanistan was the establishment of a 'Single Treasury Account' in place of the multiple accounts with different banks that the various departments of government had held. As Ghani and some of his colleagues put it,

> As different individuals had decision rights over the withdrawal from these accounts, the budgetary rules could constantly be subverted in practice. The existence of these multiple accounts also enabled various organisations to collect money in the name of the government without reporting it as part of the revenue of the state.[15]

The Finance Ministry reforms initiated by Ghani were both significant and enduring.

That said, it is important to reflect not just on the need for revenue, but also on *how* revenues might be raised. Different sources of state income can have radically different implications for resource allocation within an economy. Classically – putting aside foreign aid – one of the most important sources of revenue is taxation, that is, compulsory imposts levied by the state. The reference to 'the state' is important: too often, the extraction of funds by the Taliban from elements of the Afghan population has also been labelled 'taxation', even though a better label would be 'extortion'. Taxes come in many different shapes and sizes, and some are easier to levy than others. Direct taxes most famously include taxes on income; indirect taxes are more likely to be applied to production or consumption. In the immediate period following the overthrow of the Taliban, by far the easiest taxes to collect were customs duties levied at the border, and local power holders who controlled border crossings were positioned to do very well indeed by exercising control over these revenues rather than remitting them to the central state. In the long run, however, taxes on imports can have significant distorting effects on the allocation of resources domestically,[16] since they disrupt the competitive incentive to invest in activities where a country's comparative advantage is greatest, or comparative disadvantage least. Beyond taxation, it is also possible to fund state activity through internal borrowing (typically through the issuing of government bonds), which may be an appropriate way to fund capital investment in facilities such as schools and hospitals where the benefit of the investment will be shared by a wider range of beneficiaries than simply current taxpayers. Where revenues from taxation are exceeded by expenditure, the state budget is classically seen to be in 'deficit', with the gap covered by either foreign aid, borrowing, or what one scholar called 'income from the public printing press',[17] namely, the printing of money. The risk to which this gives rise is that of inflation, that is, a general rise in the price level in response to more money being in circulation. One of Afghanistan's main achievements since 2001 has been to avoid large-scale inflation, not least because foreign aid has been available to cover a substantial budget deficit. The inflation rate in 2017–2018 was just 4.4 per cent.[18]

In the long run, however, this reliance on foreign funds to cover deficits is unlikely to be sustainable; as Rubin has argued, 'If the state cannot sustain the recurrent costs of its security forces, its stability will be at risk. Nor can any state long survive the funding of its army and police by foreign powers'.[19] Progress has certainly been made in this area. Tax revenue as a percentage of the gross domestic product (GDP) rose from 4 per cent in 2004 to 10 per cent in 2015, while net overseas development assistance declined from 44 per cent of the gross national income in 2004 to 22 per cent in 2015.[20] Nonetheless, there is still a very long way to go: as a United States Institute of Peace report notes,

> In 2017 (Afghan fiscal year 1396), donor grants amounted to $3,863 million, covering 62 percent of total budgetary expenditures; domestic revenues funded only 38 percent… Thus, for the foreseeable future, and barring a break-through in reconciliation and an end to or at least a substantial reduction in the level of conflict, Afghanistan will remain highly aid dependent. By the same token, any sudden sharp decline in aid would have disastrous consequences and precipitate a fiscal collapse – most likely accompanied by severe, unmanageable political, security, and economic problems.[21]

A further crucial element in state budgeting is determining *what* activities will be supported through government spending. To a degree, the departmental structure of the government sets some minimum requirements for the funding of activities, but if all funding requests from all agencies were totalled, the sum would likely exceed available revenues by a wide margin. Determination of strategic priorities in Afghanistan constitutionally resides with the president and in practical terms is likely to involve key advisers to the president as well. That said, one (semi) 'insider' account of policy discussion in the Karzai cabinet points to the need for caution in assuming that such discussion would necessarily be well informed or rational[22]; in a neopatrimonial system, budgets are as much a tool for the building of political support as for the realisation of public policy priorities. In the worst cases, this can result in what has been called 'auction-based budgeting', where 'resources are provided on the basis of who is willing to pay' – in other words, 'a system of handing out resources to the highest bidder'.[23] Furthermore, the Afghan budget system mirrors the state more broadly in being highly centralised, and this has ramifications for how engaged with the budgetary process ordinary people, and administrators at the provincial level, actually feel.[24]

The shape of an economy is determined not just by fiscal policy, but also by monetary policy, which refers to regulation of the supply of money in order to provide a stable basis for economic life more broadly. Money has a number of different functions within an economy. It is a crucial medium of exchange, permitting transactions far more sophisticated than mere barter exchange of goods can facilitate; it has played this role since ancient times. It is also a store of value – provided that the value of a currency is not being eroded by inflation. This is where control of the money supply is essential. In countries devastated by war, there is quite a history of hyperinflation,[25] that is, monumental price increases generated by a combination of a rapidly increasing money supply and an increase in the velocity of circulation of money as consumers come to recognise the irrationality of holding cash when its purchasing power is rapidly declining. The *afghani* was introduced as the Afghan currency in 1925, and from 1939, the Central Bank, known as Da Afghanistan Bank, enjoyed a monopoly on the issue of banknotes.[26] But by the 1990s, this had broken down, and various versions of the *afghani* were in circulation.[27] The introduction (with assistance from informal *hawala* currency traders[28]) of a new *afghani* (AFN), and the monetary discipline displayed in Afghanistan since the introduction of the new *afghani*, have been two of the main successes of economic transition since 2001.

For major infrastructure projects, foreign aid remains centrally important. But the revival of an economy depends also upon the development of mechanisms by which savings can be mobilised in order to support productive investment. Historically, a great deal of economic activity in Afghanistan has derived from the private sector,[29] but the difficulty in securing loans for the purchase of capital equipment in the 1980s and 1990s had a very significant dampening effect on the economy. The mobilisation of savings has classically been a key role of banks. As a result, after 2001, significant attention was paid to finding ways of reviving the banking system. An effective system of private banks also had much to offer in allowing the more efficient tracking of salary payments and other transactions which in the long run could form part of a domestic tax base. It proved difficult, however, to make progress, not least because of the challenge of security, especially outside Kabul: as key policy-makers put it, 'Many branches of the Central Bank remained effectively under the control of local commanders and provincial governors'.[30] Significant banks did emerge, notably the Bank-e Millie, the Afghanistan International Bank, the Azizi Bank and the Ghazanfar Bank. The most widely known, however, proved to be the Kabul Bank, and for all the wrong reasons.

Since the business model of a successful bank requires it to make loans as well as hold deposits, a typical bank will not have on hand enough cash (so called 'liquid assets') to pay all depositors should they simultaneously demand the return of their money. Since this contingency is quite unlikely, it is typically not a problem. But it does become a problem if a collapse in confidence leads to a 'run' on the bank, with large numbers of depositors queuing for refunds. This happened to the Kabul Bank in September 2010. It turned out that the Kabul Bank, rather than making *commercial* loans calculated to generate a profitable return for the bank and its depositors, had in effect been 'gifting' deposits to friends of the management, some of whom were most unlikely ever to be in a position to repay them in full or in some cases even in part. To all intents and purposes, it had been run as a Ponzi scheme, comparable to that conducted for some decades by the notorious American fraudster Bernie Madoff.[31] Yet as one might expect in a neopatrimonial system, some of those who benefited nicely from the Kabul Bank's lending largesse were also close to the president, including his brother Mahmoud Karzai. State intervention, followed by a large-scale bailout to the tune of $825 million (much of it ultimately supplied by the US), proved necessary.[32] The chairman and chief executive officer of the Kabul Bank, Sher Khan Farnood and Khalilullah Ferozi, were treated relatively gently, at least until Ashraf Ghani became president[33]; and attempts were made by the Palace to shift the blame away from the perpetrators and onto the local regulators, who were both under-resourced and the targets of deliberate deceit.[34] The High Office of Oversight and Anti-Corruption, chaired by a diehard Karzai loyalist, Azizullah Lodin, declined to cooperate in an investigation of the fraud conducted by the Independent Joint Anti-Corruption Monitoring and Evaluation Committee, something the Committee noted with obvious distaste in its report.[35] The Kabul Bank scandal continues to cast a long shadow.

In many countries, a key measure of the state's economic achievement is the existence of high levels of employment. This is indisputably a matter of great concern for Afghans, given the close connections between employment and well-being. The *Afghanistan Living Conditions Survey 2016–17* found that 39.5 per cent of the population was not gainfully employed, the nationwide unemployment rate was 23.9 per cent, underemployment afflicted a further 15.6 per cent of the labour force and the youth unemployment rate was 30.7 per cent. Not surprisingly, given these data, 54.5 per cent of the population was assessed as living below the national poverty line,[36] and this was affirmed by a 2019 report, drawing on data from the *Living Conditions Survey*, that found that in 2016–2017, 51.7 per cent of Afghans lived in 'multidimensional poverty', defined by reference to 'education, health, living standards, work, and shocks'.[37] The attitudinal consequences of unemployment and underemployment were identified by The Asia Foundation in the report on its 2018 survey of opinion that we noted earlier in this chapter. The dilemma for any Afghan government is that it has relatively few instruments at its disposal to stimulate the labour market. Indeed, given the significance of networks in Afghanistan, any image of a freely functioning labour 'market' needs to be taken with a grain of salt. It is often social rather than market relations that provide Afghans with opportunities to secure their livelihoods.[38] And of course, a great deal of work in Afghanistan takes place outside the realm of employment relations, notably in subsistence agriculture, and in the enormous amount of work carried out by women in an unremunerated household environment.

Businessmen, entrepreneurs and the state

As Afghanistan is a country at the centre of many trading routes, trans-regional commerce and trade have historically been central to both the politics and the economy of the country. However, the development of a formal private sector that can generate revenues for the state and work as a driver of economic growth has faced numerous challenges. According to a 2019 OECD (Organisation for Economic Co-operation and Development) report, the development of the private sector as an engine of economic growth faces three major challenges. First, Afghanistan's economy remains highly informal, with 80 per cent of total economic activity remaining outside the formal economy. ('Informal' activity is not necessarily 'illicit' activity, such as opium cultivation: rather, it is typically activity undertaken by unregistered actors marked by opaque operations, a reluctance to pay tax and little interest in complying with regulatory frameworks.) This means that most economic activities are beyond the reach of government economic policies and programmes. Second, access to finance remains extremely limited. Widespread informality and low trust in banks mean that only two per cent of businesses access financial services provided by banks. Third, government institutions struggle to provide the necessary public services that can stimulate and encourage business activities.[39]

The reasons behind the limited development of Afghanistan's formal private sector are partly historical and partly the result of nearly four decades of war and instability. The first efforts to create conditions for the development of a modern private sector were initiated following the declaration of Afghanistan's independence in 1919. Parallel to the opening of diplomatic missions with several countries, a number of Afghans, usually those connected to the royal family, also found an opportunity to travel internationally and engage in trade with other countries. During the 1920s, the Rafiq Company was established by Sardar Mohammad Rafiq Khan, a member of the ruling family.[40] It was during the 1930s that a small group of powerful businessmen and entrepreneurs emerged in the country. After Nadir Shah came to power in 1929, the Musaheban family entered into an alliance with a small number of businessmen and entrepreneurs who played an important role in the development of a semi-private sector economy.[41] The most influential person in this group was Abdul Majid Zabuli, who had inherited his wealth through his family trade in Central Asia and Moscow. He had spent some time in the Soviet Union. He was living in Berlin when Nadir Khan took the throne. Upon the invitation of the King, he returned to Kabul, where in 1933, he led the foundation of Bank-e Milli as a *sherkat-e sahami* or joint stock company with shares held by the government as well as a number of businessmen. Zabuli became the chairman of the bank and also the minister of national economy through the 1930s.[42] Bank-e Milli facilitated the accumulation of capital, which was invested in about 50 other enterprises in the export and import sectors as well as a small number of agriculture and manufacturing companies. Private individuals were offered the opportunity to buy shares in these companies. Until 1938, when Da Afghanistan Bank was established, Bank-e Milli also controlled monetary and financial policies such as exchange rates.[43]

Bank-e Milli and its subsidiary companies are often regarded as the first private enterprises in Afghanistan. However, as Jonathan Lee argues, the policies pursued by Zabuli were 'the antithesis of a free market economy and were more akin to Soviet state monopolies. They encouraged price fixing, corruption and tax evasion as well as smuggling and a flourishing black market. The shirkats concentrated most of the nation's wealth in the hands of the ruling elite and contributed significantly to widening the already vast gap between rich and poor'.[44] Notwithstanding their inherent limitations as agents of a free market economy, these enterprises lost even more of their limited potential as significant private actors as a result of the nationalisation policies of Prime Minister Daoud in the 1950s. Subsequently, the Soviet-backed PDPA regime attempted to create a Soviet style state-led economy in the 1980s, before the civil strife of the 1990s crippled the formal private sector almost entirely.

In the period after the overthrow of the Taliban regime in 2001, the relative stability in major cities and the formal shift towards a market economy in the 2004 constitution created the basic conditions for revival of the private sector in the country. However, the transition from the state-led economy, which was profoundly disrupted by more than two decades of instability, to a liberal market economy was confronted with many challenges. Initially, two separate institutions competed to represent the private sector. The first institution was the Afghanistan Chamber of Commerce and Industries (ACCI), which inherited a role as an agency of the state to manage and control the private sector according to the 1980s Soviet-style state-led economy. According to its historical role, the chamber would include representatives of the private sector, but its president was appointed by the Ministry of Commerce and Industry. In 2004, the Afghanistan International Chamber of Commerce (AICC), emerged as a rival institution with support from the US and other international donors. The ACCI and the AICC competed with one another as representative of the country's private sector. The rivalries between the two chambers were also reflected in two different donor approaches. The Gesellschaft für technische Zusammenarbeit (or GTZ), the official German development agency, provided support and funding to the ACCI, which it sought to reform. By contrast, the US Agency for International Development (USAID) was opposed to the ACCI, seeing it as a relic of the Soviet-style planned economy. Instead, USAID supported the AICC as a business association that was independent of government control.[45]

In 2005, the government decided to resolve the tensions by appointing a commission to reform the chambers. After a lengthy process of negotiations between the two chambers, in 2007, they merged into a single body. The reformed ACCI would consist of a general assembly of representatives of the private sectors from the provinces. The general assembly then elected its board of directors.[46] Since the merger, the ACCI has emerged as the leading membership-based organisation of the Afghan private sector. Promoting a free market economy, it has advocated for the interests of the business community in the country. However, the organisation was also dominated by powerful political and business interests. For example, Mahmoud Karzai, brother of President Hamid Karzai, was a founder of the AICC and subsequently became a member of the board of directors of the ACCI. Sher Khan Farnood, of Kabul Bank fame, became chairman of the ACCI. Mahmoud Karzai and a range of other politically connected businessmen, including Mohammad Fahim, a brother of Qasim Fahim, the country's first vice-president, were also shareholders of Kabul Bank. Indeed, as Grant McLeod put it, a 2012 forensic audit of the Kabul Bank collapse provided 'details regarding the mechanics and beneficiaries of the fraud, which read like a who's who of the Afghan elite'.[47]

Notwithstanding the endemic corruption that pervaded relations between major businesses and the state, which was clearly demonstrated by the Kabul Bank crisis, Afghanistan's private sector grew significantly. Foreign aid and military spending, as well as private investment, expanded opportunities for small as well as major investments in the economy. The telecommunications sector serves as a good example. In 2002, except for a limited number of fixed-line connections in the cities, the telecommunications sector was virtually non-existent. By 2014, the sector had attracted billions of dollars in investment in four major GSM and two fixed-line operators. The sector had created an estimated 130,000 jobs and radically transformed the socio-economic and cultural environment of the country.[48] The four major private companies were Roshan, MTN, Etisalat and Afghan Wireless Communication Company.

In addition to these major companies, a range of other private enterprises also emerged. A significant number of entrepreneurs emerged in construction, logistics and private security, linking into the 'war economy' created by the presence of tens of thousands of foreign military forces. A number of entrepreneurs grew rich as a result of the bubble that the war economy created. For example, Hikmatullah Shadman, the son of a schoolteacher from the province of Kandahar, earned more than $160 million through trucking contracts with US military forces.[49] However, after the 2014 departure of most of the foreign forces and the collapse of the war economy, many businesses that had grown to meet the demands of the foreign military forces faced major challenges. Insecurity resulting from growing insurgent and criminal activity, as well as political uncertainty, slowed down investment. Often, the small and medium enterprises that lacked access to government resources were the first to be crippled by intense competition for what contracts were left, as well as by rising insecurity and criminal activity. As early as 2012, investment slowed down and many began to invest their capital in other countries.[50] Initially, the capital flight was triggered by the uncertainty that resulted from President Obama's announcement of his intention to withdraw US troops from the country by the end of 2014. The departure of US and NATO forces would dramatically reduce foreign military and aid spending, which were major drivers of growth in services, logistics and construction sectors. Furthermore, the withdrawal of foreign forces also created profound political and security uncertainty over the capacity of the Afghan government forces to fight the resurgent Taliban. In 2014, the combined effects of political, security and economic uncertainties proved to be devastating for the private sector. These resulted in unprecedented capital flight out of the country. There are no reliable figures for the total outflow of capital since most such transfers take place through informal cash transfers such as *hawala*, the informal remittance system that typically operates outside the formal financial and banking systems. Nonetheless, some estimates offer an indication of the magnitudes of the financial outflow from the country. In August 2014, Dr Omar Zakhilwal, the then minister of finance, estimated that the political crisis over the outcome of the presidential elections had cost the Afghan economy $6 billion in capital flight. The same month, the Finance Ministry declared that customs revenues, the source of nearly half of Afghanistan's domestic income, had declined by 25 per cent.[51] Capital flight continued well into 2016, when the economy minister, Abdul Sattar Murad, estimated that about $80 billion had been withdrawn from the country.[52] Some businessmen who had exploitable business and family connections moved their capital to Western countries. Others invested in countries around Afghanistan. One of the most popular investment destinations was the United Arab Emirates. Other attractive destinations include neighbouring Iran, Pakistan and the Central Asian republics. Turkey also became a popular investment destination for many middle-class families. A combination of capital flight and decline in investment as well as spending significantly slowed down the growth of Afghanistan. In 2014, annual GDP growth fell to 1.3 per cent, from 14.4 per cent in 2012.[53]

Afghan agriculture and the rural economy

A principal focus of economic analysis is the 'real' economy, the realm of production and trade of goods and services (as opposed to activity in the realm of finance, important though that may be). A common categorisation divides the real economy into primary, secondary and tertiary sectors, concerned, respectively, with agriculture and extractive industries, manufacturing and the supply of services. In modernising economies, the importance of services in adding value to gross domestic product tends to grow over time at the expense of agriculture, and Afghanistan is no exception[54]; agriculture as a proportion of gross domestic product declined from 71 per cent in 1994 to 24 per cent in 2013.[55] Nonetheless, the agricultural sector remains an extremely important part of the Afghan economy. While Afghanistan's rugged landscape means that only 12 per cent of its land is arable, and Afghan agriculture suffered serious damage in the 1980s,[56] the agricultural sector is a significant source of employment and workforce participation; as noted in Chapter 1, 71.3 per cent of Afghans live in rural areas, and agriculture employs around 40 per cent of the total workforce. Cereal crops are the dominant product of the agricultural sector, especially wheat. However, the agricultural sector is also fragile, and Afghanistan is marked by high levels of food insecurity, chronically affecting around 2.2 million people according to a 2018 study. The same study forecasts that cereal imports of 3.3 million tonnes would be required in 2018–2019, with wheat production declining by 18 per cent, from 4,280,000 tonnes in 2017 to a projected 3,500,000 tonnes in 2018, largely as a result of dry weather.[57]

Afghanistan, although a very poor country, has largely succeeded in avoiding the scourge of famine. The last severe case was in 1972, where one official of the Ministry of Agriculture in Kabul notoriously remarked that it was hardly a grave problem if the peasants ate grass, adding 'They're beasts. They're used to it'.[58] Modern scholarship on famines also emphasises the importance of an understanding of entitlements: famines are not necessarily the product simply of food shortages, but rather of certain categories of people being unable to access food.[59] But that said, ensuring that agricultural systems work effectively is very important from the point of view of securing livelihoods in both rural areas *and* urban areas, since cities do not feed themselves. Agricultural systems in this sense reflect the complex interplay of a range of different factors: the ownership and management of land; the mobilisation of the labour force, especially for the purposes of planting and harvesting of crops; the establishment and maintenance of appropriate irrigation systems so that water is put to productive use rather than wasted; the availability of high-quality seeds in order to support high-yield crops; and adequate access both to safe fertilisers and to mechanisms of pest control in order to prevent crops being devastated by locusts and other insects. Because of this complexity, a top-down approach to agricultural policy runs the risk of overlooking the tacit knowledge that Afghan farmers have developed over a long period of time about their operational environment.[60]

One virtually essential prerequisite to investment in agriculture is a sufficient degree of certainty about land title; in the absence of such certainty, a prudent investor is unlikely to make the necessary commitment of resources. Land title issues are extremely complex,[61] not just because of population displacement and the consequent phenomenon of occupants being in 'adverse possession', but because of the diverse kinds of land titles that historically have existed in Afghanistan – government, public, private, communal, or religious – with significant regional variation.[62] Land disputes are very common: some relate to inheritance, others turn on issues of access, others relate to the location of boundaries and some go the fundamental question of ownership. Ownership disputes can easily be marked by 'bad faith', where a powerful player attempts to use the law to obtain another's property by fraud.[63] A 2015 study concluded that 'Today, less than ten percent of rural property is covered by legal deeds. Archived records are also often outdated and inaccurate'.[64] Land has historically been used as collateral for loans, secured by a mortgage (*gerawi*),[65] and this can also give rise to disputes. What are sometimes characterised as 'land disputes' can have deeper political dimensions.[66] For example, in 2010 in the province of Wardak, houses of Hazaras were set on fire by ethnic Pushtun nomads (*kuchis*) demanding access to lands the Hazaras occupied. Foschini recorded eyewitness testimony that the nomads arrived in the Daimirdad district 'en masse, maybe a thousand of them, a hundred riding horses, thirty to forty on motorcycles, others in pickups' and that when they reached the Tezak valley at 5.20 a.m., the first thing they did was burn the houses, at which point 'the whole population evacuated Daimirdad'. Foschini observed that 'it seems clear that Kuchis never owned, or even seriously claimed to own, land in the district or utilized its territory as pasture'.[67]

It is one thing to produce a crop; it is another thing entirely to ensure that what is produced is effectively harvested, put into saleable form, drawn to the attention of potential purchasers through marketing, and transported so that it can actually be used by the buyer. While some horticultural products are not especially vulnerable to spoilage at different points in this chain, that is by no means true of all produce. Mechanised equipment is increasingly being used in Afghan agriculture, but credit for its purchase may be difficult for farmers to obtain, and poor road surfaces, as well as seasonal deterioration in weather, can interfere with the transportation of goods to market, especially if markets beyond Afghanistan are being contemplated. Some high-value Afghan products such as saffron and dried fruits are very suitable for export, and to this end, the Ghani government launched a 'National Air Corridor Program' to subsidise the cost of cargo flights to major regional markets, notably India, China, Turkey and Europe.[68] It remains to be seen how effective this will be, but already there are some promising signs in terms of the increase of exports by air. In December 2018, President Ghani also inaugurated the so-called 'Lapis Lazuli' route for land transit to Europe via Turkmenistan and Azerbaijan.

The agricultural sector is relevant to the concerns of a number of different ministries, with two in particular standing out: the Ministry of Agriculture and Irrigation and Livestock and the Ministry of Rural Rehabilitation and Development. The Ministry of Agriculture and Irrigation and Livestock has amassed considerable technical expertise and has established an administrative presence at both provincial and *woleswali* (district) levels. In fiscal year 2018, it spent fully 95 per cent of its development budget, a level of spending which it claimed to be 'unprecedented in the ministry's history'. The funds were spent on irrigation projects such as irrigation canals, implementation of gardening development projects, reforestations, and natural resources, distribution of improved wheat seeds and fertilizers for farmers, development of saffron industry, cotton cultivation and development, distribution of gardens and greenhouses, distribution of animal food and grass for drought-affected livestock holders, expansion of investigative farms, implementation of infrastructural projects such as quarantine port networks, and other infrastructural projects.[69]

The focus of the Ministry of Rural Rehabilitation and Development is more broadly on rural communities, not simply those involved in agricultural activity, but of course there is some overlap. These ministries' focus has been significantly on the nurturing of markets as a way of protecting livelihoods more broadly, and there is no doubt that markets are important. But their importance as a practical reality can be overstated[70]: significant forms of economic activity in the rural sector are more complex than one would expect in a 'civil economy' dominated by legal market activity.[71] Subsistence production remains important,[72] as do networks[73]; indeed, one of the most effective poverty alleviation mechanisms in Afghanistan has come in the form of norms of reciprocity within complex affinity networks.

The Ministry of Rural Rehabilitation and Development also administered one of the most ambitious public policy programs in Afghanistan, namely, the National Solidarity Program (NSP), which ran from 2003 to 2017, when it was succeeded by the Citizen Charter Program. The NSP was very much the brainchild of Ashraf Ghani and was focused on bringing development to villages and remote areas. Funded by international donors, it saw roughly $1.5 billion disbursed during its lifetime, via 85,918 sub-projects completed. Its most imaginative dimension came with the establishment of Community Development Councils responsible for identifying and managing the sub-projects; during the life of the NSP, some 35,075 councils were elected, with the overwhelming majority receiving some finance.[74] Community grants, wrote two observers, 'will put decision-making in the hands of communities, enable the state to bypass warlord structures to provide resources to communities directly, and promote the development of community-level democracy and decision-making as the basis for a more democratic polity'.[75] A 2013 evaluation of the NSP conducted for the World Bank did not go so far, and offered a range of conclusions:

> NSP improves the access of villagers to basic utilities … NSP also increases access to education, health care, and counseling services for women … NSP impacts the economic perceptions and optimism of villagers, particularly women … NSP impacts the structure of local governance by substantially increasing the proportion of local assemblies that contain at least one woman member.

But that said,

> after project completion, male villagers are less likely to be satisfied with the work of local leaders and are more likely to disagree with recent decisions and actions of village leaders ... there is no overall evidence of a discernible impact of NSP on social cohesion.[76]

Agriculture is one area where there is some scope for useful 'technical assistance', that is, non-financial aid, but it is important to distinguish between different forms of technical assistance. One common form is training and advising, and in recent years, this kind of assistance has been strongly criticised, on the grounds that it may not produce sustainable change, and can be very expensive to implement, not least because of high salary costs involved in employing outside advisers. It is also debatable whether training and advising is what Afghan farmers need. Experts who have visited Afghan farms in the past have often been struck by the rationality of farmers, who, seeking to survive in what is quite a tough environment, tend to develop an acute understanding of farming techniques. Where technical assistance can be useful is in introducing new strains of seeds which can increase crop yields and in the supply of improved fertilisers and pesticides that are friendlier to the environment than some first-generation chemical additives had been. Nonetheless, like any forms of aid, technical assistance needs to be understood as a social intervention, and in the absence of a detailed understanding of social complexity, there is a risk either that an intervention will have negative consequences or that it will deliver less than was promised or expected, raising real questions about whether it constituted an appropriate use of scarce resources.[77]

Nuance in macro policy settings is also extremely important, and insufficiently nuanced policies may have unintended and severely damaging consequences. One instructive example comes from the early years after the fall of the Taliban regime, when under the auspices of the World Food Program, 'massive food distribution continued despite a lack of coordination with the government'. When a bumper harvest of wheat was produced in 2003,

> many farmers found that its market price was so depressed that the cost of harvesting was not warranted. Consequently, the wheat was left to rot ... The result was that the farmers, in order to survive, had to draw their own conclusions as to how best to earn a living by growing crops that could earn them the maximum revenue regardless of state or Islamic law, which both clearly forbid growing opium.[78]

There has since been some debate about the extent to which food aid distribution, as opposed to other considerations such as water availability, shaped the farmers' decisions[79]; but the broader point stands that complex problems require solutions that are assembled with a genuine awareness of the complexities involved.

Environmental factors are also extremely important determinants of the prospects for Afghan agriculture. Many parts of Afghanistan experience harsh weather, with very cold winters and very hot summers. The existence of the Hindu Kush mountain range bifurcating the country from northeast to southwest means that rivers in Afghanistan are often fed by melting snows and flow at great speed for a short period of time in spring, only to go dry once the supply of melting snow has been exhausted. The interplay between planting and irrigation means that unusual weather can have a disruptive effect on agricultural output. Furthermore, whilst climate change is a global phenomenon,[80] its effects are being felt in Afghanistan in diverse ways. Afghanistan has long been prone to experience earthquakes, simply as a result of its location near shifting tectonic plates; but it is increasingly vulnerable to flooding and landslides. Apart from the tragic human consequences, these impose economic costs through both the disruption of economic activities and the destruction of capital assets; and Afghanistan's relatively weak disaster-response capability adds to the problem. A detailed 2016 study stated that

> the main negative impact of climate change in Afghanistan in the future will be increased drought risk – with increased flood risk being of secondary concern. Annual droughts in many parts of the country will likely become the norm by 2030, rather than being a temporary or cyclical event. This will mostly be due to higher temperatures leading to higher evapo-transpiration and higher crop and livestock water demand.

It also concluded that

> Temperatures in Afghanistan are expected to increase more than the global average … this warming is expected to occur fairly uniformly throughout the year, but will vary geographically – with the most severe warming occurring in the mountainous Central Highlands and Hindu Kush areas.[81]

This study provides a useful reminder that Afghanistan is not just affected by problems of conflict, but is exposed to risks that it shares with a wide range of other countries. Much attention in the climate change sphere has focused on states faced with an existential threat because of rising sea levels, states such as the Maldives, the Republic of the Marshall Islands and Kiribati. But many more states face crippling threats to the well-being and livelihoods of significant elements of their populations, and in Afghanistan, climate change is likely to be a driver of forced migration. Afghanistan is already experiencing significant movement from rural areas to towns and cities, with consequent development of informal settlements and slums. Ashraf Ghani has made the point that every day, the Afghan population becomes younger and more urbanised. Furthermore, in the central highlands of Afghanistan, there is a strong tradition of labour migration amongst members of the Hazara ethnic group which is only likely to be accentuated by climate change.[82] In certain circumstances, out-migration can be a positive development – if, for example, mechanisation and technical change in agriculture are leading to a fall in the demand for manual labour of a kind that could give rise to serious unemployment issues in a particular locality. But it can also be a marker of social crisis to which exit appears a rational response.

Afghanistan has now experienced decades of forced migration,[83] and to the extent that labour is an important factor of production, this is highly disruptive of economic life. At the very least it interferes with the development of specific occupational skills, a process that economists call 'human capital formation'; and forced migration can also fragment networks and connections on which people may depend to secure even casual employment. Some forced migration is in the form of internal displacement, which, as we noted in the previous chapter, is currently very significant in scale in Afghanistan. A study by Susanne Schmeidl estimated the population of 'internally displaced persons' (IDPs) at the end of 2016 to be 1.5 million.[84] Other migration, however, comes in the form of the return to Afghanistan, not altogether voluntarily, of refugees long based in Pakistan or Iran for whom the political climate in those countries has become markedly less welcoming. (Iran has become particularly dangerous, with young refugees at risk of being virtually press-ganged into the so-called 'Fatemiyoun', companies assembled by the Iranian Revolutionary Guards for deployment in theatres such as Syria.[85]) Reflecting shifting interactions of 'push' and 'pull' factors, recent annual totals of returnees have fluctuated dramatically: 16,995 in 2014, 58,460 in 2015, 372,577 in 2016, 58,817 in 2017 and 15,699 in 2018.[86] There have also been involuntary deportations to Afghanistan from European states of Afghan asylum seekers, many premised on the highly suspect claim that the individuals concerned come from 'safe' parts of Afghanistan. There is mounting evidence, however, that these returnees face huge difficulties on return and leave Afghanistan again quite quickly[87]; they are certainly not a reliable source of replacement human capital.

This brings us to a final point pertinent to agriculture in the Afghan economy. Rural Afghanistan is not simply a venue for agricultural, horticultural and pastoral life, with towns and villages providing support for those involved directly in the primary sector. It is also the venue for competition and contestation between the Afghan government and its enemies; and significant parts of rural Afghanistan might best be described as war zones. This impacts on economic life in multiple ways. Crops and irrigation systems can be targeted as a way of clearing territory of potentially hostile forces: the Soviet Union did this in the 1980s and the Taliban in the 1990s. But even if such attacks are not occurring, the *possibility* that they might occur has ramifications for the willingness of people to commit scarce resources to activities that might prove vulnerable. This tends to militate in favour of short-term thinking and the pursuit of immediate returns – quite possibly of illicit provenance – rather than investment for the long run. Keynes's comment that in the long run we are all dead resonates with many Afghans.[88]

The political economy of opium cultivation

In Article 7 of Afghanistan's 2004 Constitution, one can find a prohibition on 'intoxicants' (*muskirat*). It has not proved at all effective. In particular, since the 1980s, the illicit cultivation and trade of opium have steadily increased, creating significant spill-over effects for the legal economy as well as for the politics and society of the country. Afghanistan's opium economy is a multi-faceted phenomenon, involving a range of domestic and international factors. On the one hand, the expansion and proliferation of the drug economy has involved a gradual criminalisation of the country's economy, which serves the interests of transnational crime networks, as well as terrorist and insurgent groups, and undermines the legitimacy of the state.[89] Furthermore, despite international efforts at prohibition,[90] persistently high international demand for narcotics is also key to understanding the durability of the drug economy in the country. On the other, after decades of instability, opium cultivation also became attractive for farmers as a coping mechanism in conditions of extreme socio-economic insecurity. Opium is a high-value and relatively drought-resistant crop that can yield higher income when compared to wheat and other similar crops,[91] although most of the income goes not to farmers and farm labourers, but to those higher up in the supply-chain.

These factors are central to the persistence and sheer magnitude of the drug economy in the country. In 2018, the United Nations (UN) estimated that the value and production of opium were significantly lower as compared to 2017. For example, the land under cultivation decreased from 328,000 hectares to 263,000 hectares, and the overall production dropped from 9000 to 6400 metric tons. As a result, the total value of the opium produced in the country at farm gate rate declined from $1.4 billion to $0.6 billion.[92] Nonetheless, the value of the opiate increases significantly once it leaves the farms. In 2017, the UN estimated that the total value of opiates, including revenues generated from the production of heroin and transport to the borders of the country, was somewhere between $4.1 billion and $6.6 billion, which amounted to 20 to 32 per cent of the GDP of the country. During the same year, the entire legal agricultural sector was estimated to account for 23 per cent of the GDP,[93] although as we noted earlier, cereal crops involve a vastly greater volume of physical output than that associated with the opium poppy.

The drug economy also flourishes because it serves the interests of the powerful. Over the years, in addition to farmers who often receive a small share of the revenues, a range of groups have developed deep interests in the cultivation and trade of the crop. These include insurgent groups, political and criminal networks that often transcend political and ideological divides, and transnational mafia. The confluence of the interests of these various sectors in the drug economy is particularly strong in Helmand, which is often the source of more than half of the opiates produced in the country. In 2017, a UN report found powerful groups, including the Taliban and others who are aligned with the local government, were benefiting from taxing the crop:

According to the interviewees, 'the powerful', which referred mainly to local powerholders in Hilmand province, accrued 36 per cent of all opium taxes collected, the Taliban 35 per cent, generic insurgency/anti-government groups 18 per cent and 'others' 12 per cent. If the same groupings collected a similar share from the value of the opiate economy (including the farm-gate value) this would correspond to US$ 78–124 million for 'the powerful', US$ 76–121 million for the Taliban, US$ 40–63 million for generic anti-government/insurgency groups and US$ 25–41 million for 'others'.[94]

The bar chart in Figure 4.1 gives a clear picture of the expansion of opium cultivation.

To explore how opium became such an important element of Afghanistan's economy, it is useful to draw a distinction between cultivation and production of opium before and after the 1979 Soviet invasion of Afghanistan. Cultivation of opium for local and private consumption has a long history in Afghanistan. It was used in certain regions of the country for medicinal purposes. However, cultivation of poppy as a commodity for trade and export has a more recent history and is centrally related to the collapse of the country's formal economy during the years of war. Opium as an export commodity first emerged in the 1930s. Mohammad Hashim Khan, prime minister of Afghanistan from 1929 to 1946, oversaw the development of opium as a licit export commodity. Opium served an important purpose in boosting exports and generating revenues for the Musaheban rulers who had sought to shift government revenue

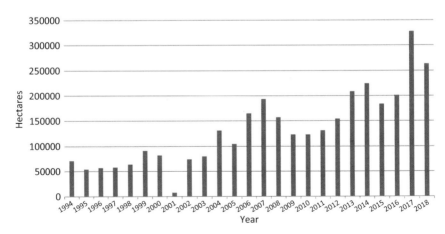

FIGURE 4.1 Level of opium cultivation in Afghanistan (From *Afghanistan Opium Survey 2018: Cultivation and Production*, United Nations Office on Drugs and Crime and Ministry of Counter Narcotics, Kabul, Islamic Republic of Afghanistan, November 2018.)

sources from taxing the rural population to taxing trade and foreign exports. Furthermore, the government in Kabul was also seeking to access medicinal opiates from international markets. In Kabul, the Government Opium Company, which was a monopoly established by Bank-e Milli, was responsible for the trade and export of opium. Local government officials at district levels would buy raw opium from farmers who were licensed by the government to cultivate the crop. The company first began exporting raw opium in 1935 to Germany, and subsequently to a number of other countries, including the Soviet Union, France and the United States.[95] However, the sector was not that significant. According to a 1949 UN report, in 1932, opium was cultivated on 3846 hectares of land, which produced an estimated 74.5 tons.[96]

The export of opium as a licit commodity faced a number of challenges, including the absence of adequate legal frameworks that would comply with international standards and conventions. Afghanistan had not ratified the 1912 *International Opium Convention*, since the foreign policy of the country was controlled by the British at that time. On 21 June 1935, the government acceded to the 1931 *Convention for Limiting the Manufacture and Regulating the Distribution of Narcotic Drugs*. However, the government faced major challenges in complying with the provisions of the conventions, which among other things, required signatory states to declare estimates of licit narcotics produced or consumed in their territories.[97] Furthermore, by the 1940s, the government was also losing its ability to maintain control over cultivation and production of drugs in the country. As the demand for opium increased, the cultivation of opium spread to areas that were not effectively controlled by the state.[98] The inability to control production of opium also affected Afghanistan's relations with major powers. This was particularly important for the country's efforts to attract aid and development assistance from the United States. Thus, Afghanistan acceded to the *International Opium Convention* on 5 May 1944, and the first prohibition was declared in 1945 by Hashim Khan. However, the ban was not enforced, which meant that opium continued to be cultivated in many parts of the country. During the 1950s, the country encountered further international pressure to take effective measures against the cultivation and production of opium. In 1958, Prime Minister Daoud declared a new ban on the cultivation of opium across the country. This time, the new ban was enforced with coercion, particularly in the province of Badakhshan, which had emerged as a major centre of poppy cultivation in the country. As Bradford argues, the coercive enforcement of the ban was also relatively easy to implement in Badakhshan, as the majority of its population were Tajiks and other smaller minorities. A similar ban in Pushtun majority provinces, which were the support bases of the Musaheban, had the potential to provoke anti-government rebellions.[99]

Despite its initial success, the 1958 ban also failed to end the cultivation and trade in narcotics. Throughout the 1960s and 1970s, opium continued to be cultivated in Afghanistan. During this period, Kabul became a major destination in the so-called 'hippie trail', with young Western tourists visiting Afghanistan in increasing numbers. Strange as it may now seem, Afghanistan in the 1960s was seen as a relaxed place, in which the local authorities observed foreign visitors with a degree of bemusement, but with a 'live-and-let-live' attitude. In fact, the Afghan government was quite concerned about the impact of these tourists,[100] not least because of the numbers of deaths from overdoses, to which gravestones in the European cemetery (*Qabr-e gureh*) in Kabul bore witness; but Afghan governments in those times also had other problems to address, and it was the eruption of turmoil in Afghanistan and Iran at the end of the 1970s that brought an end to the problem, rather than any specific public policy response.

The 1979 Soviet invasion of Afghanistan and the subsequent war and violence provided a conducive environment for the spread of poppy cultivation in many more regions of the country. The instability and violence disrupted the traditional patterns of economic relations, and the Soviet military used scorched-earth tactics against the *Mujahideen* by destroying crops and irrigation canals. As the traditional sources of livelihoods were disrupted, many farmers turned to opium for its high value in the market. A number of *Mujahideen* commanders and organisations also turned to trading in opium as a source of additional revenues to boost their political and military powers. The most notable of these were Gulbuddin Hekmatyar of the *Hezb-e Islami*, to a lesser degree Pir Sayed Ahmad Gailani, the leader of National Islamic Front of Afghanistan, and militia leader Esmatullah Muslim. Hekmatyar's *Hezb-e Islami* controlled opium refineries in Pakistan.[101] According to Rubin, Hekmatyar was 'the only leader to exploit opium profits systematically as a basis for a hierarchically organized party and conventional army'.[102] Esmatullah Muslim, a member of the Achakzai tribe from the border town of Spin Boldak in Kandahar, became a major figure in the narcotics trade on the pro-government side. A former military officer, Muslim first joined the anti-Soviet resistance in 1979 before switching sides to become a commander of a major government militia force in the south of the country. Relying on the networks of his Achakzai tribe that lived on both sides of the border between Pakistan and Afghanistan, Muslim became one of the first to combine gains derived from drug economy to strengthen his political influence.[103]

Another major figure to emerge during this period was Mullah Nasim Akhundzada, a commander of the *Harakat-e Inqilab* in Musa Qala district of Helmand province. Akhundzada systematically encouraged the cultivation of poppy in areas under his control. He set production quotas for the farmers and made advance payments to poppy growers at the time of cultivation. In 1989, he even required all farmers under his control to cultivate poppy in 50 per cent of their lands.[104] Subsequently, the advance payments by commanders and drug traffickers to farmers became a key driver of the spread of opium cultivation across the country. In the absence of formal credit systems, drug traffickers became a main source of credit for many farmers.

During the 1990s, poppy cultivation spread to other parts of the country as many more local power brokers and farmers were attracted to the benefits of the crop. A World Bank study attributed the rise to a range of factors: changing world market conditions, the collapse of governance, the relationship between drugs and arms, rural pauperisation, comparative advantage, and market development.[105] Poppy cultivation continued to grow after the emergence of the Taliban in 1994. In fact, the first few years of the Taliban rule even facilitated the cultivation and trade of narcotics. The Taliban's success in establishing a monopoly over the highways and dismantling checkpoints set up by the former *Mujahideen* militias created a more favourable environment for drug trade on a national scale. Furthermore, the Taliban collected *zakat*, a 10 per cent Islamic tax on the farmers as well as traders, which brought up to $200 million to their treasury.[106] In 1994, poppy cultivation had covered 71,500 hectares, which produced an estimated 3400 tons. By 1999, the area under cultivation had increased to 91,000 hectares and the production had reached 4600 tons.[107]

In July 2000, the Taliban declared a complete ban on cultivation of poppies across the country. The ban has been hailed as one of the most successful counternarcotics measures, as it brought down the size of land covered by poppy cultivation to only 8000 hectares. The Taliban's ban was likely to have been motivated by a number of factors, chief among them being a desire to increase their international legitimacy. Although by 1999, the movement had seized control of more than 90 per cent of the country, a combination of its draconian domestic policies and its alliance with international terrorist groups such as Al-Qaeda meant that it could not achieve much success in gaining international recognition. Only Pakistan, Saudi Arabia and the United Arab Emirates had recognised the Taliban. In this context, a major success in banning opium seemed a tool for significantly increasing its legitimacy internationally. However, the Taliban did not survive long enough to gain any legitimacy from the policy shift. Furthermore, it has also been suggested that the Taliban's policy may have been driven by economic calculations rather than a desire to seek international legitimacy. During the 1990s, the price of opium had steadily declined as a result of annual increases in production. The ban by the Taliban resulted to a 10-fold increase in opium prices in the country.[108] It can be argued that in the process of enforcing the ban, the Taliban also consolidated their monopoly over the production and trade of narcotics by eliminating rival networks.

In 2001, although poppy cultivation was at a historically low rate, after the fall of the Taliban, there were multiple challenges in maintaining a national ban on poppy cultivation. Afghanistan's Counter Narcotics Law of December 2005 provided a comprehensive framework for the prosecution of traffickers, but the Afghan government lacked the institutional capacity to enforce a nationwide ban and was dominated by networks of political and militia leaders that did not share an interest in eliminating the drug economy. Similarly, the international actors, including the United States and NATO, initially did not see counternarcotics as a priority. Furthermore, the underlying drivers of the drug economy, which included widespread poverty, well-developed national and transnational criminal networks and a weak or non-existent law enforcement capacity, were present across the country. Since narcotics played important roles in rural livelihoods[109] as well as providing finance for important political networks, an aggressive campaign could also negatively impact counterterrorism and counterinsurgency operations by driving local communities and power holders into the arms of the Taliban. These competing priorities meant that the counternarcotics strategy frequently changed its focus. For the first few years, major actors, particularly the United States, took a hands-off approach, as they prioritised political and security stabilisation. Only the British took a more active interest by assisting in the establishment of the Counter Narcotics Directorate as part of the National Security Council. As drug cultivation and production increased between 2004 and 2009, major actors, including the United States took a more active approach by integrating counter narcotics in counterterrorism and counterinsurgency operations. During this period, the US and NATO military forces were actively deployed in physical eradication of poppy fields as well as interdictions of drugs being trafficked. The Directorate of Counter Narcotics in Kabul was also upgraded to become a full-fledged ministry in 2005. After these interventions failed to produce results, in 2009, the US shifted its focus towards less coercive measures, focusing on programmes that aimed to create alternative livelihoods for farmers in the licit sector of the Afghan economy. It also aimed to incentivise provincial officials through a scheme that rewarded provincial governments with development funds if they could demonstrate their provinces were free from poppy cultivation. The new strategy was devised as part of President Obama's 2009 military and civilian surge that aimed to counter the Taliban insurgency through active deployment of aid and civilian personnel across the country.[110]

By 2017, the United States alone had spent $8.62 billion in various counternarcotics programmes in the country.[111] In November that year, the US military force in Afghanistan launched an aerial campaign, code-named Iron Tempest, to destroy drug laboratories in many provinces of Afghanistan. The objective of the campaign was clear. US military officials estimated that the Taliban were generating up to $200 million annually from the drug trade and operating up to 500 drug laboratories under their own control. Initially, US military commanders claimed that in 200 aerial strikes, they had deprived the Taliban of up to $45 million in income. But by the end of 2018, after it became clear the campaign was ineffective, the US military quietly dropped the plan.[112] Mansfield, a leading analyst of the country's drug economy, conducted research using satellite imaging together with data collected through field research interviews to assess the effectiveness of the aerial campaign. The research showed that most of the strikes targeted mud houses that were not active drug laboratories at the times of the attacks. Consequently, 'the destruction of these facilities had a negligible effect on the Taliban's finances, exacted little toll on drug trafficking organisations, and served to alienate the rural population in and around the areas where airstrikes were deployed'.[113] The failure of the Iron Tempest campaign illustrates the complexity of eliminating the drug economy that is now so deeply ingrained in the dynamics of insecurity, the insurgency, and the socio-economic challenges facing Afghanistan.

Afghanistan and the global economy

Residents of what is now Afghanistan were part of the global economy well before the emergence of anything like a system of states. It was only in the sixteenth and seventeenth centuries, and then predominantly in Europe, that territorially bounded units began to take shape in place of the heteronomous patterns of rule that had prevailed up to that point. In Central Asia, walled cities supplied the core of a number of political units, and the authority of rulers tended to erode as one moved away from the compounds in which they could exercise power with a reasonable degree of security, at least in the face of external rather than dynastic threats. Trade, however, was a vibrant activity – not just old, but positively ancient. Robert Crews has argued that 'The history of trade networks tying the region to faraway places dates back long before the caravan routes linking the Roman Empire and Han China, a network of corridors for the movement of all manner of commodities, later referred to as the "Silk Road"'[114]; and Shah Mahmoud Hanifi writes that 'Kabul, Peshawar, and Qandahar are ancient market settings between one and two thousand years of age. In a long-term historical perspective, Kabul, Peshawar, and Qandahar have combined in varying proportions exchange, finance, storage, and consumption activities'.[115] Afghanistan has not suddenly found itself part of the global economy; rather, the ancestors of present-day Afghans were frequently involved in trade, commerce and mercantile activity in a very intimate fashion. It is not surprising that many Afghans remain heavily involved in trading activity.[116]

The development of a modern system of states did, however, have one significant ramification for Afghanistan. It gave a salience to its status as a *landlocked* state which hardly made sense at a time when borders and boundaries were fluid rather than fixed. While the idea of a border as a marker of jurisdiction can be traced back at least to the Peace of Westphalia of 1648 in Europe, the idea of a border as an effective device for controlling the movement of merchandise and people came later and in a more ragged fashion,[117] not least because borders in this sense require elaborate bureaucratic mechanisms to exercise physical control over transit and to identify who and what is entitled to cross a border, and who and what is not. There are 43 landlocked states at present, and for most such states, their landlocked status gives rise to no special problems. Afghanistan, however, is different. Afghanistan historically positioned itself at the forefront of those states arguing for rights of transit under international law,[118] but it remains the case that 'a general right of transit is difficult to sustain'.[119] Afghanistan's historically tense relations with Pakistan exposed it to the risk that Pakistan might see the interdiction of Afghan trade through Pakistan as a source of leverage on political issues; and Pakistan did not hesitate to flex its muscles when relations with

Afghanistan hit their nadir in the early 1960s. A solution, of sorts, came with the 1965 Afghanistan-Pakistan Transit Trade Agreement, updated in 2010, but problems remained, and transit trade through Pakistan has been declining as new transport routes and air corridors via Iran, Central Asia and India have opened.

If there are potential difficulties in coping with a fraught regional environment, one way of addressing them is to try to become involved with a wider range of actors. This was a strategy pursued by Prime Minister Daoud between 1953 and 1963, in the context of Soviet-American rivalry. The United States had been interested in project-support opportunities from the late 1940s, most famously in the Helmand valley, where ambitious water management projects took shape.[120] Soviet economic involvement also began at this time. Much has been written about Soviet aid to Daoud's government, but a significant development came before this, as the emergence of the Pushtunistan dispute complicated the export of Afghan goods via Karachi. As Henry S. Bradsher noted,

> In July 1950 the Soviet Union signed a four-year trade agreement with Afghanistan to barter Soviet petroleum products, cotton cloth, sugar, and other commodities for Afghan wool, furs, raw cotton, fruit and nuts. It also provided duty-free transit for Afghan goods and gave Kabul a politically high currency exchange rate.[121]

Soviet investment in Afghanistan was to continue following the death of Stalin in March 1953 and was reinforced by the ideas of 'peaceful coexistence' and of a 'Zone of Peace' linking socialist and developing countries that Soviet leader Nikita S. Khrushchev set out to promote.[122] But there were also significant limits on how far the USSR was prepared to go in engaging economically with Afghanistan. Most strikingly, even following the Soviet invasion of Afghanistan in December 1979, the Soviet Union made no real attempt to integrate Afghanistan economically with other states in the Soviet sphere of influence. Indeed, Afghanistan never became a member of the Soviet-run Council for Mutual Economic Assistance, more commonly known as COMECON; and acquired observer status in the Council only in 1986, the very year in which the Soviet Politburo under the leadership of Mikhail Gorbachev took the decision in principle to withdraw from Afghanistan.

By this time, of course, Afghanistan was a severely disrupted state, and disrupted states are rarely attractive partners for economic integration. On the contrary, processes of trade and engagement with disrupted states are likely to be accompanied by very high transactions costs, of a kind that will deter all but the most adventurous investors, whether state or private. While the US energy company UNOCAL sought to engage with the Taliban with a view to building pipelines between Turkmenistan and South Asia via Afghanistan, in 1998, it suspended its activities for the simple reason that lenders had deemed the scheme unfinanceable given the risks involved.[123] For shrewd investors, risk is a political as well as purely economic idea.

In this sense, the re-establishment of the degree of political order after 2001 had a significant economic as well as political dimension. President Karzai was not an economist by training and for much of his presidency seemed content to leave the focus on economic issues to other political actors. President Ghani, by contrast, had served as a senior social scientist at the World Bank before returning to Afghanistan and had written his doctoral dissertation at Columbia University on the topic of production and domination in Afghanistan between 1747 and 2001. Unsurprisingly, he had developed a very clear vision of how Afghanistan's positioning of itself within the global economy might be used to advance the cause of political and economic reconstruction. A detailed account of this vision was offered by Ghani in a discussion at the Council on Foreign Relations in New York in March 2015. He emphasised three particular areas of opportunity[124]:

> Well, in terms of opportunities, the first is our location. Our location for 200 years has been a disadvantage. For three millennia, our location was a phenomenal advantage because we were at the centre of the circle lapis lazuli road, all roads led to us. And then, we were marginalized. Now in the next 25 years, Asia is going to become the largest continental economy. What happened in the United States in 1869 when the continental rail-roads were integrated is very likely to happen in Asia in the next 25 years. Without Afghanistan, central Asia, south Asia, East Asia and west Asia will not be connected, so this is our first advantage … Our goal is to become a transit country, for transport, for power transmission, for gas pipelines, for fiber optics. It's a networked approach to the economy because this will create massive jobs and opportunities … Second, we have water. We are the source, the headwater source for all our neighbors, but only 10 per cent of our water is utilized … Harnessing this water is the critical driver now of bringing prosperity to agriculture and the value chains and land utilization … The third asset is our mineral wealth … In 10 years, we can be the largest producer of copper and iron in the world.

Despite all the distractions which he faced as president, Dr Ghani kept his eyes firmly focussed on optimising the exploitation of Afghanistan's location. Apart from the National Air Corridor Program, the most important development in this respect has related to the coming on-stream of the expanded Chabahar port in the Iranian province of Sistan-Baluchistan. India invested heavily in this project and formally took over port operations in December 2018.[125] Somewhat remarkably, in November 2018, the United States agreed to exempt Chabahar from sanctions against Iran, in recognition of the importance of the Chabahar port for the economic development of Afghanistan.[126] From Afghanistan's point of view, the primary significance of Chabahar is that it provides an alternative to Pakistani ports such as Karachi or Gwadar for the export of merchandise from Afghanistan. It also provides an avenue for imports to reach Afghanistan as well, and this opens the possibility of Afghanistan's securing easier access to capital equipment which it is currently unable to produce domestically. In the long run, however, its greatest significance may simply lie in the weakening of Pakistan's capacity to wreak havoc economically for Afghanistan should it be inclined to do so.[127] This, in turn, would set the scene for a more level playing field for the negotiation of regional economic integration arrangements.

Southwest Asia is currently witnessing a range of significant economic developments, not least because of China's 'Belt and Road' initiative, and the spinoff 'China-Pakistan Economic Corridor'.[128] In the long run, this may threaten Afghanistan's crossroads position by allowing Pakistan to transport goods via China to destinations in Central Asia and beyond, but much will depend on how the initiative evolves. In the meantime, Afghanistan has been active in seeking to engage with regional organisations with an economic focus, although its memberships are best seen as facilitators for future regional engagement than evidence of achievements already attained. Notably, it has been a member since 1992 of the Economic Cooperation Organization, a member since 2007 of the South Asian Association for Regional Cooperation and an observer since 2012 in the Shanghai Cooperation Organisation. Its focus, however, has not been simply regional, and Afghanistan affirmed its commitment to a rules-based international trading order when it became a member on 29 July 2016 of the World Trade Organization. The World Trade Organization came into existence on 1 January 1995 as successor to the 1948 General Agreement on Tariffs and Trade and serves not only as custodian of the ideal of free international trade, but also offers dispute resolution mechanisms that can be employed by members objecting to the actions of other member-states.[129]

The current patterns of Afghanistan's external trade point to a position of ongoing fragility. In 2017, imports greatly exceeded exports, contributing to a deficit in net trade in goods and services worth US$6.972 billion.[130] According to World Trade Organization figures, Afghanistan, in 2017, had a GDP valued at US$20.889 billion and a GDP per capita of US$591. Merchandise exports for 2017 totalled just US$780 million. In 2016, agricultural products made up 73.3 per cent of merchandise exports. The three main destination countries for such exports were Pakistan (47.5 per cent), India (38.6 per cent) and Iran (3.2 per cent).[131] Sustained trade deficits can be covered in a number of ways. One is through capital inflow, in Afghanistan's case in the form of aid, although foreign capital investment is an alternative. Another is through the depreciation of the foreign exchange rate of one's currency. The effect of such depreciation is to make one's exports cheaper for foreign buyers, and imports more expensive for domestic purchasers, which, other things being equal, should help to reduce the difference in value of exports and imports. But that said, in the real world, things are rarely equal, and other factors may come into play. Notably, policy settings that make imports more expensive may be politically unpopular if significant elements of the population see the imports involved not as luxury goods, but as staple necessities. The value of the *afghani* against the US dollar has depreciated, but relatively gently, since its launch. In October 2002, a dollar would buy 43 *afghanis*. By January 2019, a dollar would buy 75 *afghanis*.

There is no doubt that expansions in global trade have been amongst the most significant contributors to improved standards of living, but equally, it is important to recognise that there are potential threats to international trade that could materialise to the disadvantage of significant numbers of Afghans. One is simply the re-emergence of global protectionism. Until recently, this was seen as highly unlikely, but several developments have occurred that point to the need for caution. One has been the stalling of multilateral trade negotiations, notably, the Doha Round; and a proliferation of 'bilateral' or 'regional' free trade agreements which are better seen as 'preferential trade agreements'.[132] Another has been the broadly protectionist orientation of the United States under the Trump Administration, especially in its relations with China. If a fully fledged 'trade war' were to break out between these two major actors, the ramifications would most likely be felt by most other trading states as well, via a slump in the volume of trade globally. A second potential threat to Afghanistan's trade could arise at the regional level, either through deliberate measures by Pakistan to exploit Afghanistan's vulnerability as a landlocked state, or through an escalation in conflict between India and Pakistan that could affect Afghan exports. A third potential threat could arise domestically in Afghanistan, if established producers were to make use of their networks in order to secure protection from the state against competition from imports. This may not be a major problem at present, but it could become more serious in the future.[133]

Of course, as our earlier discussion of opium made clear, not all of Afghanistan's trade is legal. In fact, two forms of illegal trade have potentially been very significant for Afghanistan. One is smuggling: the illicit movement of goods in order to avoid the imposition of customs duties is a very old phenomenon; indeed, Rudyard Kipling wrote a poem – *A Smuggler's Song* – about it.[134] With a porous border historically existing between Afghanistan and Pakistan, at different stages a lively smugglers' trade has seen goods being transported across the border from Afghanistan to Pakistan by smugglers for sale, free of duty, in smugglers' markets. One of the authors, travelling by car from Jalalabad to Peshawar via the Khyber Pass in 1998, found himself behind a truck carrying new televisions; given the Taliban restrictions on media in Afghanistan at the time, the televisions were certainly not intended for sale in Afghanistan. Afghan governments have no interest in seeing the smuggling trade flourish, as it can only complicate the already-fraught relationship with Pakistan, but there is always a risk that smugglers will add to the problem of corruption in Afghanistan by bribing those officials who could cause them trouble. This is even more the case where the other form of illegal trade, namely, in narcotics, comes into play. The profits that drug traffickers can derive tend to be extremely large, and it is entirely rational from their point of view to spend some of them as a lubricant for the operation of their trade.

Finally, Afghanistan's economic trajectory and prospects are inseparably connected to the impact on Afghanistan of the wider phenomenon of globalisation, which we discuss in more detail in the next chapter. What is very clear, however, is that international economic relations have been transformed by globalisation, for Afghanistan as for other states in the international system. The international economic order is no longer largely paper-based; finance now substantially involves real-time activity in a world of electronic communications. This has given rise to great benefits, by reducing the costs associated with a vast range of economic transactions, and the advantages for businesses in poor countries operating on thin profit margins can be very considerable. It does, however, inject a high degree of volatility into international economic relations, especially when computer algorithms are available to trigger the sale of assets the prices of which appeared to be declining. The world has witnessed volatility before, but for different reasons. The contagion which saw the Great Depression spread around the world from 1929 had much to do with the existence of the gold standard, which limited flexibility in the realm of monetary policy. But the end of the gold standard did not mean the end of financial instability, as was demonstrated with the spread of the Asian Financial Crisis from July 1997 and the Global Financial Crisis in 2008. Business failures, or the collapse of asset price bubbles,[135] can have complex effects that spread to even remote parts of the world. There is no reason for thinking that in a globalising world, Afghanistan will prove itself to be immune from such forces.

Notes

1 Adam Smith, *An Inquiry into the Nature and Causes of the Wealth of Nations* (London: Nelson & Sons, 1873) pp. 6–7. For Mandeville's earlier formulation, from 1729–1732, see Bernard Mandeville, *The Fable of The Bees, Or Private Vices, Publick Benefits* (Indianapolis: Liberty Fund, 1988).

2 Lionel Robbins, *An Essay on the Nature and Significance of Economic Science* (London: Macmillan, 1945) p. 16.

3 For discussion of some complexities surrounding these issues, see János Kornai, *The Socialist System: The Political Economy of Communism* (Princeton: Princeton University Press, 1992); Lisa Herzog, *Inventing the Market: Smith, Hegel and Political Theory* (Oxford: Oxford University Press, 2013); William J. Baumol, *The Free-Market Innovation Machine: Analyzing the Growth Miracle of Capitalism* (Princeton: Princeton University Press, 2002).

4 See Ashley Jackson and Giulia Minoia, 'Political and Economic Life in Afghanistan: Networks of Access', *Asian Survey*, vol. 58, no. 6, November-December 2018, pp. 1090–1110.

5 *A Survey of the Afghan People: Afghanistan in 2018* (Kabul: The Asia Foundation, 2018) p. 68.

6 See William Maley, 'Realising the minimal state: The case of Afghanistan', *Agenda*, vol. 3, no. 2, 1996, pp. 261–264.

7 See Ashraf Ghani, Clare Lockhart and Michael Carnahan, *Closing the Sovereignty Gap: An Approach to State-Building* (London: Working Paper no. 253, Overseas Development Institute, September 2005); Peter Blunt, Farid Mamundzay, Nader Yama, and Hamidullah Afghan, 'Policy paradigms, subnational governance and the state sovereignty gap in Afghanistan', *Progress in Development Studies*, vol. 15, no. 3, July 2015, pp. 270–285.

8 Kenneth Katzman and Clayton Thomas, *Afghanistan: Post-Taliban Governance, Security, and U.S. Policy* (Washington, DC: Congressional Research Service, 13 December 2017) p. ii.

9 *Net official development assistance and official aid received (constant 2015 US$): Afghanistan* (Washington, DC: The World Bank, 2018).

10 *Aid Effectiveness in Afghanistan: A Research Study by ATR Consulting* (Kabul: Oxfam and Swedish Committee for Afghanistan, March 2018) p. 27.

11 Nematullah Bizhan, 'State-building in Afghanistan: Aid, politics, and state capacity', *Asian Survey*, vol. 58, no. 6, November–December 2018, pp. 973–994 at p. 981.

12 See Paul Seabright, 'Conflicts of objectives and task allocation in aid agencies', in Bertin Martens, Uwe Mummert, Peter Murrell and Paul Seabright, *The Institutional Economics of Foreign Aid* (Cambridge: Cambridge University Press, 2002) pp. 34–68.

13 Nematullah Bizhan, *Aid Paradoxes in Afghanistan: Building and Undermining the State* (London: Routledge, 2018) pp. 139–141.

14 John Maynard Keynes, *The General Theory of Employment, Interest and Money* (London: Macmillan, 1973).

15 Ashraf Ghani, Clare Lockhart, Nargis Nehan and Baqer Massoud, 'The budget as the linchpin of the state: Lessons from Afghanistan', in James K. Boyce and Madalene O'Donnell (eds.), *Peace and the Public Purse: Economic Policies for Postwar Statebuilding* (Boulder: Lynne Rienner, 2007) pp. 153–183 at p. 168.

16 See W.M. Corden, *The Theory of Protection* (Oxford: Oxford University Press, 1971); W. Max Corden, *Trade Policy and Economic Welfare* (Oxford: Oxford University Press, 1997).

17 See Hugh Dalton, *Principles of Public Finance* (London: George Routledge & Sons, 1946) pp. 184–191.

18 *Afghanistan Statistical Yearbook 2017–18* (Kabul: National Statistics and Information Authority, Islamic Republic of Afghanistan, August 2018) p. ii.

19 Barnett R. Rubin, 'Constructing sovereignty for security', *Survival*, vol. 7, no. 4, Winter 2005, pp. 93–106 at p. 99.

20 Nematullah Bizhan, *Building Legitimacy and State Capacity in Protracted Fragility: The Case of Afghanistan* (London and Oxford: LSE-Oxford Commission on State Fragility, Growth and Development, 2018) p. 16.

21 William A. Byrd and Shah Zaman Farahi, *Improving Afghanistan's Public Finances in 2017–2019: Raising Revenue and Reforming the Budget* (Washington, DC: Special Report no. 424, United States Institute of Peace, April 2018) p. 2.

22 Peter Blunt, Farid Mamundzay and Muqtader Nasery, 'The long and the short of policy pantomime in Afghanistan', *Progress in Development Studies*, vol. 17, no. 1, January 2017, pp. 67–88.

23 *The Blight of Auction-Based Budgeting: What is it and how can we deal with it?* (Washington, DC: Development Practice Note, Institute for State Effectiveness, September 2017) p. 2.

24 See Nematullah Bizhan and Ferhat Emil with Haroon Nayebkhail, *Bringing the State Closer to the People: Deconcentrating Planning and Budgeting in Afghanistan* (Kabul: Afghanistan Research and Evaluation Unit, July 2016); Aureo de Toledo Gomes, 'Statebuilding and the politics of budgeting in Afghanistan', *Journal of Intervention and Statebuilding*, vol. 11, no. 4, 2017, pp. 511–528.

25 See Phillip Cagan, 'The monetary dynamics of hyperinflation', in Milton Friedman, *Studies in the Quantity Theory of Money* (Chicago: University of Chicago Press, 1956) pp. 25–117. To give a sense of what this can involve, Cagan notes (at p. 26) that in the hyperinflation in Hungary from August 1945 to July 1946, the ratio of prices at the end to those at the beginning was 3.81×10^{27}.

26 Maxwell J. Fry, *The Afghan Economy: Money, Finance, and the Critical Constraints to Economic Development* (Leiden: E.J. Brill, 1974) pp. 112, 109.

27 See Barnett R. Rubin, 'The political economy of war and peace in Afghanistan', *World Development*, vol. 28, no. 10, October 2000, pp. 1789–1803 at p. 1793. The situation in which multiple currencies compete with each other has potential advantages,

but also disadvantages. For different perspectives, see F.A. Hayek, *New Studies in Philosophy, Politics, Economics and the History of Ideas* (London: Routledge & Kegan Paul, 1978) pp. 218–231; Lance Girton and Don Roper, 'Theory and implications of currency substitution', *Journal of Money, Credit and Banking*, vol. 13, no. 1, February 1981, pp. 12–30.

28 See Ghani, Lockhart, Nehan and Massoud, 'The budget as the linchpin of the state', pp. 163–164. On the *hawala* system more generally, see Samuel Munzele Maimbo, *The Money Exchange Dealers of Kabul: A Study of the Hawala System in Afghanistan* (Washington, DC: World Bank Working Paper no. 13, The World Bank, 2003); Edwina A. Thompson, *Trust is the Coin of the Realm: Lessons from the Money Men in Afghanistan* (Karachi: Oxford University Press, 2011).

29 See Horst Nägler, *Privatinitiative beim Industrieaufbau in Afghanistan* (Düsseldorf: Bertelsmann Universitätsverlag, 1971).

30 Ghani, Lockhart, Nehan and Massoud, 'The Budget as the Linchpin of the State', p. 165.

31 See Colleen P. Eren, *Bernie Madoff and the Crisis: The Public Trial of Capitalism* (Stanford: Stanford University Press, 2017).

32 James Fontanella-Khan and Robin Wigglesworth, 'Kabul steps in to stop run on biggest bank', *The Financial Times*, September 6, 2010.

33 See Jon Boone, 'The Financial Scandal that Broke Afghanistan's Kabul Bank', *The Guardian*, 17 June 2011. In November 2015, the Government actually signed a property deal with Ferozi, apparently in the hope of recovering missing funds: see Emma Graham-Harrison, 'Afghan Government Signs Huge Property Deal with Shamed Ex-Banker', *The Guardian*, 6 November 2015. In the face of negative publicity, President Ghani nullified the deal: see Grant McLeod, *Responding to Corruption and the Kabul Bank Collapse* (Washington, DC: Special Report no. 398, United States Institute of Peace, December 2016) p. 10. Farnood died in prison in August 2018.

34 See Joshua Partlow, *A Kingdom of Their Own: The Family Karzai and the Afghan Disaster* (New York: Alfred A. Knopf, 2016) pp. 234–255; Abdul Qadeer Fitrat, *The Tragedy of Kabul Bank* (New York: Page, 2018).

35 Independent Joint Anti-Corruption Monitoring and Evaluation Committee, *Report of the Public Inquiry into the Kabul Bank Crisis* (Kabul: Independent Joint Anti-Corruption Monitoring and Evaluation Committee, 2012) p. 3.

36 *Afghanistan Living Conditions Survey 2016–17: Analysis Report* (Kabul: Central Statistics Organization, Islamic Republic of Afghanistan, 2018) pp. iv, v.

37 See *Afghanistan Multidimensional Poverty Index 2016–2017: Report and Analysis* (Kabul: National Statistics and Information Authority, Islamic Republic of Afghanistan, 2019) pp. vi–vii.

38 See Paula Kantor and Adam Pain, *Securing Life and Livelihoods in Afghanistan: The Role of Social Relationships* (Kabul: Afghanistan Research and Evaluation Unit, December 2010).

39 *Boosting Private Sector Development and Entrepreneurship in Afghanistan* (Paris: Eurasia Competitiveness Programme, OECD, 2019) p. 23; See also Richard Ghiasy, Jiayi Zhou and Henrik Hallgren *Afghanistan's Private Sector: Status and Ways Forward* (Stockholm: SIPRI and NIR–Näringslivets Internationella Råd, October 2015).

40 Mir Muhammad Siddiq Farhang, *Afghanistan dar panj qarn-e akhir* (Peshawar: Ehsanullah Mayar, 1988) p. 437.

41 The phenomenon of intimate relations between rulers and businessmen has been a common one in developing countries: see, for example, Andrew MacIntyre, *Business and Politics in Indonesia* (Sydney: Allen & Unwin, 1991); Andrew MacIntyre (ed.), *Business and Government in Industrialising Asia* (Ithaca: Cornell University Press, 1994); and Peter Searle, *The Riddle of Malaysian Capitalism: Rent-Seekers or Real Capitalists?* (Honolulu: University of Hawai'i Press, 1999).

42 For a semi-autobiographical account of the life of Abdul Majid Zabuli, see Wahid Mozhdah (ed.), *Yaddasthay-e Abdul Majid Zabuli* (Peshawar: Maiwand Publishers, 2001).

43 Jonathan L. Lee, *Afghanistan: A History from 1260 to the Present* (London: Reaktion Books, 2018) p. 516.

44 Ibid., p. 515.

45 'Dueling Afghan Chambers of Commerce', Cable Reference ID 05KABUL5118_a, U.S Embassy, Kabul, 17 December 2005.

46 *Annual Report 2010-2011* (Kabul: Afghanistan Chamber of Commerce and Industries, 2011) pp. 7–12.

47 See McLeod, *Responding to Corruption and the Kabul Bank Collapse*, p. 3.

48 *ICT Economic Impact Assessment* (Kabul: Altai Consulting Company and USAID, July 2014) p. 7.

49 Matthieu Aikins, 'The Bidding War: How a Young Afghan Military Contractor became Spectacularly Rich,' *The New Yorker*, 28 February 2016.

50 Matthew Green, 'Afghanistan Acts to Curb Flight of Capital', *The Financial Times*, 19 March 2012.

51 'Wazir-e maliyah Afghanistan: bohran-e entekhabat panj milliard ba eqtesad-e ma sadamah zadah,' *BBC Persian Service,* 25 August 2014; 'Tolani shodan-e rawand-e entekhabat baais-e kahish-e dar amadhai dakhili shoda ast,' *BBC Persian Service*, 4 August 2014.

52 'Capital flight result of inadequate facilities: MoE,' *The Afghanistan Times*, 24 May 2016.

53 *The Economic Disaster Behind Afghanistan's Mounting Human Crisis* (Brussels: International Crisis Group, 3 October 2016).

54 See Bizhan, *Building legitimacy and state capacity in protracted fragility*, p. 28.

55 Izabela Leao, Mansur Ahmed and Anuja Kar, *Jobs from Agriculture in Afghanistan* (Washington, DC: International Development in Focus, World Bank, 2018) p. 9.

56 See Grant M. Farr and Azam Gul, 'Afghan agricultural production: 1978–1982', *Journal of South Asian and Middle Eastern Studies,* vol. 8, no. 1, 1984, pp. 65–79; *The Agricultural Survey of Afghanistan: First Report* (Peshawar: Swedish Committee for Afghanistan, 1988).

57 *Country Briefs: Afghanistan* (Rome: Global Information and Early Warning System, Food and Agriculture Organization, 21 June 2018). The idea of food security is itself a complex one, with multiple dimensions. For some discussion, see Andrew Pinney and Scott Ronchini, 'Food security in Afghanistan after 2001: From assessment to analysis and interpretation to response', in Adam Pain and Jacky Sutton (eds.), *Reconstructing Agriculture in Afghanistan* (Rugby: Practical Action Publishing, 2007) pp. 119–164.

58 Michael Barry, *Afghanistan* (Paris: Éditions du Seuil, 1974) p. 182.

59 See Amartya Sen, *Poverty and Famines: An Essay on Entitlement and Deprivation* (Oxford: Oxford University Press, 1982).

60 See Ian Christoplos, *Out of Step? Agricultural Policy and Afghan Livelihoods* (Kabul: Afghanistan Research and Evaluation Unit, May 2004). On the importance of local understanding more generally, see James C. Scott, *Seeing Like a State: How Certain Schemes to Improve the Human Condition Have Failed* (New Haven: Yale University Press, 1998).

61 For background, see Liz Alden Wily, *Land, People, and the State in Afghanistan: 2002–2012* (Kabul: Afghanistan Research and Evaluation Unit, February 2013).

62 See Liz Alden Wily, *Land Rights in Crisis: Restoring Tenure Security in Afghanistan* (Kabul: Afghanistan Research and Evaluation Unit, March 2003) pp. 3–4.

63 Colin Deschamps and Alan Roe, *Land Conflict in Afghanistan: Building Capacity to Address Vulnerability* (Kabul: Afghanistan Research and Evaluation Unit, April 2009) pp. 6–9.

64 *An Introduction to the Property Law of Afghanistan* (Stanford: Afghanistan Legal Education Project, Stanford Law School, 2015) p. 153.

65 See Niamatullah Ibrahimi, *The Hazaras and the Afghan State: Rebellion, Exclusion, and the Struggle for Recognition* (London: Hurst & Co., 2017) p. 104.

66 See Andrea Chiovenda and Melissa Chiovenda, 'The spectre of the "arrivant": Hauntology of an interethnic conflict in Afghanistan', *Asian Anthropology*, vol. 17, no. 3, 2018, pp. 165–184 at pp. 173–174.

67 Fabrizio Foschini, *The Kuchi-Hazara Conflict, Again* (Kabul: Afghanistan Analysts Network, 27 May 2010).

68 'Air Cargo Route Opens from Northern Afghanistan to Turkey, Europe', *Reuters*, 10 January 2019.

69 *MAIL Spends 95 Percent Development Budget* (Kabul: Ministry of Agriculture and Irrigation and Livestock, 19 December 2018).

70 See Adam Pain and Danielle Huot, 'Challenges of late development in Afghanistan: The transformation that did not happen', *Asian Survey*, vol. 58, no. 6, November–December 2018, pp. 1111–1135.

71 See Richard Rose, 'Toward a civil economy', *Journal of Democracy*, vol. 3, no. 2, April 1992, pp. 13–26 at p. 14.

72 Paula Kantor and Adam Pain, *Running Out of Options: Tracing Rural Afghan Livelihoods* (Kabul: Afghanistan Research and Evaluation Unit, January 2011).

73 See Jackson and Minoia, 'Political and Economic Life in Afghanistan: Networks of Access'.

74 *The Evaluation of the 'National Solidarity Program' in Afghanistan* (Kabul: Center for Regional and Strategic Studies, 18 March 2017).

75 Nicholas Leader and Mohammed Haneef Atmar, 'Political projects: Reform, aid and the state in Afghanistan', in Antonio Donini, Norah Niland and Karin Wermester (eds.), *Nation-Building Unraveled? Aid, Peace and Justice in Afghanistan* (Bloomfield: Kumarian Press, 2004) pp. 166–186 at p. 172.

76 Andrew Beath, Fotini Christia and Ruben Enikolopov, *Randomized Impact Evaluation of Afghanistan's National Solidarity Program: Final Report* (Kabul: World Bank, 1 July 2013) pp. ix–xi. See also Andrew Beath, Fotini Christia and Ruben Enikolopov, 'The national solidarity programme: Assessing the effects of community-driven development in Afghanistan', *International Peacekeeping*, vol. 22, no. 4, August 2015, pp. 302–320. For earlier appraisals of the NSP, see Inger W. Boesen, *From Subjects to Citizens: Local Participation in the National Solidarity Programme* (Kabul: Afghanistan Research and Evaluation Unit, August 2004); Yama Torabi, *Assessing the NSP: The Role of Accountability in Reconstruction* (Kabul: Integrity Watch Afghanistan, 2007).

77 For further discussion of some of these issues, see Doug Porter, Bryant Allen and Gaye Thompson, *Development in Practice: Paved with Good Intentions* (London: Routledge, 1991).

78 Ashraf Ghani and Clare Lockhart, *Fixing Failed States: A Framework for Rebuilding a Fractured World* (New York: Oxford University Press, 2008) p. 214.

79 Charlotte Dufour and Annelies Borrel, 'Towards a public nutrition response in Afghanistan: Evolutions in nutritional assessment and response', in Adam Pain and Jacky Sutton (eds.), *Reconstructing Agriculture in Afghanistan* (Rugby: Practical Action Publishing, 2007) pp. 93–118 at p. 113.

80 See Tony Eggleton, *A Short Introduction to Climate Change* (Cambridge: Cambridge University Press, 2012).

81 *Climate Change in Afghanistan: What does it Mean for Rural Livelihoods and Food Security?* (Kabul: World Food Programme, United Nations Environment Programme, and National Environmental Protection Agency, November 2016) pp. 50, 52.

82 See Alessandro Monsutti, *War and Migration: Social Networks and Economic Strategies of the Hazaras of Afghanistan* (New York: Routledge, 2005).

83 See Susanne Schmeidl and William Maley, 'The case of the Afghan refugee popula-tion: Finding durable solutions in contested transitions', in Howard Adelman (ed.), *Protracted Displacement in Asia: No Place to Call Home* (Aldershot: Ashgate, 2008) pp. 131–179.

84 Susanne Schmeidl, 'Internal displacement in Afghanistan: The tip of the iceberg', in Srinjoy Bose, Nishank Motwani and William Maley (eds.), *Afghanistan – Challenges and Prospects* (London: Routledge, 2018) pp. 169–187 at p. 169.

85 See Ali M. Latifi, 'How Iran Recruited Afghan Refugees to Fight Assad's War', *The New York Times*, 30 June 2017; Ahmad Shuja Jamal, 'Mission accomplished? What's next for Iran's Afghan fighters in Syria?', *War on the Rocks*, 13 February 2018; Ahmad Shuja Jamal, *The Fatemiyoun Army: Reintegration into Afghan Society* (Washington, DC: Special Report no. 443, United States Institute of Peace, March 2019).

86 *Afghanistan: Voluntary Repatriation Update* (Geneva: United Nations High Commissioner for Refugees, 10 January 2019) p. 4. Interestingly, none of these figures remotely approached the scale of voluntary repatriation that followed the overthrow of the Taliban regime: 1,834,537 in 2002, 475,639 in 2003, 761,122 in 2004, and 514,090 in 2005.

87 See Liza Schuster and Nassim Majidi, 'What happens post-deportation? The experi-ence of deported Afghans', *Migration Studies*, vol. 1, no. 2, July 2013, pp. 221–240; Liza Schuster and Nassim Majidi, 'Deportation stigma and re-migration', *Journal of Ethnic and Migration Studies*, vol. 41, no. 4, 2015, pp. 635–652.

88 John Maynard Keynes, *A Tract on Monetary Reform* (London: Macmillan & Co., 1923) p. 80.

89 See Jonathan Goodhand, 'Corrupting or consolidating the peace? The drugs economy and post-conflict peacebuilding in Afghanistan,' *International Peacekeeping*, vol. 15, no. 3, June 2008, pp. 405–423; James A. Piazza, 'The opium trade and patterns of terrorism in the provinces of Afghanistan: An empirical analysis,' *Terrorism and Political Violence*, vol. 24, no. 2, April 2012, pp. 213–234; David Bewley-Taylor, 'Drug trafficking and organised crime in Afghanistan,' *The RUSI Journal*, vol. 158, no. 6, December 2013, pp. 6–17.

90 See William B. McAllister, *Drug Diplomacy in the Twentieth Century: An International History* (London: Routledge, 2000). International policy in this respect has been notoriously perverse in its consequences: Ralph Seccombe, 'Squeezing the balloon: International drugs policy', *Drug and Alcohol Review*, vol. 14, no. 3, July 1995, pp. 311–316; Ralph Seccombe, 'Troublesome boomerang: Illicit drug policy and security', *Security Dialogue*, vol. 28, no. 3, September 1997, pp. 287–299.

91 David Mansfield and Adam Pain, *Alternative Livelihoods: Substance or Slogan?* (Kabul: Afghanistan Research and Evaluation Unit, October 2005); Paul Fishstein, *Despair or Hope: Rural Livelihoods and Opium Poppy Dynamics in Afghanistan* (Kabul: Afghanistan Research and Evaluation Unit, August 2014).

92 *Afghanistan Opium Survey 2018: Cultivation and Production* (Kabul: United Nations Office on Drugs and Crime and Ministry of Counter Narcotics, Islamic Republic of Afghanistan, November 2018) p. 5.

93 *Afghanistan Opium Survey 2017: Challenges to Sustainable Development, Peace and Security* (Kabul: United Nations Office on Drugs and Crime and Ministry of Counter Narcotics, Islamic Republic of Afghanistan, May 2018) p. 13.

94 Ibid., p. 9.

95 James Tharin Bradford, *Poppies, Politics, and Power: Afghanistan and the Global History of Drugs and Diplomacy* (Ithaca: Cornell University Press, 2019) p. 59.

96 See 'Opium Production Throughout the World', *Bulletin on Narcotics*, vol. 1, no. 1, 1949, pp. 6–38.

97 See Bradford, *Poppies, Politics, and Power*, p. 57.

98 David Mansfield, *A State Built on Sand: How Opium Undermined Afghanistan* (London: Hurst & Co., 2016) p. 103.

99 See James Bradford, 'Drug control in Afghanistan: Culture, politics, and power during the 1958 Prohibition of Opium in Badakhshan', *Iranian Studies*, vol. 48, no. 2, 2015, pp. 223–248.

100 Lee, *Afghanistan: A History from 1260 to the Present.*

101 See Hazhir Teimourian, 'Drug Baron in the Border Hills', *The Times,* 25 September 1989.

102 Barnett R. Rubin, *The Fragmentation of Afghanistan: State Formation and Collapse in the International System* (New Haven: Yale University Press, 2002) p. 257.

103 Vanda Felbab-Brown 'Kicking the opium habit?: Afghanistan's drug economy and politics since the 1980s', *Conflict, Security and Development*, vol. 6, no. 2, June 2006, pp. 127–149.

104 Rubin, *The Fragmentation of Afghanistan*, p. 263.

105 Christopher Ward and William Byrd, *Afghanistan's Opium Drug Economy* (Washington, DC: Working Paper SASPR–5, The World Bank, December 2004) pp. 9–10.

106 Felbab-Brown, 'Kicking the opium habit?,' p. 137.

107 *Global Illicit Drug Trends 2001* (New York: United Nations Office for Drug Control and Crime Prevention, 2001) p. 35.

108 *Afghanistan Opium Survey 2003* (Kabul: United Nations Office on Drugs and Crime and Afghan Transition Government, Counter Narcotics Directorate 2003), p. 6.

109 See *Afghanistan—State Building, Sustaining Growth, and Reducing Poverty* (Washington, DC: The World Bank, 2005) pp. 118–119.

110 For a discussion of these changes in counternarcotics strategies, see Christopher J. Coyne, Abigail R. Hall Blanco, and Scott Burns, 'The War on Drugs in Afghanistan: Another Failed Experiment with Interdiction,' *The Independent Review*, vol. 21, no. 1, Summer 2016, pp. 95–119.

111 For an assessment of the US approaches to counternarcotics in Afghanistan see *Counternarcotics: Lessons from the U.S. Experience in Afghanistan* (Arlington: Lessons Learned Report, Special Inspector General for Afghanistan Reconstruction, June 2018).

112 W.J. Hennigan, 'The U.S. Sent Its Most Advanced Fighter Jets to Blow Up Cheap Opium Labs. Now It's Canceling the Program', *Time*, 21 February 2019.

113 David Mansfield, *Denying Revenue or Wasting Money? Assessing the Impact of the Air Campaign Against 'Drugs Labs' in Afghanistan* (London: LSE International Drug Policy Unit, April 2019) p. 8.

114 Robert D. Crews, *Afghan Modern: The History of a Global Nation* (Cambridge: Harvard University Press, 2015) p. 19. The 'Silk Road' was never a single road, but rather a complex space: see Christopher I. Beckwith, *Empires of the Silk Road: A History of Central Asia from the Bronze Age to the Present* (Princeton: Princeton University Press, 2009). See also Faiz Ahmed, *Afghanistan Rising: Islamic Law and Statecraft between the Ottoman and British Empires* (Cambridge: Harvard University Press, 2017) p. 10.

115 Shah Mahmoud Hanifi, *Connecting Histories in Afghanistan: Market Relations and State Formation on a Colonial Frontier* (Stanford: Stanford University Press, 2008) p. 6.

116 See Magnus Marsden, *Trading Worlds: Afghan Merchants Across Modern Frontiers* (London: Hurst & Co., 2016).

117 See Charles S. Maier, *Once Within Borders: Territories of Power, Wealth and Belonging since 1500* (Cambridge: Harvard University Press, 2016).

118 See Abdul Hakim Tabibi, *The Right of Transit of Land-Locked Countries: A Study of Legal and International Development of the Right of Free Access to the Sea* (Kabul: Afghan Book Company, 1970). Dr Tabibi was Minister of Justice of Afghanistan in 1965–1966, and in 1975 served as Chair of the 27th Session of the International Law Commission.

119 James Crawford, *Brownlie's Principles of Public International Law* (Oxford: Oxford University Press, 2012) p. 344.

120 See Louis Dupree, *Afghanistan* (Princeton: Princeton University Press, 1980) pp. 482–485, 499–507.

121 Henry S. Bradsher, *Afghanistan and the Soviet Union* (Durham: Duke University Press, 1985) pp. 21–22.

122 See Vendulka Kubálková and A.A. Cruickshank, *Marxism-Leninism and Theory of International Relations* (London: Routledge & Kegan Paul, 1980) pp. 161–163.

123 See William Maley, *The Afghanistan Wars* (New York: Palgrave Macmillan, 2009) pp. 204–205.

124 See 'The Road Ahead for Afghanistan', Council on Foreign Relations, New York, 26 March 2015. https://www.cfr.org/event/road-ahead-afghanistan (Text edited to omit transcription errors.)

125 'India Takes Over Iran's Strategic Chabahar Port', *Radio Free Europe/Radio Liberty*, 25 December 2018.

126 See Ayaz Gul, 'Afghans hail exemption of Iran port from US sanctions, *Voice of America*, 7 November 2018.

127 For more detailed discussion, see C. Christine Fair, 'A New Strategy for Afghanistan Begins in Iran', *The Khaama Press News Agency*, 22 November 2018.

128 See Claude Rakisits, 'A path to the sea: China's Pakistan plan', *World Affairs Journal*, Fall 2015.

129 See David A. Deese, *World Trade Politics: Power, Principles and Leadership* (New York: Routledge, 2008).

130 *Afghanistan: Net trade in goods and services (BoP, current US$)* (Washington, DC: The World Bank, 2018).

131 *Afghanistan and the WTO* (Geneva: World Trade Organization, 2018).

132 See Jagdish Bhagwati and Arvind Panagariya, 'The theory of preferential trade agreements: Historical evolution and current trends', *American Economic Review*, vol. 86, no. 2, May 1996, pp. 82–87; Jagdish Bhagwati, *Termites in the Trading System: How Preferential Agreements Undermine Free Trade* (New York: Oxford University Press, 2008).

133 See Mancur Olson, *The Logic of Collective Action: Public Goods and the Theory of Groups* (Cambridge: Harvard University Press, 1965). Given the salience of networks in a neopatrimonial system, this danger is unlikely to be ameliorated by what Trumbull has called 'legitimacy coalitions': see Gunnar Trumbull, *Strength in Numbers: The Political Power of Weak Interests* (Cambridge: Harvard University Press, 2012) pp. 22–29.

134 *Rudyard Kipling's Verse: Inclusive Edition 1885–1926* (London: Hodder & Stoughton, 1927) pp. 635–636.

135 Asset price bubbles occur when the market price of a traded asset far exceeds any intrinsic value that the asset has. The two most famous cases were Tulipmania in the Dutch Republic in 1637 and the South Sea Bubble of 1720 – although recent scholarship has raised questions as to how far out of the ordinary Tulipmania actually was: see Anne Goldgar, *Tulipmania: Money, Honor, and Knowledge in the Dutch Golden Age* (Chicago: University of Chicago Press, 2008).

5

INTERNATIONAL RELATIONS

Afghanistan is to a significant degree a hostage of its international relations and arguably has been for most if not all of its life. This is likely to remain the case for the foreseeable future. This is not to say that Afghanistan is incapable of contributing to the shaping of its future or that it is pointless for Afghanistan to invest in the development of a significant diplomatic capability. On the contrary, the more vulnerable a state is to a hostile regional and global environment, the more important it is that it optimise its capacity to protect its vital interests by peaceful means. A fundamental difficulty that Afghanistan faces relates to the asymmetry of power within the international system. Power is not as simple an idea as people sometimes think. Power is relational rather than absolute, and it is to some degree contextually determined. It is not just a matter of capacity; it is also a matter of willingness and ability to use such capacities as one might have. The exercise of power may prove to be at the expense of legitimacy.[1] Nonetheless, Afghanistan is located in a neighbourhood where adjacent states have greater military power than Afghanistan and, in some cases, more productive relations with great and powerful friends. In its more vulnerable moments, Afghanistan has become virtually a battlefield in which rivalries between different regional states have been played out. Whilst many states proclaim a commitment to a free and stable Afghanistan, in a number of cases, this has disguised the disposition to try to subordinate Afghanistan, if only with a view to preventing other states from developing a significant degree of influence in Kabul and beyond. These concerns are in keeping with the thrust of a 'realist' conception of international relations, where power is seen as a key determinant of the character of the international system.

But this takes us only so far. 'Realism' tends not to be especially sensitive to the complicating effects of domestic politics, yet political actors routinely seek to use the international connections of their state as resources to advance their own domestic political interests or as excuses for not advancing policies that they might be under domestic pressure to adopt.[2] Furthermore, Afghanistan is also constrained by a number of factors that arise from the international *system's* not simply being captured by a 'realist' model. International relations are shaped not merely by power, but also by a framework of laws, rules, norms, and institutions. Despite its current fragility, Afghanistan has a long history as an accepted state in the international system. It became a member of the League of Nations on 27 September 1934,[3] and although its neutrality during the Second World War prevented it from being a founding member of the United Nations (UN) in 1945, it was formally admitted to membership of the UN on 19 November 1946. Membership of international organisations brings with it not only rights, but obligations, specifically, fidelity to the principles embodied in the constitutional structure of the organisation itself. And above and beyond these obligations, states such as Afghanistan, by becoming a party to bilateral treaty relations with other states, or to multilateral conventions, assume responsibilities that arise from the constitutive principles of the international system, notably *pacta sunt servanda* – the requirement that promises be kept.

At a doctrinal level, the principal device by which Afghanistan sought to insulate itself from the more destructive buffetings of power politics was its specific claim to be animated by a policy of non-alignment (*bi tarafi*), sometimes also labelled neutralism or neutrality, although these terms have their own subtleties.[4] This was most obviously on display when, with some dexterity, Afghanistan managed to maintain formal neutrality during both the First and Second World Wars.[5] The advent of the Cold War, however, and particularly the emergence of competition in Third World countries between the United States (US) and the USSR,[6] made this a more difficult position to sustain. As a matter of practical reality, non-alignment came to a shuddering halt with the events of 1978–1979, but before those events, Afghanistan had been an active participant in the activities of the Non-Aligned Movement and indeed had taken part in the 1955 Bandung Conference in Soekarno's Indonesia, which many saw as the occasion on which the Non-Aligned Movement was born. That said, however, Afghanistan's non-alignment was not especially rigid. It is relatively easy to be non-aligned when one is located in a remote part of the world, of limited geostrategic significance. Afghanistan never enjoy that luxury. It had a substantial physical border with the Soviet Union, as well as a small one with China, and this meant that to some degree it would be subject to the influence of the USSR. In the context of the Cold War, its best hope was to open Afghanistan to aid from a diverse range of sources, including the United States. Thus, Afghanistan became to some degree a theatre for peaceful Cold War competition.

It remains a theatre for competition to this day, although the cast of actors has changed. The following sections outline some of the dimensions of this competition, and some of the driving forces behind Afghanistan's engagement with the wider world. The first section explores various ways in which Afghanistan's position has been or could be conceived, either by Afghans themselves or by outside observers. The second examines Afghanistan's relations with its largest regional neighbours, namely, Pakistan, India and Iran. The third looks slightly further afield, taking into account Afghanistan's relations with China, Russia and Central Asia. The fourth is concerned with Afghanistan's relations with the United States. The fifth focuses on international drivers of conflict in Afghanistan, and the final section outlines some of the important ways in which the wider phenomenon of globalisation has affected Afghanistan.

Buffer state? Graveyard of empires? Cultural crossroads? Theatre of competition?

Popular as well as scholarly understandings of Afghanistan's history and politics have been influenced at least in part by its geographic location at the intersections of three neighbouring regions: South Asia to its south and east, Iran and the Middle East to its west and Central Asia and China to its north and northeast. Since the nineteenth century, this geographic location has often been depicted as a source of negative foreign influences that turned the country into a theatre of competition and hostilities between regional and world powers. There are some important reasons for this narrative. During the nineteenth century, Anglo-Russian rivalry played a formative role in the shaping of the Afghan state. Beginning from the middle of the twentieth century, US and Soviet rivalries gradually intensified, turning the country into a major battlefield of the Cold War during the 1980s. An important feature of this power rivalry over Afghanistan is that none of the major powers succeeded in establishing permanent control over the country. Consequently, Afghanistan is often depicted not just as a theatre of competition, but as a 'highway of conquests'[7] or 'graveyard of empires'.[8] The symbolism created by the history of frequent opposition to external invaders has been deployed by groups such as the Taliban to strengthen their narratives of opposition to external influences in the country.[9]

It can also be argued that Afghanistan's geography has created major and almost-insurmountable barriers to Afghanistan's social and economic development. Collier, for one, has suggested that landlocked countries such as Afghanistan are often caught in four reinforcing development traps: conflict; dependence on natural resources; poor governance; and being landlocked with bad neighbours.[10] The argument is that each of these challenges reinforces the development barriers created by the others, thereby creating a vicious circle from which these countries cannot escape without major and long-term international assistance. For example, conflict and negative influences from neighbouring countries can impede the development of effective governance institutions, without which economic development and growth cannot be sustained. To a great extent, these challenges have indeed combined to contribute to a vicious circle of negative foreign influences and domestic instability in Afghanistan. In recent decades, these dynamics have also been reinforced by authoritarian regimes in the region that prioritise their own survival over long-term benefits of regional cooperation and peace. The authoritarian regimes that have ruled the Central Asian republics since the disintegration of the Soviet Union have prioritised the stability of the ruling regimes over any benefits that may result from greater transnational economic liberalisation and trade. Collins has argued that 'regime survival, border security, and concrete economic incentives – coming from China, not Afghanistan – will determine the foreign policies of the Central Asian states'.[11] Similarly, as we shall see, successive governments in Pakistan, obsessed with power rivalries with India, have prioritised the imposition of a client government in Kabul over regional trading relations.

But despite Afghanistan's difficult neighbourhood, its geography has not always been a source of negative foreign influences. Historically, Afghanistan's location between the regions of South Asia, Central Asia, China and the Middle East has also meant that it has served as a land bridge, connecting civilisations and cultures. Consequently, a major question of the long-term stability of the country is whether it can regain that historical role that it played along the ancient 'Silk Road' for centuries. The potential value of the revival of the historical status of Afghanistan along the 'Silk Road' has not been lost either on Afghan politicians or on national and international development policy makers. In 2010, President Karzai emphasised that Afghanistan could become a new '"Asian Roundabout," a central point of interconnection of goods, ideas, services and people in the fast expanding Asian economy'.[12] Subsequently, as we noted in the previous chapter, President Ghani, a former World Bank technocrat, became an even more passionate advocate of turning Afghanistan into an area of regional cooperation.[13]

One way in which the country might seek to overcome the negative influences of power competition is by adopting a policy of neutrality in global power rivalries. This policy was a notable source of the relative stability that the country enjoyed during the reign of King Zahir Shah from 1933 to 1973. The policy of neutrality, however, was undermined by Muhammad Daoud, first as prime minister from 1953 to 1963, and then as president from 1973 to 1978. As detailed in Chapter 2 of this book, Daoud sought to exploit the strategic location of Afghanistan between South Asia and Central Asia to attract development and military assistance from the Soviet Union and the United States, but his unsuccessful attempt to play one power against the other contributed to his own demise. Subsequently, during the 1980s, the country became a key battlefield of the Cold War, involving the Soviet Union and its allies on one side and the United States and a coalition of Western and Islamic countries on the other. There are now many obstacles to the re-establishment of Afghan neutrality, including the volatility of its environment.[14]

Afghanistan's location has already achieved renewed significance as a result of growing demand for trans-regional trade in energy between the South Asian and Central Asian regions. In recent years, the expanding economies and populations of the states of the Indian sub-continent have created a particularly high demand for new energy resources. Central Asia, which has abundant supplies of hydro-electricity and gas, is increasingly seen as a source of energy that can meet the soaring demands in Pakistan and India. A number of different projects have been conceived to transport energy from Central Asia through Afghanistan to both India and Pakistan. These include the TAPI gas pipeline, which is named after its participating countries, Turkmenistan, Afghanistan, Pakistan and India. Another major project, mentioned in Chapter 3, is TUTAP, which is also named after the participating countries: Turkmenistan, Uzbekistan, Tajikistan, Afghanistan and Pakistan. TUTAP, which is supported by major international donors such as the Asian Development Bank, is designed to allow the import of electricity from Central Asia through Afghanistan to Pakistan. Yet another major project which is supported by the World Bank is the Central Asia-South Asia power project, which is commonly known as CASA-1000, designed to transport hydroelec-tricity through a 1000 kV transmission line from Kyrgyzstan and Tajikistan to Afghanistan and Pakistan. These multi-billion-dollar projects can be important steps towards turning Afghanistan into an economic roundabout between the two regions. The government of Afghanistan expects that these projects will generate hundreds of millions of dollars in revenue for the state treasury from transit fees and create jobs and stimulate economic growth in the country.[15]

In parallel to these major economic and energy projects, the political and security components of regional cooperation have also attracted significant attention. The most notable effort to date to initiate regional cooperation on Afghanistan was the Istanbul Process on Regional Security for a Secure and Stable Afghanistan, which was launched in November 2011 in Istanbul. Central to this process was the idea that Afghanistan holds the potential to become the centre of regional cooperation; hence, it became popularly known as the 'Heart of Asia' process. For the United States and its Western allies, the initiative was part of a broader strategy of ensuring that Afghanistan would not become a battleground for a proxy war after the planned withdrawal of US and NATO forces in 2014. The process included all countries around Afghanistan as members and more than 20 Western countries and leading donor agencies as supporters, including major international donor agencies that financed trans-regional energy projects, such as the World Bank and the Asian Development Bank.[16] Despite significant tensions and distrust between participating coun-tries, the process led to several high-level ministerial meetings and articulation of areas of cooperation in a wide range of areas, including counterterrorism and counternarcotics. The Heart of Asia process became a significant platform for regional cooperation on Afghanistan with several meetings at the level of ministers and senior government officials held over several years. What is dis-tinctive about the process is that despite significant regional tensions, the gov-ernment of Afghanistan was given the leading role in setting the agendas and shaping issues for discussion among the participating countries. However, the process failed to achieve the overall goal of achieving a regional consensus on a *political* settlement in Afghanistan.[17] This meant that security and regional geo-strategic rivalries involving Afghanistan's immediate neighbours have continued to overshadow the potential benefits of successful regional cooperation over Afghanistan.

Afghanistan, Pakistan, India and Iran

Afghanistan's relations with Pakistan have been fraught with tension for decades, in part reflecting the reality that Pakistan itself is a deeply troubled state.[18] When it was created by the partition of the sub-continent in 1947, it had the benefit of mature leadership by two very eminent figures: Muhammad Ali Jinnah, revered to this day as the single most important driving force behind the creation of Pakistan, and its first governor-general; and Liaquat Ali Khan, who was the first prime minister of Pakistan, although he is now largely forgotten.[19] Unfortunately, Jinnah was already frail at the time of Pakistan's independence, and died in September 1948, while Liaquat was assassinated in Rawalpindi in October 1951. Thus, barely four years after independence, Pakistan had lost the two steadiest hands in its political leadership, and it was not long before the military intervened in Pakistani politics, leading it to play a political role, which the military in neighbouring India never sought to assume. The military first intervened directly in politics in 1958 when General Ayub Khan seized power, and this set the scene for subsequent phases of military rule – from 1958 to 1962, 1969 to 1972, 1977 to 1988, and 1999 to 2007. These military interventions in politics proved to be at the expense of a statesmanlike civilian political elite; on occasion, they saw the military looking to alliances with radical Islamist groups as a source of legitimacy[20]; and they gave a disproportionate role in politics to a force with a vested interest in preserving its privileged position[21] by playing up threats to the state, both external and internal – with the powerful Inter-Services Intelligence Directorate (ISI) a key player from the 1980s.[22] But this was by no means Pakistan's only problem. It fractured, traumatically, in 1971 when 'East Pakistan' broke away to form the new state of Bangladesh,[23] and witnessing this catastrophe had a searing effect on a whole generation of Pakistani politicians and generals. And this in turn set the scene for a decade of 'Islamisation' after General Zia ul-Haq took power in 1977. Ordinary Pakistanis are not notably radical in religious terms, and Islamist parties have typically not performed well electorally, but from the 1980s onwards, Pakistan was afflicted by increasing levels of sectarian violence,[24] a burgeoning jihadist rhetoric and debate over the very nature of Pakistan as a state,[25] the instrumentalisation of religion by the military[26] and the emergence eventually of a particularly nasty Pakistani Taliban movement that directed extreme violence against its perceived enemies.[27]

As far as Afghanistan's troubled relations with Pakistan from 1947 were concerned, certain Afghan leaders, especially Muhammad Daoud, were at least as much to blame as their Pakistani counterparts, since Afghanistan's irredentist claims to the border areas of Pakistan were never going to be acceptable to

Pakistan's leaders and had little chance of securing active support in the wider world either. Afghanistan's 'Pushtunistan' claims had one further insidious effect. When the Soviet invasion of Afghanistan turned Pakistan into a frontline state in the Cold War, with Afghan resistance parties mobilising amongst refugees on Pakistani territory, Pakistan proved wary of providing much support to Afghan nationalists. The result, however, as noted earlier, was that the ISI gave by far the most support to Islamist groups that by virtue of their belief in a global Islamic community (*ummah*) seemed less likely to revive a purely territorial dispute in the future. This benefited groups such as the *Hezb-e Islami* of Hekmatyar, but arguably did Pakistan little good in the long run, since the unpopularity of the *Hezb-e Islami* amongst ordinary Afghans meant that Pakistan did not benefit as much as it should have from its contribution as a generous host for millions of Afghan refugees.[28] While it was an open secret that Pakistan was supporting the *Mujahideen*, it sought to deny it. As former US Secretary of State, George P. Shultz wrote of the 1988 Geneva Accords, 'I heard the president ask Zia how he would handle the fact that they would be violating their agreement. Zia replied that they would "just lie about it. We've been denying our activities there for eight years"'.[29]

Had Pakistan been prepared in 1992 simply to work with any Afghan government that emerged through a genuine intra-Afghan process, the history of the following decades might well have been very different, and the long history of tense relations between Afghanistan and Pakistan might have been brought to a conclusion. But it was given virtually a free hand by the US to do what it wanted,[30] and by overplaying its hand, Pakistan lost the goodwill that it had built up as a host for Afghan refugees and for elements of the Afghan resistance and set the scene for the difficulties that prevail to this day. This overplaying came first in its support for Hekmatyar, and then in its redirection of support to the Taliban.[31] The problem proved particularly serious once the Taliban took over Kabul and was well captured in an observation made by the foreign minister of Pakistan, Abdul Sattar: 'Islamabad failed to foresee that the Taliban were internationally perceived to be the creation of Pakistan... As the only friend of the Taliban, Pakistan was blamed for their policies'.[32] The dilemma for Pakistan was that it was in a position to cripple the Taliban regime altogether, but not in a position to control its activities on a day-to-day basis. This persisted right up to the commencement by the United States of Operation Enduring Freedom in October 2001. Something of a hiatus followed, since the Taliban had been scattered, but from 2003, Pakistan resumed support for the Afghan Taliban, setting the scene for what has been called a 'two-track' Pakistani approach to Afghanistan,[33] with professions of support for measures against terrorism running alongside covert support for the Taliban movement and its terrorist tactics. Even Pakistani President Musharraf, as we noted earlier, stated that 'There is no doubt Afghan militants are supported from Pakistani soil. The problem that you have in your region is because support is provided from our side'.[34] This alone provided more than adequate justification for demands that Pakistan take action to block such support; but a great deal of evidence went further and suggested official Pakistani involvement.[35] A range of factors account for Pakistan's approach, but the dominant factor has been a desire to minimise Indian influence in Afghanistan[36] – although as even a former ISI director-general, Asad Durrani, has pointed out, the 'Indian factor in Afghanistan has been highly exaggerated in Pakistan'.[37] This 'creeping invasion'[38] of Afghanistan virtually guarantees tense bilateral relations, since it implies a desire to limit Afghanistan's standing as a sovereign state. As a former Pakistani ambassador to the US has candidly put it, Pakistan could play a positive role in promoting peace negotiations over Afghanistan, 'provided it changes its ultimate goal – in place since the 1970s – of installing an Islamist, Pashtun, pro-Pakistan, anti-Indian government in Kabul'.[39] At present, there is little to suggest that such a change is at all likely.

India's historical ties with Afghanistan are very long-standing. In part, this reflects one of the peculiarities of the partition process in 1947: that whilst Pakistan was indisputably a 'new' state, the 'Dominion of India' was well positioned to claim ownership of a great deal of the cultural heritage of the subcontinent, including those related to the historical period of Muslim rule in India which had established commonalities of identity with residents of what came to be known as Afghanistan. But beyond this, there was also a Cold War dimension to the India-Afghanistan relationship after 1947. While Pakistan developed a complex, but elaborate relationship with the United States,[40] India found its anti-colonial rhetoric of the 1950s, particularly associated with diplomat and some-time Defence Minister V.K. Krishna Menon,[41] much more warmly welcomed in Moscow than in Washington. Given the tensions between India and Pakistan to which we will turn shortly, India was more than happy to develop a cordial relationship with Afghanistan, although Pakistani fears that this would trap Pakistan militarily in a pincer between India and Afghanistan did not materialise during the India-Pakistan conflicts in 1965 and 1971. In the 1960s, there was also a great deal of Indian cultural influence in Afghanistan through cinema, and Prime Minister Indira Gandhi visited Afghanistan in June 1969 and July 1976.

The long-standing Indian relationship with the Soviet Union explained in large measure the mild Indian response to the Soviet invasion of Afghanistan. At the time of the invasion, an election was about to be held for the 7th Lok Sabha (lower house of parliament), and while the response to the invasion of the outgoing government under Prime Minister Charan Singh was strongly critical, India then took a starkly different direction when Indira Gandhi returned to the prime ministership once the results of the January 1980 election were tallied. As a recent study put it, 'The U-turn sent a shock wave both within and outside India. In one stroke, Gandhi had alienated substantial parts of the world, including many Afghans, as well as Indians'.[42] Another observer described India's posture as an 'utterly self-serving position, in which moral considerations were subordinated to the dictates of pragmatism'.[43] As things turned out, it was not even an especially effective pragmatism: change in the USSR itself left India scrambling to respond to the Soviets' desire to exit Afghanistan.

India did, however, find an opportunity to regain some influence in Afghanistan when Pakistan opted to support forces such as the *Hezb-e Islami* of Hekmatyar, and the Taliban. More moderate forces were prepared to put aside their memories of Indian support for the likes of Babrak Karmal and Najibullah in order to find friends in their resistance to Pakistan's proxies. Thus, the Afghan Embassy in New Delhi remained in the hands of the Taliban's opponents. Furthermore, India had little love for the Taliban, especially after the hijacking to Kandahar in December 1999 of Indian Airlines flight IC814.[44] India's opportunities for influence mounted with the overthrow of the Taliban regime in 2001, but despite insinuations to the contrary from Islamabad, India's approach was a measured one rather than one designed to create a springboard for covert action against Pakistan. This did not prevent the Indian Embassy in Kabul from coming under terrorist attack in July 2008 and October 2009 by the Pakistan-based Haqqani network, one of the key components of the Taliban, but on the whole, Indian aid to Afghanistan, the centrepiece of the reinvigorated relationship, proceeded without too much difficulty. India's internal challenges militate against its easily achieving the influence that a China is capable of exercising,[45] but its aid to Afghanistan has been diverse, sophisticated and substantial, especially when measured in terms of purchasing power,[46] and covers humanitarian needs, small-scale community-level projects and major infrastructural development.

Afghanistan has been a victim of the historically tense relations between India and Pakistan. Unfortunately, there is little to suggest that a resolution of the fundamental tensions that divide these two powers is in the offing. There have been very significant wars or major armed conflicts between India and Pakistan in 1948, 1965, 1971 and 1999, and a major ongoing dispute exists over the troubled territory of Kashmir.[47] In addition, both India and Pakistan are nuclear-weapons states, although neither is a party to the 1968 Non-Proliferation Treaty. One could argue that this has established a degree of deterrence that works against major war between the two states, but the downsides are that if deterrence fails, the consequences would be catastrophic; and that the existence of deterrence can encourage the nurturing of proxies or surrogates engaging in terrorist attacks, such as the November 2008 killings carried out in Mumbai by members of the Pakistan-based terrorist group *Lashkar-e-Toiba*.

Afghanistan's relations with Iran give rise to quite different challenges from those that spring from the relationships with Pakistan and India. Developments in Iran have long had an influence of sorts on politics and society in Afghanistan; one commentator even went so far as to credit the Shah of Iran for triggering the April 1978 coup in Afghanistan,[48] through his pressuring Daoud to crack down on Marxist groups. Iranian influence has persisted ever since the Islamic Revolution of January 1979 resulted in the overthrow of the Shah and the establishment of an anti-American theocratic regime initially led by the Shiite religious figure Ayatollah Ruhollah Khomeini.[49] The Iranian regime, for more than four decades, has been repressive and autocratic, but not totalitarian: different strands of thinking about Islamic rule have long been present within the religious elite and articulated by different power centres within a notably complex political system[50]; and this has affected Iran's foreign relations, which have often been justified in Islamic terms, but manifest a strong streak of pragmatism. But equally significant have been four decades of tension in relations between Iran and the United States: this tension has pervaded many spheres of Iranian foreign policy and defied all efforts to bring it to a halt.[51]

Both Shiite identity and geopolitical calculations have contributed to Iranian approaches to Afghanistan.[52] Iran's geopolitical objectives in Afghanistan have never been as far-reaching as those of Pakistan, since it has no realistic expectation of being able to dominate the country through the installation of proxies in the heights of power in Kabul. Tehran uses a number of instruments to appeal to different constituencies in Afghanistan. It has drawn on a particular interpretation of Shiite political Islam to increase its influence among the Shiite minority in Afghanistan, especially the Hazara community, which has its own complex politics, involving not just religious ideologues, but followers of secular ideologies such as Maoism.[53] During the 1980s, Tehran exercised particularly high influence among the Shiite *Mujahideen* groups, when its support proved instrumental in empowering Islamist *Mujahideen* groups over secular and nationalist groups. But there were significant tensions between Tehran's emphasis on Shiite political Islam and an underlying current of ethnic nationalism among the Hazaras, which surfaced particularly strongly in the formation of *Hezb-e Wahdat Islami* in Bamiyan in 1989.[54] Nonetheless, Iran did project some sense of protective responsibility towards the Afghan Shia and very nearly went to war with the Taliban in August 1998 after a massacre of Hazaras in Mazar-e Sharif that also saw Pakistani extremists killing staff of the Iranian consulate.[55] Beyond the Shia, Tehran has also drawn on shared language and culture to build rapport with diverse Persian-speaking communities in Afghanistan and Tajikistan. Furthermore, in its anti-Western rhetoric and agenda, it also finds shared interests with groups such as the Taliban and Hekmatyar's *Hezb-e Islami*. In 1997, Iran gave refuge to Hekmatyar, and he stayed there until 2002. Subsequently, Iran has provided support to both state and non-state actors, ranging from provision of cash to staff of the presidential palace,[56] to supplying arms to factions of the Taliban.[57]

This is not to say that Iran has lacked geopolitical interests in Afghanistan. On the contrary, Afghanistan has been to some degree a theatre for rivalry between Iran and other powers antagonistic to it. The pre-eminent source of regional tension contributing to this problem has been the relationship – or lack of it – between Iran and Saudi Arabia. It is far too simplistic to see this as simply a manifestation of tensions between Sunni and Shia; there are significant economic, political, and cultural dimensions to the tension as well. On the whole, Afghanistan has avoided becoming a battleground of the kind that Yemen has been in recent years, with the devastating human consequences that have accompanied that conflict. One reason for this, paradoxically, is that a more active Iranian role in Afghanistan would be likely to dissuade Washington from taking steps to eliminate its footprint on the ground in Afghanistan, something which Tehran would almost certainly like to see happen as long as it did not result in chaos in Afghanistan and a spillover of chaos into Iranian territory. Iran has invested heavily in 'educational' facilities with a distinct religious bent, especially in Kabul and Herat, but it is highly debatable whether these have succeeded in winning as much influence as some circles in Iran might wish. Of course, very large numbers of Afghan refugees, probably in the millions, remain in Iran; but not all feel warmly towards their hosts.

The mere reality of Iran's physical proximity to Afghanistan means that, like Pakistan, it will be an enduring component of Afghanistan's strategic environment. But what kind of component it will prove to be is heavily dependent upon a range of considerations that are beyond Afghanistan's control. The most important by far of these is the future of the relationship between Iran and the United States, which is presently poor given the Trump Administration's unilateral abrogation of the July 2015 'Joint Comprehensive Plan of Action' designed to address nuclear development in Iran. At various times in the last four decades in both Washington and Tehran there have been political leaders prepared to explore the possibility of developing a different kind of relationship between the two states. Unfortunately, the presence of these leaderships has not necessarily coincided, but two factors have worked to some degree to insulate Afghanistan from the danger of entanglement in this wider relationship. First, Iran has on the whole been a constructive rather than a destructive player in Afghanistan,[58] something which the United States was prepared to recognise at the time of the 2001 Bonn conference. This has allowed Afghanistan to be quarantined to a degree from wider US-Iranian tensions, although this may not last. Second, while Iran has supported forces such as Hezbollah in Lebanon and the Houthis in Yemen, it is not a state given to expansionist territorial aggression: as Ansari has put it, 'Iran has been on the strategic defensive for two hundred years'.[59]

Thus far, we have largely focused on Afghanistan's bilateral relations with Pakistan, India and Iran, as well as on the bilateral tensions that have long marked the relationship between Pakistan and India. Beyond this, however, it is necessary to take into account how Afghanistan's *region* in an overarching sense impinges on Afghanistan's foreign relations. This is a slightly more complex issue than might initially appear to be the case. The very nature of a 'region' is itself open for debate. Is it a geographical notion? Or a cultural notion? Or a notion to be defined in terms of complex interdependencies? Or in terms of 'regional security complexes', a topic on which a burgeoning literature has developed?[60] Or in terms of the existence of 'regional organisations' or 'regional institutions'? From these complexities, several points flow. One is that the boundaries of regions may be fluid rather than fixed. Another is that the significance or character of 'regions' may change over time: in the light of the collapse of the Soviet Union, Central Asia in the 21st century is a different space from what it was for much of the 20th century.[61]

But an even greater complication is that no matter how Afghanistan's region is specifically defined, it is beyond doubt that it is severely afflicted by distrust between a number of the key states that make it up.[62] Almost two decades ago, a group of commentators including Ashraf Ghani argued that the Afghan conflict formed 'the core of a regional conflict formation' and identified a range of steps that might be taken in response.[63] But little has been achieved since, and it is worth reflecting on why that has been the case. Two recent analyses, touched on earlier, shed light on the problem. Harpviken and Tadjbakhsh conclude a recent book by arguing that

> Afghanistan is not an integral part of any regional security complex, but rather is surrounded by three regional complexes, each with a distinct conflictual dynamic. Afghanistan constitutes a sub-complex of its own, but even if peripheral to the dynamic of the three surrounding regions, it is the unwilling host of conflicts and tensions rooted within each of those.[64]

In a study which is complementary rather than competing, Motwani details the array of multiple, interlocking security dilemmas and strategic challenges that afflict the region.[65] The implication of these analyses is that the development through diplomatic means of a regional approach equal to the task of solving Afghanistan's regional difficulties is an undertaking of awesome complexity.

Afghanistan, China, Russia and Central Asia

In mapping the complexities of Afghanistan's region, it is tempting simply to focus on the Indo-Pakistan relationship, which supplies complexities aplenty for an observer's delectation. But this would offer an unduly simplified picture of what is an even more challenging space. The presence of China and Russia in reasonable proximity to Afghanistan injects further layers of difficulty, grounded in both the histories of these states, and in their interests as inhabitants of an international system in which the power of the United States in *relative* terms is declining while the power of other states is rising – China and possibly Russia among them.

China has only a tiny border with Afghanistan – abutting the isolated Wakhan corridor in Afghanistan's northeastern province of Badakhshan[66] – but it has a political significance for Afghanistan that exceeds its geographical importance. In 1965, the Chinese Defence Minister, Lin Biao, published a much-discussed text, *Long Live the Victory of People's War*, which was widely interpreted as encouraging revolutionary uprisings in poor countries, and this radical message found listeners in many parts of the world – including Afghanistan, where the Maoist *Shula-i Jawid* ('Eternal Flame') party developed a complex constituency including a number of Hazara intellectuals.[67] Nonetheless, Afghanistan only became a matter of significant *strategic* concern for China following the December 1979 Soviet invasion.[68] To understand why, it is necessary to see the invasion within the wider context of rivalry between the Soviet Union and China for leadership within the 'communist world'. Following the death of Soviet leader Stalin in

March 1953, relations between the new leadership of the Communist Party of the Soviet Union under Nikita S. Khrushchev, and the leadership of the Chinese Communist Party chaired by Mao Zedong, became increasingly tense, on both political and ideological grounds. Khrushchev's policy of 'De-Stalinisation', inaugurated with his so-called 'Secret Speech' on 'The cult of personality and its consequences' (*O kul'te lichnosti i ego posledstviiakh*) at the 20th Congress of the Communist Party of the Soviet Union in February 1956, left Communist leaders such as the Chinese heavily exposed by undermining the foundations of their legitimacy claims; and in Peking's view, this contributed directly to events such as the 1956 Hungarian Revolution.[69] The split between Moscow and Peking flared dramatically at a November 1960 conference of communist parties in Bucharest, and it was to be one of the dominant features of international politics throughout the 1960s and 1970s,[70] although China's introversion as a result of its so-called 'Great Proletarian Cultural Revolution'[71] from 1965 to 1976 to some degree kept the dispute under control. Sino-Soviet relations were still fraught at the time of the Soviet invasion of Afghanistan, and China located the invasion in the context of wider rivalry with the Soviet Union in the so-called 'Third World', and specifically of suspicion of Soviet interventionism, not least because of the December 1978 invasion of 'Democratic Kampuchea' by Moscow's ally Vietnam, which displaced the Khmer Rouge regime that Beijing had supported.[72] Very specifically, China identified Afghanistan as a 'regional conflict' that would need to be resolved to its satisfaction before any Sino-Soviet rapprochement could occur,[73] and it was only in 1989, following the Soviet withdrawal from Afghanistan, that 'party-to-party' relations were restored between the Chinese Communist Party and the Communist Party of the Soviet Union. As a result of the dramatic internal reforms initiated by Deng Xiaoping from 1978,[74] China is a very different power now from what it was then, and it faces a range of complex challenges.[75] Nonetheless, its interests in Afghanistan have been expanding,[76] and three areas in particular deserve to be noted.

First, China under President Xi Jinping now has significant economic interests in Afghanistan's region, not least because of the 'Belt and Road' initiative noted in the previous chapter. As a result of economic liberalisation in China, Chinese foreign investment has expanded dramatically in areas where it was previously a marginal player, such as Africa and the Pacific. Afghanistan has also become a focus of such endeavours, albeit on a scale constrained by security issues, especially in the area of minerals extraction, through the work of the Metallurgical Corporation of China, and in the area of energy resources, through the China National Petroleum Company.[77] (Afghanistan is richly endowed with minerals ranging from gemstones to rare earths.[78]) These areas of potential investment give China a modest – but non-trivial – interest in a stable and secure Afghanistan.[79] Second, China has no desire to witness any spillover into western China of radical or extremist forces and is wary to the point of paranoia about radicalisation of the Uighur Muslim population in the Autonomous Region of Xinjiang. Unlike Hui Muslims who are found throughout China, the Uighurs have been viewed as a serious threat to the dominant position of both the Han Chinese and the Communist Party. China long pursued a 'Strike Hard' policy to address the possibility of Uighur separatism and has recently elevated its repression to even greater heights.[80] The Taliban before September 2001 had attempted to connect with a range of Muslim groups in different places; these included not only Chechens from Russia, but also Uighurs from Xinjiang. This is not something the Chinese leadership would want to see repeated. Third, China has geostrategic interests in Central Asia. The establishment of the Shanghai Cooperation Organization in June 2001 saw China position itself to pursue a more active role in this part of the world, and the Shanghai Cooperation Organization fortuitously provided a framework within which it could seek to block any attempt by the US to build a sphere of influence in Central Asia after September 2001. It has proved to be a more significant part of the landscape than either Washington's 'New Silk Road' idea or the 'Commonwealth of Independent States' that was formed at the time of the USSR's disintegration.[81]

The Russian Federation also has ongoing interests in Afghanistan, but of a character quite different from those of China. As principal successor to the Soviet Union, Russia carries the burden of the 1980s more heavily than the other countries that were once part of the USSR, and this limits its disposition to become directly or heavily involved in Afghanistan's affairs. Nonetheless, Russia in recent times has also proved to be a somewhat unpredictable power, and this needs to be taken into account when assessing what kinds of roles it might play in the future. There are a number of reasons why this is the case. The first relates to the decline of democratic forces in Russia in the last two decades in particular and the rise of autocratic, personalised politics associated with the dominance of one figure, Vladimir Putin. A former security operative, Putin has not hesitated to manipulate the political system and mobilise the powers of the state in order to consolidate his personal position.[82] Under Putin, prominent opposition figures have found themselves under threat, such as Aleksei Navalny, subject to multiple malicious prosecutions, and Boris Nemtsov, assassinated in February 2015[83]; other critics of Putin, such as Anna Politkovskaia, Aleksandr Litvinenko and Boris Berezovskii have perished at home and abroad in suspicious circumstances. As a result in part of the development of autocratic tendencies in Russia, the hopes for a durable rapprochement between East and West[84] that accompanied the disintegration of the Soviet Union have fallen well short of being realised; on the contrary, tensions have developed across a wide range of issue areas.[85]

Nourzhanov has argued that 'Russia does not have a cogent and detailed Afghanistan strategy. Its specific policy actions are mostly reactive, undertaken in the context of the global geopolitical situation, resource limitations, and changing security threats'.[86] The mere fact that Russia has developed an autocratic domestic power structure does not mean that it will act recklessly abroad; much will depend upon the disposition of the autocrat of the apex of the system. Here, the evidence is mixed and so are the implications for Afghanistan. Russia has used its armed forces beyond its borders, in both Georgia and Ukraine, although it remains a matter of debate whether these exercises in power projection should be seen as methodical or impulsive.[87] It is highly unlikely that Afghanistan has anything to fear of this kind. More pertinently, the US *Report on the Investigation into Russian Interference in the 2016 Presidential Election* (the 'Mueller Report') concluded that the 'Russian government interfered in the 2016 presidential election in sweeping and systematic fashion'[88]; and doubtless it could attempt to manipulate an Afghan presidential election as well, through the spread of 'disinformation' via Afghanistan's vibrant electronic and social media networks – although whether it would be worth the effort is another question. What is rather more likely is a certain amount of *ad hoc* mischief-making by Russia, with a view both to discomforting the United States and keeping its foot in the door as Afghanistan's political future takes shape. An example of Russia's arguably playing such a role was its hosting of a meeting between Afghan Taliban and a range of Afghan politicians at odds with President Ashraf Ghani at a Kremlin-owned hotel in February 2019.[89] If one turns to the question of what Russia's fundamental interests in Afghanistan might be, it is hard to find many beyond thwarting the spread of 'Islamic State' (Daesh),[90] countering the narcotics trade and maintaining the broad stability of the Central Asian states, formerly part of the Soviet Union, that lie between Afghanistan and the Russian Federation itself.[91] But the states of Central Asia now enjoy agency of their own, although to varying degrees; they are not simply tools or clones of Moscow.

The various states of Central Asia have been heavily preoccupied for decades with consolidating their own independence and institutions, which have often had a dictatorial or quasi-dictatorial character. Kazakhstan, Kyrgyzstan and Tajikistan all have interests in a stable Afghanistan, but are not major players in its foreign relations, although they form part of a potential corridor for exports from Afghanistan and are central to ideas of expanded Central Asian cooperation.[92] Turkmenistan, whilst touted as a potential partner for Afghanistan in the export of oil and gas to South Asia (the so-called 'TAPI' project), and part of the 'Lapis Lazuli' road transport route, has been an especially closed society, notably because of the rule from 1991 to 2006 of Saparmurat Niyazov, whose repressive dictatorship was bolstered by a massive cult of personality, which persisted following Niyazov's death when Gurbanguly Berdimukhamedov became president. Outside the economic sphere, there is little basis for vigorous cooperation between Afghanistan and Turkmenistan, despite the existence of a Turkman minority within Afghanistan. The same is not the case, however, with the state of Uzbekistan. Following the death in 2016 of the longstanding dictator Islam Karimov, who had been somewhat isolated following a gruesome massacre of protestors in Andijan in 2005 and who had expelled US forces based in his country, his successor Shavkat Mirziyoyev has been internationally much more engaged, including with respect to Afghanistan,[93] and could potentially play a role in facilitating negotiations between different Afghan political forces. Geography ordains that these states have relationships with Afghanistan; how these relationships evolve is a matter for ongoing observation.

Afghanistan and the United States

The relationship between Afghanistan and the United States is by far the most important of Afghanistan's positive international linkages. This is not to say that it has been an untroubled relationship. On the contrary, all too often relationships that one might expect to be extremely close on the basis of shared interest have proved to be quite difficult to manage, and the US–Afghanistan relationship is no exception.[94] One of the key contributors to this difficulty is the fundamentally asymmetrical character of the relationship. On the one hand, the idea of the sovereign equality of states has played a central role in constituting the international system since 1945. The wording of the Charter of the United Nations deliberately set out to dispel the notion of varying levels of 'civilisation' among states[95] that prevailed during the life of the League of Nations and which helped explain the tepid response to events such as the Italian invasion of Abyssinia in October 1935. At a practical level, however, considerations of power have often trumped the theory of sovereign equality of states,[96] and this has applied to the US–Afghanistan relationship as well. As long as a substantial proportion of the Afghan state budget is covered by US taxpayers' funds, the United States will expect to have a say, and a substantial say, on the question of how such funds are to be used. This has the potential to give rise to a situation in which Afghanistan functions as a 'quasi-state', with a high level of 'juridical' sovereignty, but a lower level of 'empirical' sovereignty.[97] Such circumstances are tailor-made to produce tension between Washington and Kabul. In part, this is because differences in perspective on a range of issues are almost inevitable, but it is also because Afghan rulers, keen not to be seen as twenty-first-century examples of Shah Shuja, are incentivised to seek to control the more symbolic dimensions of social and political life where they genuinely can make a difference.

The asymmetry of power between the United States and Afghanistan is one of the factors that helps explain the on-again, off-again character of US engagement with Afghanistan. Global powers tend to have global interests, and at any given moment, there are likely to be plenty of distractions that prevent the leadership of the United States from giving its full attention to a small state – except if circumstances contrive to make that state, at least momentarily, of overwhelming importance to Washington, as occurred in late 2001 where Afghanistan was concerned. For the United States to concentrate on Afghanistan has been the exception rather than the rule. In the 1950s and 1960s, it tended to lavish more attention on relations with its Cold War ally Pakistan than Afghanistan. This of course changed when the Soviet invasion of Afghanistan in December 1979 put an end to the era of detente with the Soviet Union; and as detailed earlier, through the period of the Reagan Administration, aid flowed to various components of the Afghan resistance. The Soviet withdrawal from Afghanistan, however, led Washington's attention to drift,[98] and this became much more patent during the Clinton administration, when amongst Afghans, there was a palpable sense of having been abandoned by their erstwhile US allies.[99] Memories of this period have haunted a generation of Afghan political leaders, and for this reason, dealing with Afghan elites after 2001 was always a task likely to demand considerable sensitivity.

The burden of US domestic politics on the US-Afghanistan relationship is also significant. Any US president is likely to be crafting policy towards Afghanistan with one eye towards domestic political consequences. Constitutionally, a president is limited to two terms of four years, but the temptation is great for a first-term president to devise policies that will not adversely affect his or her prospects of re-election. Furthermore, the scheduling of 'mid-term' Congressional elections two years into a president's term may be a very significant factor shaping policy towards foreign conflict zones, especially if a president is committed to a domestic agenda which can only be implemented if Congress is prepared to pass necessary legislation. President Lyndon B. Johnson (1963–1969) found that the Vietnam War diminished his authority, presenting him domestically with challenges that to a degree blighted his days in the White House,[100] and led to his withdrawal from the 1968 presidential race. When Barack Obama became president in January 2009, it was very clear that he had no desire to re-live Johnson's unhappy experience. No US president will want to be trapped in a quagmire.[101] But nor will a president want to be the leader on hand if an ignominious collapse occurs in an allied state of a kind that in April 1975 produced devastating images from South Vietnam as helicopters evacuated the last personnel from the roof of the US Embassy.[102] Here, a calculation that comes into play is the need to avoid reputational damage to the United States, since such damage harms the *power* of the United States as well.

It is also the case that the US policymaking process is marked by serious pathologies. It is easy to associate these with the chaotic leadership 'style' of President Donald J. Trump, especially given the high level of personnel turnover within his Administration and the exodus of mature and experienced professionals from the Administration's ranks. But even before Trump became president, both memoir literature and political science analysis had pointed to major problems in US policymaking. These include ineffective coordination of different goals and different agencies tasked with pursuing them; significant problems of effective implementation of policy; on occasion, indifferent understanding of the complexities of the environments in which the United States was required to operate; and a mismatch between needs and resources to meet those needs, as well as a poor understanding of how US approaches would be viewed by others. A particular problem in Afghanistan arises from the tendency to see the United States as all-powerful. When, therefore, things go wrong, even sophisticated observers can be inclined to come up with conspiratorial explanations of why this would be the case, based on alleged US bad faith, rather than simply recognise the inadequacies of the US as a power. President Karzai was somewhat prone to think this way during his second term in office from 2009 to 2014; President Ghani, long a resident of Washington, DC, had considerably more experience with US policy processes, but equally grounds for feeling on occasion exasperated with the inadequacies of the US approach to his country.

One of the greatest misfortunes that befell Afghanistan after 2001 was the US invasion of Iraq in March 2003. No event in the decades after the September 11 attacks did more to distract attention from Afghanistan's needs and ongoing difficulties. Driven by the simplistic ideologies of unrealistic 'realists' in the Bush administration, the invasion rapidly saw the US out of its depth, both politically and militarily.[103] As an official report put it, 'The liberation model – in which a rapid transfer of power to Iraqi authorities would enable U.S. troops to depart 90 days after the regime's fall – broke down almost immediately after the invasion. Neither the U.S. military nor the civilian leadership was prepared for the complete disintegration of Iraq's government and the subsequent loss of law and order. The looting and chaos it engendered destroyed plans for a rapid transfer of power'.[104] One of the most important rules of thumb for an international actor is that it should not act in such a way as to expose the limits of its own power or capacity. This was precisely what the United States managed to do in Iraq, in full measure. Afghanistan fell victim to some of the consequences, as two observations by well-placed US officials make clear. Admiral Michael G. Mullen, Chairman of the US Joint Chiefs of Staff, stated in 2007 that 'In Afghanistan we do what we can. In Iraq we do what we must'.[105] From the Bush administration's point of view, the Afghan theatre of operations had taken a back seat to the Iraqi theatre of operations. This was recognised by the very level-headed US Secretary of Defense, Dr Robert M. Gates, who in his memoirs wrote that 'As much as President Bush detested the notion, our later challenges in Afghanistan, especially the return of the Taliban in force by the time I became defense secretary, were, I believe, significantly compounded by the invasion of Iraq'.[106]

What Kabul saw as Washington's maladroit handling of Pakistan also injected friction into the US-Afghanistan relationship. A number of President Karzai's objections to American policy were ill conceived, but it is hard not to sympathise with his frustration at being told by US officials that they knew how to handle Pakistan at the very time that Pakistan's meddling in Afghanistan was growing and growing. A real dilemma was of course at play. The US found itself dependent logistically on cooperation from Pakistan to allow it to supply US ground troops in Afghanistan, a problem that was only exacerbated when President Karimov expelled US forces from Uzbekistan. Furthermore, a generation of US policymakers had internalised the argument, sedulously peddled by Pakistan, that any real pressure on Pakistan could precipitate an internal collapse and the rise of a fundamentalist regime with nuclear weapons. The result, however, was a deteriorating situation in Afghanistan with US soldiers, Afghan soldiers and Afghan civilians dying because of the duplicity of Washington's erstwhile 'ally' to Afghanistan's east. President Trump addressed this in a speech in August 2017: 'For its part, Pakistan often gives safe haven to agents of chaos, violence, and terror... We can no longer be silent about Pakistan's safe havens for terrorist organizations, the Taliban, and other groups that pose a threat to the region and beyond... We have been paying Pakistan billions and billions of dollars at the same time they are housing the very terrorists that we are fighting. But that will have to change, and that will change immediately'.[107] Unfortunately, there is little evidence that it did, and by late 2018, the Trump Administration had shifted to a very different approach, namely, engaging directly with the Taliban in the absence of the Afghan government, although this approach ultimately fell apart in September 2019, something we discuss in more detail in the concluding chapter.

In the previous chapter, we discussed the scale of US aid to Afghanistan since 2001, but noted that there have been significant problems of aid delivery and coordination. This is not to deny the dedication to Afghanistan and its people of a very large number of Americans, but simply to recognise a rather painful reality. US aid was slow in getting off the ground. A study by the Center on International Cooperation at New York University demonstrated that while US$5.2 billion had been pledged for Afghanistan in January 2002, the total funds committed by May 2003 came to only US$2.6 billion, reconstruction disbursements came to only US$1.6 billion and the value of projects actually completed was only US$192 million.[108] But once aid monies began to flow on a more substantial scale, other problems began to surface, namely that the combination of bureaucratic complexity, and the pressure to spend, rapidly fuelled corruption.[109] Sub-contracting offered fresh opportunities for the exploitation of aid.[110] Many specific failings have been identified and documented by the Office of the US Special Inspector General for Afghanistan Reconstruction, established by the *National Defense Authorization Act* for Fiscal Year (FY) 2008, which reports quarterly to the US Congress.[111]

Of course, the US and Afghanistan on 30 September 2014 signed a formal 'Security and Defence Cooperation Agreement', but what such an agreement constitutes in practice may differ from what its wording seems to say. For all the talk by the Taliban about 'foreign occupation', it remains the case that since the end of 2014, the number of US troops in Afghanistan has been relatively small, standing in early 2019 at around 14,000.[112] This figure can be compared with over 55,000 in Japan, 35,000 in Germany and 25,000 in South Korea.[113] Furthermore, US troops in Afghanistan are overwhelmingly involved in training and support roles, rather than active combat. It is not so much US *troops* that alarm the Taliban, but other critical capabilities that the United States continues to share with Afghanistan, such as air power and intelligence. Depriving the Afghan government of access to such force-multipliers would be a very significant achievement for the Taliban and could even be sufficient to trigger a breakdown in operational capacity of the armed forces if it led to defections by entire units.

Afghanistan has a significant diplomatic relationship with the United States; indeed, the United States' Embassy in Kabul is one of its biggest anywhere in the world. Diplomatic relations were initially established on 4 May 1935, and from 1942 to 1948 a resident Legation was in place, which was then elevated to the status of an Embassy. As noted earlier, the US was significantly involved in providing assistance to Afghanistan from the 1950s. But following the murder in Kabul in February 1979 of Ambassador Adolph ('Spike') Dubs, the diplomatic relationship was downgraded, and with fears of mayhem following the withdrawal of Soviet troops, the US Embassy was closed in 1989 and did not reopen until the beginning of 2002. Most US ambassadors since then have been career diplomats – non-career 'political' appointees, often receiving ambassadorships in recognition of active support for successful presidential candidates, rarely aspire to serve in trouble spots. The main exception was Dr Zalmay Khalilzad who served as US Ambassador from 2003 to 2005 and was by training an academic, originally from Afghanistan.[114] A partial exception was retired Lieutenant-General Karl W. Eikenberry who served from 2009 to 2011 and had been Commander, Combined Forces Command-Afghanistan from 2005 to 2007. In addition, in 2009–2010, the energetic US diplomat Richard Holbrooke was appointed by US Secretary of State Hillary Clinton as 'Special Representative for Afghanistan and Pakistan', which gave him a roving brief to address a range of transnational issues pertinent to Afghanistan's future. However, his mission was tragically cut short in December 2010 when he died suddenly of a ruptured aorta, and while it is doubtful whether he exercised much influence over the White House or the Pentagon,[115] he probably carried more weight than any of his successors. Holbrooke's abrasive temperament also contributed to the suspicion of President Karzai that Holbrooke and the United States were keen to see him ejected from office.[116] The office of special representative was finally disestablished in June 2017.

The eminent historian Sir Michael Howard once observed that 'States are cold monsters that mate for convenience and self-protection, not love'.[117] This is something which has always worried Afghan leaders. As noted earlier, despite all the assistance that US administrations have provided at various times to Afghans, their experience of having been abandoned to their own devices or to the tender mercies of their neighbours is rich and unsettling. This needs to be borne in mind when one assesses the ways in which political actors in Kabul respond to US initiatives. Many, furthermore, have been witnesses to US inconsistency in other parts of the world. In April 1975, the US Ambassador to Cambodia, John Gunther Dean, wrote to the Cambodian political leader Prince Sisowath Sirik Matak with an offer to transport him to freedom as Khmer Rouge forces descended on the capital Phnom Penh. Sirik Matak famously responded that he could not leave 'in such a cowardly fashion', and that 'I have committed this mistake of believing in you, the Americans'.[118] In a chilling account of the end of the Vietnam War, one American official used the term 'Decent Interval' to describe what the US was seeking[119] – best understood as an interval between US withdrawal and regime collapse that was long enough to disguise US responsibility for failure. And as recently as December 2018, President Trump was seen as undercutting commitments by the United States to Kurds in Syria.[120] Afghans fear being caught in a similar situation.

This provides much of the context for the tensions between Washington and Kabul that became apparent when the United States commenced direct discussions with the Taliban in Doha[121] following the appointment of Dr Zalmay Khalilzad as US Special Representative for Afghanistan Reconciliation in

September 2018. As far back as 1996, Khalilzad had advocated engagement with the Taliban: in an article published shortly after they seized Kabul, he wrote

> once order is established, concerns such as good government, economic reconstruction and education will rise to the fore...The Taliban does not practice the anti-US style of fundamentalism practiced by Iran...The departure of...Osama bin Laden, the Saudi financier of various anti-US terrorist groups, from Afghanistan indicates some common interest between the United States and the Taliban.[122]

These naïve views may not have been held strongly against him, but nor had they been forgotten. More seriously, in 2019, a detailed plan for an interim government including the Taliban, reportedly authored by a former US official, was circulated widely in Kabul. President Ghani, formerly a professor at Johns Hopkins University in Baltimore, responded with characteristic force: 'Afghans do not accept an interim government – not today, not tomorrow, not in a hundred years...Whoever comes up with such stupid ideas – a few former officials that I wouldn't even accept as my students – should think again'.[123] Most seriously of all, the Afghan government was not given a place at the table, hauntingly reminiscent of the exclusion of the Czechoslovak representatives from the discussions on the future of their country held in Munich in September 1938.[124] Senior Afghan officials made little effort to hide their scepticism about Dr Khalilzad's motives,[125] and the Afghan National Security Adviser (and former Ambassador to the United States), Hamdullah Mohib, spoke so critically about US policy during a visit to the US[126] that thereafter, US officials, doubtless acting under instruction from Washington, began walking out of meetings in Kabul that Mohib was attending.[127] The chill that blighted relations between the United States and Afghanistan towards the end of the Karzai presidency had returned, with Arctic force. What its long-term consequences might be was less obvious, and the abandonment by President Trump in September 2019 of attempts to negotiate with the Taliban certainly opened the door for a warming in the relations between Washington and Kabul.

International drivers of conflict in Afghanistan

Lasting for more than four decades, the conflict in Afghanistan is one of most protracted conflicts of the modern era. A range of domestic and international factors are responsible for the protracted nature of the conflict. Some have pointed to the centralised model of the Afghan state that was built by Amir Abdul Rahman Khan as a key factor in creating persistent tensions between state and society and between various social and ethnic groups. Other explanations have highlighted various forms of traditional divisions in the country, including ideological conflicts between elite groups and a socio-economic and cultural divide between the cities and rural countryside.[128] While these domestic divisions are undoubtedly significant drivers of conflict and instability, a fuller explanation must focus on how domestic dynamics intersect with international influences. One way to examine the conflict in Afghanistan is by locating it in a wider context of regional and global politics and security. As Rubin and Armstrong put it,[129]

> Several networks have linked Afghanistan to a wider arc of conflict, or a regional conflict formation, stretching from Moscow to Dubai. Networks of armed groups, often covertly aided by neighboring states, link the conflict within Afghanistan to violence in Kashmir, Chechnya, Tajikistan, Kyrgyzstan, and Uzbekistan. Networks of narcotics traffickers collaborating with armed groups, link Afghan poppy fields to global markets via Pakistan, Iran, and Central Asia. Networks of traders, more benignly, seek access to buy and sell their goods, even when profit requires avoidance of customs regulations. Cross-border social ties among the region's various ethnic and religious groups underpin all of these networks.

The present regional and global power competition over Afghanistan is reminiscent of the so-called 'Great Game' of the nineteenth century that had some formative impact on the Afghan state. As discussed in the second chapter, global power rivalries played a significant role, in complicated ways, in fomenting instability and undermining periods of relative stability in the country. During the twentieth century, the country remained the most stable country in the region, as its ruling elites consciously attempted to reduce the impact of foreign influence in the country. As the interests of global powers in Afghanistan waxed, regional countries also saw Afghanistan as a field for the projection of power and competitive rivalries. However, the present competition for influence over Afghanistan is significantly different from that which it encountered in the nineteenth century. The contemporary regional competition for influence brings together a range of complex alliance relationships that also intersect with domestic power politics. Countries in the region attempt to exert influence in Afghanistan for a number of reasons. However, the objectives and level of influence of each country's policy in Afghanistan vary significantly. Drawing on Stedman's[130] typology of spoilers in peace processes, Motwani and Bose have drawn distinctions between *limited*, *greedy* and *total spoilers*. Limited spoilers pursue goals and priorities that are largely compatible with those of the government of Afghanistan and hence may only engage in tactical interference to increase their bargaining position with Kabul. Greedy spoilers share limited interests with Kabul and consequently are likely to engage in more destabilising interference if they are not confronted with strong reactions. Finally, total spoilers pursue objectives that are in outright and fundamental conflict with the government of Afghanistan and hence may even engage in policies that push the government in Kabul to submit to the spoilers' interests or that seek to overthrow it.[131]

At a basic level, each country in the region has important reasons to take measures that reduce the impact of the conflict in Afghanistan on its own territories. One way in which they could do this is to minimise interaction by seeking to enforce strict controls over the border with Afghanistan. The Central Asian countries of Tajikistan, Uzbekistan and Turkmenistan have pursued such policies for most of the period since the 1990s. However, many regional states have also engaged in actively supporting one warring faction against the others. Some neighbouring countries have nurtured tactical or strategic relations with Afghan groups and communities that live across their immediate borders. For example, Pakistan has traditionally exerted greater influence in areas adjacent to the Durand Line, which runs through the heart of Pushtun-dominated territories in both countries. The Central Asian republics of Turkmenistan, Uzbekistan and Tajikistan have higher stakes in maintaining ties with groups that are dominant in Afghanistan's northern and northeastern provinces that are adjacent to their borders. Similarly, Iran has traditionally maintained closer ties with powerful actors in the western provinces of Herat, Farah and Nimroz.

However, the motivation of countries in influencing Afghanistan's politics often goes beyond simply mitigating the effects of the war and instability on their own territories. For example, during the 1990s, Tehran became a major player in the proxy war, and in the period after 2001, it has even established some relations with the leadership of the Taliban, with which it found a common interest in countering the US military presence in the region.[132] Since the late 1970s, Pakistan has exercised the greatest level of influence on the politics and security dynamics of Afghanistan. Pakistan's policies in Afghanistan have been driven by a number of domestic and regional factors. Historically, the fear generated by Pushtun nationalism, particularly the irredentist claim promoted by Daoud Khan and Afghan Pushtun nationalists with respect to Pakistan's Pushtun tribal areas and territories, created deep anxieties among Pakistani military and political elites about the prospects of a Pushtun nationalist state in Afghanistan. The effect of this fear is palpable given Pakistan's vulnerabilities to ethnic and separatist movements, particularly after the 1971 formation of Bangladesh out of what used to be East Pakistan. Subsequently, the country has been struggling with a myriad of ethnic and tribal movements that seek either autonomy or outright independence. In this context, the revival of separatist nationalism among the Pushtuns of Pakistan could pose a serious threat to the territorial integrity of the country. However, a more important reason for Pakistan's interference in Afghanistan has been its rivalry with India, a state which has traditionally maintained good relations with the governments in Kabul. During the 1980s, when Pakistan hosted and supported the anti-Soviet *Mujahideen* groups, India maintained good ties with the PDPA regime in Kabul. In 1992, when Dr Najibullah found his hold over power uncertain, he sent his family to New Delhi. Subsequently, India also established good relations with the Rabbani government during the 1990s, while Pakistan supported

Hekmatyar's *Hezb-e Islami*, and subsequently the Taliban after 1994. Pakistani military planners supported the Taliban even though they knew the devastating effect the movement and its draconian policies had on Afghanistan and its people. In the words of Pervez Musharraf,

> The peace that they brought to Afghanistan was the peace of the graveyard. Nevertheless, we still supported them, for geostrategic reasons. If we had broken with them, that would have created a new enemy on our western border, or a vacuum of power there into which might have stepped the Northern Alliance, comprising anti-Pakistan elements. The Northern Alliance was supported by Russia, India, and Iran.[133]

In the period after 2001, as we noted earlier, India became a significant donor to Afghanistan's reconstruction[134] – the fifth largest donor to Afghanistan's reconstruction globally, and by far the most generous country to Afghanistan in the region. In the meantime, Pakistan also established formal relations with the government in Kabul and committed to providing assistance to a relatively smaller number of projects. However, Pakistan's formal policy in Afghanistan was overshadowed by its creeping invasion through supporting proxy groups such as the Taliban. Pakistani military and intelligence officials claimed that India was using its influence in Afghanistan to threaten Pakistan. Pervez Musharraf, the military general who ruled Pakistan after a coup in 1999 until 2008, later admitted that Pakistan was using militant groups as proxies to counter Indian influence in Afghanistan.[135] As a result of the critical role played by the various components of the Taliban movement, the leadership groups of the movement became known as the 'Quetta Shura', the 'Peshawar Shura' and the 'Miran Shah Shura' after Pakistani cities of the same names in the provinces of Baluchistan and Khyber Pakhtunkhwa. The Quetta Shura, which is led by the overall leader of the movement, in theory provides the overall leadership for the group. The Haqqani Network, which is led by the Miran Shah Shura, is also known for particularly strong ties to Pakistan's intelligence agency, the ISI.[136]

Since the 1980s, the weakness of state authority in Afghanistan, and interference by foreign actors, have led to a proliferation of violent non-state actors that have also become significant players in the conflict in Afghanistan. The anti-Soviet jihad attracted thousands of volunteers from a number of Muslim countries. While initially many of these volunteers worked as part of local organisations, over time some of them formed their own transnational entities. Furthermore, while some of them were motivated to support the *Mujahideen* against the Soviet Union, others followed their own agendas for which Afghanistan became a staging ground. The most significant such actor was the Al-Qaeda network founded by Osama Bin Laden. Other similar groups include the Islamic Movement of Uzbekistan, Chechens, and ethnic Uighurs from China, as well as Pakistani militant groups that were primarily focused on the conflict in Kashmir. The most recent such group to emerge was the 'Islamic State – Khorasan province', which was formed in 2014 after some factions of Afghan and Pakistani Taliban pledged allegiance to Abu Bakr Al Baghdadi, the leader of the Islamic State in Iraq.[137] In 2018, President Ghani claimed that there were '21 international terrorist groups' operating in the country.[138] Some of these non-state actors are instrumentally used by global and regional powers. Since the 1980s, different countries have engaged in tactical relationships with these groups to pursue their interests in Afghanistan. That said, as the history of many of these violent groups demonstrates, they can also develop high levels of autonomy and may even turn against their sponsors.

The impact of globalisation

At the beginning of the third decade of the twenty-first century, the cycle of domestic and external drivers of instability and violence in Afghanistan appears to be far from broken. A resurgent Taliban with safe havens in Pakistan, combined with deep elite divisions in Kabul, continue to pose serious threats to the political stability of the country. Yet while the record of international intervention in terms of building a capable state, promoting democracy and triggering socio-economic recovery remains extremely uncertain, the post-2001 international intervention has left vastly more enduring effects on Afghanistan by exposing its society to the forces of globalisation.

The idea of globalisation, which has now generated a mountainous literature, is complex and multidimensional,[139] intimately connected with the idea of networks, but in this case, transnational networks rather than domestic networks of the kind that we discussed in Chapter 3.[140] Networks can bring together all sorts of actors, ranging from government officials to civil society activists to violent extremists, which is one reason why the phenomenon of globalisation has evoked ambivalent reactions. Grewal has argued that 'globalisation is best understood as the emergence and consolidation of transnational and international networks that link people – or groups of people, including entire countries – through the use of shared coordinating standards'.[141] These are longer-term processes, which James Mittelman famously argued would lead to 'compression of time and space',[142] where events in some parts of the world impact swiftly on what happens in other places. Since the 1990s, globalisation has been a hotly contested topic, with scholars and researchers exploring the novelty of contemporary transnational connections and their impacts on the politics, economy and culture of different societies.[143] As a set of complex processes that involve transnational economic, social, cultural and political influences, the impact of globalisation on poor and war-torn countries has also raised significant issues and concerns. On the one hand, economic globalisation and increased political interdependence have the potential to reduce conflict by increasing the opportunity costs of conflict and increasing incentives for peace. On the other hand, closer integration with global economies can also expose poorly developed economies to competition from more developed rivals and to boom-and-bust cycles in the global economy.[144] It is generally recognised that whether a country benefits from globalisation also depends on the circumstances under which it joins the globalising processes. Effective state institutions with well-developed regulatory frameworks that can manage globalisation processes and distribute the benefits of connectivity more broadly are widely recognised as central to the success of globalisation in these countries.[145]

One can argue that Afghanistan has been at the receiving end of many of the dark and destabilising forces of globalisation.[146] These include transnational violent terrorist groups such as Al-Qaeda in the 1990s and the so-called Islamic State-Khorasan Province since 2014. Furthermore, transnational drug and other criminal networks have linked Afghanistan's economy to a global network of illicit trade that extends across several countries. Consequently, as Mendel argues, such transnational forces, which are underpinned by globalisation, have been central to the upheaval the country has experienced since the 1980s. He notes that 'there are strong echoes of representations of African states in representations of Afghanistan. Afghanistan's sovereignty is often described in terms of a lack of connectivity and this is often held to be key to the problems in the state. However, in both the African states discussed and in Afghanistan, this sovereignty is configured not by an absence of connections but by an excess of them'.[147] In the period since 2001, however, Afghanistan's experience with globalisation has also been qualitatively different. During this period, the country was exposed to globalisation as a result of a set of conscious policies of the government and its international donor agencies. At the centre of these strategies was the programme of economic and trade liberalisation that followed the post-2001 international intervention. These policies have raised questions that echo broader debates about the benefits and challenges of globalisation in poor and underdeveloped economies. In Kabul, as part of its top-down liberalisation policy, the government privatised dozens of state-own enterprises. Critics have argued that the rush to privatise before creating the necessary institutional and security environment for private investment was like 'putting the cart before the horse'.[148] For the foreseeable future, security and political uncertainties, as well as the limited capacity of the state to provide an appropriate regulatory environment, are likely to prevent the country from benefiting fully from the processes of economic and trade globalisation.

However, globalisation, at its basic level conceived as compression of time and space, has had a dramatically transformative impact on Afghanistan. The effects of such transformative changes can be seen in different aspects of the politics, culture and economy of the country. Some emerging aspects of these changes deserve to be highlighted here. In 2001, when the Taliban regime was overthrown, Afghanistan was an extremely isolated country. As a result of a virtually non-existent transport and communication infrastructure, various regions of Afghanistan were extremely disconnected from one another and from the rest of the world. In the absence of a basic communication infrastructure, the flow of information and socio-economic exchanges between various regions of the country and between the country and the rest of the world were also extremely limited. In the following years, the country witnessed an explosive growth in communication and mass media. In 2001, the Taliban had banned the use of the Internet in Afghanistan.[149] Subsequently, investment by the private sector as well as the government has significantly expanded Internet services across the country. These include major investments in a national fibre-optic network that has connected 23 provinces of the country. By 2017, it was estimated that 12 per cent of the population of the country had access to the Internet, including 9 per cent who were active social media users.[150] In 2018, government officials estimated that up to 9.7 million people had access to the Internet.[151] In the meantime, Afghanistan also experienced explosive growth in its mass media and broadcasting sector. Beginning with only one national radio channel in 2001, which the Taliban named Radio Sharia and used as a propaganda channel, Afghanistan quickly established one of the most dynamic and pluralistic media landscapes in the region. In 2015, the country's national broadcaster, the Radio and Television of Afghanistan with its 22 provincial channels, competed with 174 radio stations and 68 private television networks.[152] Parallel to these rapid changes in media and communication, Afghanistan has witnessed the rise of a new generation of internationally connected social and political activists, entrepreneurs, journalists and civil society leaders.

As in other societies, the expansion of mass media and communication services has also been exploited by the Taliban and other violent groups. These groups have used the Internet and social media platforms to spread their own narratives of violent insurgency.[153] However, these services are likely to empower broader segments of the population by exposing them to diverse world views. According to the annual surveys of The Asia Foundation, the number of people who have said they get their news from television and the Internet has been rapidly growing. For example, the number of people who reported using television as a source of news increased from 58.3 per cent in 2014 to 68.7 per cent in 2018. The shift towards the Internet as a source of information has been even more dramatic. The number of people who reported using the Internet as a source of news and information increased from just 3.3 per cent in 2013 to 16.8 per cent in 2018. Mobile phones have also emerged as an essential household item, with 89.5 per cent of the people reporting access to at least one mobile phone in their families.[154]

One way in which these changes will impact Afghanistan is by creating conditions for long-term bottom-up modernisation. Since the time of Amanullah Khan in the 1920s, Afghanistan's modernist elites in Kabul lacked a popular constituency for their reforms. Top-down programmes of modernisation were frequently faced with violent opposition from conservative segments of the populations who feared that rapid modernising changes would affect their local customs and traditions. With the rapid expansion of a globally connected and educated generation from across the country, these dynamics are likely to change significantly. Afghans truly live in a new world.

Notes

1 See Christian Reus-Smit, *American Power and World Order* (Oxford: Polity Press, 2004).

2 See Robert D. Putnam, 'Diplomacy and domestic politics: The logic of two-level games', *International Organization*, vol. 42, no. 3, Summer 1988, pp. 427–460.

3 See Manley O. Hudson, 'Afghanistan, Ecuador and the Soviet Union in the League of Nations', *American Journal of International Law*, vol. 29, no. 1, January 1935, pp. 109–116 at pp. 110–111.

4 For more detailed discussion, see Louis Dupree, 'Myth and reality in Afghan "Neutralism"', *Central Asian Survey*, vol. 7, no. 2–3, 1988, pp. 145–151.

5 See Ludwig W. Adamec, *Afghanistan's Foreign Affairs to the Mid-Twentieth Century: Relations With the USSR, Germany, and Britain* (Tucson: University of Arizona Press, 1974).

6 See Jerry F. Hough, *The Struggle for the Third World: Soviet Debates and American Options* (Washington, DC: The Brookings Institution, 1986).

7 Arnold Fletcher, *Afghanistan: Highway of Conquest* (Ithaca: Cornell University Press, 1965).

8 Milton Bearden, 'Afghanistan, graveyard of empires', *Foreign Affairs*, vol. 80, no. 6, November–December 2001, pp. 17–30.

9 See Thomas H. Johnson, *Taliban Narratives: The Use and Power of Stories in the Afghanistan Conflict* (London: Hurst & Co., 2017).

10 See Paul Collier, *The Bottom Billion: Why the Poorest Countries Are Failing and What Can Be Done About It* (Oxford: Oxford University Press, 2007).

11 Kathleen Collins, 'The limits of cooperation: Central Asia, Afghanistan, and the new silk road', *Asia Policy*, no. 17, January 2014, pp. 18–26.

12 See President Hamid Karzai's speech at the International Kabul Conference on Afghanistan, 20 July 2010.

13 For a detailed demonstration of this point, see 'A Conversation with Mohammad Ashraf Ghani', Council on Foreign Relations, New York, 21 September 2017. https://www.cfr.org/event/conversation-mohammad-ashraf-ghani

14 See Nasir A. Andisha, *Neutrality in Afghanistan's Foreign Policy* (Washington, DC: Special Report no. 360, United States Institute of Peace, March 2015); Nasir A. Andisha, 'Neutrality and its place in Afghanistan's foreign policy', in Srinjoy Bose, Nishank Motwani and William Maley (eds.), *Afghanistan – Challenges and Prospects* (London: Routledge, 2018) pp. 241–259.

15 For more detail on the background of TUTAP and CASA-1000 and their anticipated benefits for Afghanistan, see Mohsin Amin, *Power to the People: How to extend Afghans' access to electricity* (Kabul: Afghanistan Analysts Network, 3 February 2015).

16 See Marissa Quie, 'The Istanbul Process: Prospects for regional connectivity in the heart of Asia,' *Asia Europe Journal*, vol. 12, no. 3, September 2014, pp. 285–300.

17 See Richard Ghiasy and Maihan Saeedi, *The Heart of Asia Process at a Juncture: An Analysis of Impediments to Further Progress* (Kabul: Afghan Institute for Strategic Studies, June 2014).

18 See Ian Talbot, *Pakistan: A New History* (New York: Columbia University Press, 2012); Ayesha Jalal, *The Struggle for Pakistan: A Muslim Homeland and Global Politics* (Cambridge: Harvard University Press, 2014).

19 See Muhammad Reza Kazimi, *Liaquat Ali Khan: His Life and Work* (Karachi: Oxford University Press, 2003).

20 For further discussion, see Hasan-Askari Rizvi, *Military, State and Society in Pakistan* (Basingstoke: Macmillan, 2000) pp. 170–173; Vali Nasr, 'Military rule, Islamism and democracy in Pakistan', *The Middle East Journal*, vol. 58, no. 2, Spring 2004, pp. 195–209; Aqil Shah, *The Army and Democracy: Military Politics in Pakistan* (Cambridge: Harvard University Press, 2014); S. Paul Kapur, *Jihad as Grand Strategy: Islamist Militancy, National Security and the Pakistani State* (New York: Oxford University Press, 2017).

21 See Ayesha Siddiqa, *Military, Inc.: Inside Pakistan's Military Economy* (Karachi: Oxford University Press, 2007).

22 Shuja Nawaz, *Crossed Swords: Pakistan, Its Army, and the Wars Within* (Karachi: Oxford University Press, 2008) p. 373.

23 See G.W. Choudhary, *The Last Days of United Pakistan* (Perth: University of Western Australia Press, 1974).

24 See Muhammad Qasim Zaman, 'Sectarianism in Pakistan: The radicalization of Shi'i and Sunni identities', *Modern Asian Studies*, vol. 32, no. 3, July 1998, pp. 689–716; S.V.R. Nasr, 'The rise of Sunni militancy in Pakistan: The changing role of Islamism and the Ulama in society and politics', *Modern Asian Studies*, vol. 34, no. 1, January 2000, pp. 139–180; S.V.R. Nasr, 'International politics, domestic imperatives, and identity mobilization: Sectarianism in Pakistan, 1979–1998', *Comparative Politics*, vol. 32, no. 2, January 2000, pp. 171–190.

25 See Farzana Shaikh, *Making Sense of Pakistan* (New York: Columbia University Press, 2009); Samina Yasmeen, *Jihad and Dawah: Evolving Narratives of Lashkar-e Taiba and Jamat ud Dawah* (London: Hurst & Co., 2017); C. Christine Fair, *In Their Own Words: Understanding Lashkar-e-Tayyaba* (London: Hurst & Co., 2018).

26 See C. Christine Fair, *Fighting to the End: The Pakistan Army's Way of War* (New York: Oxford University Press, 2014).

27 See Muhammad Qasim Zaman, *Islam in Pakistan: A History* (Princeton: Princeton University Press, 2018) pp. 244–251. For an earlier discussion of Pakistan's vulnerability to a Taliban-like force, see William Maley, 'Talibanisation and Pakistan', in *Talibanisation: Extremism and Regional Instability in South and Central Asia* (Berlin: Conflict Prevention Network: Stiftung Wissenschaft und Politik, 2001) pp. 53–74.

28 See Daniel A. Kronenfeld, 'Afghan refugees in Pakistan: Not all refugees, not always in Pakistan, not necessarily Afghan?', *Journal of Refugee Studies*, vol. 21, no. 1, March 2008, pp. 43–63.

29 George P. Shultz, *Turmoil and Triumph: My Years as Secretary of State* (New York: Scribner's, 1993) p. 1091. The US president at the time was Ronald Reagan.

30 See Steve Coll, *Ghost Wars: The Secret History of the CIA, Afghanistan and Bin Laden, from the Soviet Invasion to September 10, 2001* (London: Penguin, 2005); Roy Gutman, *How We Missed the Story: Osama Bin Laden, the Taliban, and the Hijacking of Afghanistan* (Washington, DC: United States Institute of Peace Press, 2013).

31 See Anthony Davis, 'How the Taliban became a military force', in William Maley (ed.), *Fundamentalism Reborn? Afghanistan and the Taliban* (London: Hurst & Co., 1998) pp. 43–71.

32 Abdul Sattar, *Pakistan's Foreign Policy 1947–2005* (Karachi: Oxford University Press, 2007) p. 227.

33 Marvin G. Weinbaum and Jonathan B. Harder, 'Pakistan's Afghan policies and their consequences', *Contemporary South Asia*, vol. 16, no. 1, March 2008, pp. 25–38 at p. 27.

34 See Taimoor Shah and Carlotta Gall, 'Afghan Rebels Find Aid in Pakistan, Musharraf Admits', *The New York Times*, 13 August 2007.

35 Seth G. Jones, 'Pakistan's dangerous game', *Survival*, vol. 49, no. 1, Spring 2007, pp. 15–32 at p. 15. See also Seth G. Jones, *Counterinsurgency in Afghanistan* (Santa Monica: RAND National Defence Research Institute, 2008); Seth G. Jones, *In the Graveyard of Empires: America's War in Afghanistan* (New York: W.W. Norton, 2009); Shaun Gregory, 'The ISI and the war on terrorism', *Studies in Conflict and Terrorism*, vol. 30, no. 12, 2007, pp. 1013–1031; Matt Waldman, *The Sun in the Sky: The Relationship Between Pakistan's ISI and Afghan Insurgents* (London: Discussion Paper no. 18, Crisis States Research Centre, London School of Economics and Political Science, June 2010); Carlotta Gall, *The Wrong Enemy: America in Afghanistan, 2001–2014* (New York: Houghton Mifflin Harcourt, 2014); Steve Coll, *Directorate S: The C.I.A. and America's Secret Wars in Afghanistan and Pakistan* (New York: Penguin Press, 2018).

36 See Frédéric Grare, *Pakistan-Afghanistan Relations in the Post-9/11 Era* (Washington, DC: Carnegie Endowment for International Peace, 2006) pp. 8–15; Ashley J. Tellis, *Pakistan and the War on Terror: Conflicted Goals, Compromised Performance* (Washington, DC: Carnegie Endowment for International Peace, 2008) p. 12.

37 Asad Durrani, *Pakistan Adrift: Navigating Troubled Waters* (Chennai: Westland Publications, 2018) p. 190.

38 On the applicability of this label, see William Maley, 'Confronting creeping invasions: Afghanistan, the UN and the world community', in K. Warikoo (ed.), *The Afghanistan Crisis: Issues and Perspectives* (New Delhi: Bhavana Books, 2002) pp. 256–274; William Maley, Afghanistan: An historical and geographical appraisal', *International Review of the Red Cross*, vol. 92, no. 880, December 2010, pp. 859–876 at p. 875.

39 Husain Haqqani, 'Don't trust the Taliban's promises', *Foreignpolicy.com*, 7 February 2019.

40 See Shirin Tahir-Kheli, *The United States and Pakistan: The Evolution of an Influence Relationship* (New York: Praeger, 1982); Dennis Kux, *The United States and Pakistan 1947–2000: Disenchanted Allies* (Washington, DC: Woodrow Wilson Center Press, 2001).

41 See Ian Hall, '"Mephistopheles in a Saville Row Suit": V.K. Krishna Menon and the West', in Ian Hall (ed.), *Radicals and Reactionaries in Twentieth Century International Thought* (New York: Palgrave, 2015) pp. 191–216.

42 Avinash Paliwal, *My Enemy's Enemy: India in Afghanistan from the Soviet Invasion to the US Withdrawal* (London: Hurst & Co., 2017) p. 49.

43 Amin Saikal, 'The regional politics of the Afghan crisis', in Amin Saikal and William Maley (eds.), *The Soviet Withdrawal from Afghanistan* (Cambridge: Cambridge University Press, 1989) pp. 52–66 at p. 57.

44 See Neelesh Misra, *173 Hours in Captivity: The Hijacking of IC814* (New Delhi: HarperCollins, 2000).

45 See Sandy Gordon, *India's Rise as an Asian Power: Nation, Neighborhood, and Region* (Washington, DC; Georgetown University Press, 2014).

46 See Rani D. Mullen, *India in Afghanistan: Understanding Development Assistance by Emerging Donors to Conflict-Affected Countries* (Washington, DC: The Stimson Center, August 2017).

47 See Sumit Ganguly, *Conflict Unending: India-Pakistan Tensions since 1947* (Washington, DC: Woodrow Wilson Center Press, 2001).

48 Selig S. Harrison, 'The Shah, Not Kremlin, Touched Off Afghan Coup', *The Washington Post*, 13 May 1979.

49 See Zalmay Khalilzad and Cheryl Benard, *The Government of God: Iran's Islamic Republic* (New York: Columbia University Press, 1984); Amin Saikal, *The Rise and Fall of the Shah: Iran from Autocracy to Religious Rule* (Princeton: Princeton University Press, 2009).

50 See Anoushiravan Ehteshami, *Iran: Stuck in Transition* (New York and London: Routledge, 2017) pp. 32–114; Amin Saikal, *Iran Rising: The Survival and Future of the Islamic Republic* (Princeton: Princeton University Press, 2019).

51 For some discussion, see Trita Parsi, *Treacherous Alliance: The Secret Dealings of Israel, Iran, and the United States* (New Haven: Yale University Press, 2007); Ali M. Ansari, *Confronting Iran: The Failure of American Foreign Policy and the Next Great Conflict in the Middle East* (New York: Basic Books, 2006); Trita Parsi, *A Single Roll of the Dice: Obama's Diplomacy with Iran* (New Haven: Yale University Press, 2012).

52 See Anwar-ul-Haq Ahady, 'Saudi Arabia, Iran and the conflict in Afghanistan', in William Maley (ed.), *Fundamentalism Reborn? Afghanistan and the Taliban* (London: Hurst & Co., 1998) pp. 117–134.

53 See Niamatullah Ibrahimi, *The Hazaras and the Afghan State: Rebellion, Exclusion, and the Struggle for Recognition* (London: Hurst & Co., 2017); also Robert Leroy Canfield,

Faction and Conversion in a Plural Society: Religious Alignments in the Hindu Kush (Ann Arbor: Anthropological Papers no. 50, Museum of Anthropology, University of Michigan, 1973); David Busby Edwards, 'The evolution of Shi'i political dissent in Afghanistan', in Juan R.I. Cole and Nikkie R. Keddie (eds.), *Shi'ism, and Social Protest* (New Haven: Yale University Press, 1986) pp. 201–229; Rolf Bindemann, *Religion und Politik bei den schi'itischen Hazâra in Afghanistan, Iran und Pakistan* (Berlin: Das Arabische Buch, 1987); Kristian Berg Harpviken, *Political Mobilization among the Hazara of Afghanistan: 1978–1992* (Oslo: Report no. 9, Department of Sociology, University of Oslo, 1996).

54 See Niamatullah Ibrahimi, *The Dissipation of Political Capital among Afghanistan's Hazaras: 2001–2009* (London: Working Paper no. 51, Crisis States Research Centre, London School of Economics and Political Science, June 2009).

55 See *Afghanistan: The Massacre in Mazar-i Sharif* (New York: Human Rights Watch, 1998); Rupert Colville, 'One Massacre That Didn't Grab the World's Attention', *International Herald Tribune*, 7 August 1999; Ahmed Rashid, *Taliban: Militant Islam, Oil and Fundamentalism in Central Asia* (New Haven: Yale University Press, 2000) p. 73.

56 Dexter Filkins, 'Iran Is Said to Give Top Karzai Aide Cash by the Bagful', *The New York Times*, 23 October 2010.

57 Shahram Akbarzadeh, 'Iran's policy towards Afghanistan: In the shadow of the United States', *Journal of Asian Security and International Affairs*, vol. 1, no. 1, 2014, pp. 63–78.

58 See Bruce Koepke, *Iran's Policy on Afghanistan: The Evolution of Strategic Pragmatism* (Stockholm: Stockholm International Peace Research Institute, September 2013).

59 Ansari, *Confronting Iran*, p. 240.

60 See Barry Buzan, 'Regional security complex theory in the post-Cold War world', in Fredrick Söderbaum and Timothy M. Shaw (eds.), *Theories of New Regionalism: A Palgrave Reader* (London: Palgrave Macmillan, 2003) pp. 140–159.

61 See Robert L. Canfield, 'Restructuring in greater central Asia: Changing political configurations', *Asian Survey*, vol. 32, no. 10, October 1992, pp. 875–887.

62 See William Maley, 'Afghanistan and its region', in J. Alexander Thier (ed.), *The Future of Afghanistan* (Washington, DC: United States Institute of Peace, 2009) pp. 81–91.

63 See Barnett R. Rubin, Ashraf Ghani, William Maley, Ahmed Rashid, and Olivier Roy, *Afghanistan: Reconstruction and Peacebuilding in a Regional Framework* (Bern: KOFF Peacebuilding Reports 1/2001, Swiss Peace Foundation, 2001) p. 1.

64 Kristian Berg Harpviken and Shahrbanou Tadjbakhsh, *A Rock Between Hard Places: Afghanistan as an Arena of Regional Insecurity* (London: Hurst & Co., 2016) p. 156.

65 Nishank Motwani, 'Afghanistan and the regional insecurity contagion', in Srinjoy Bose, Nishank Motwani and William Maley (eds.), *Afghanistan – Challenges and Prospects* (London: Routledge, 2018) pp. 219–240.

66 On this area and its peoples, see M. Nazif Shahrani, *The Kirghiz and Wakhi of Afghanistan: Adaptation to Closed Frontiers and War* (Seattle: University of Washington Press, 2002).

67 See Niamatullah Ibrahimi, *Ideology without Leadership: The Rise and Decline of Maoism in Afghanistan* (Kabul: AAN Thematic Report no.03/2012, Afghanistan Analysts Network, August 2012).

68 Gerald Segal, 'China and Afghanistan', *Asian Survey*, vol. 21, no. 11, November 1981, pp. 1158–1174. See also Yaacov Y.I. Vertzberger, *China's Southwestern Strategy: Encirclement and Counterencirclement* (New York: Praeger, 1985) pp. 105–107.

69 See Tibor Meray, *Thirteen Days That Shook the Kremlin: Imre Nagy and the Hungarian Revolution* (New York: Praeger, 1959); Charles Gati, *Hungary and the Soviet Bloc* (Durham: Duke University Press, 1986); Charles Gati, *Failed Illusions: Moscow, Washington, Budapest, and the 1956 Hungarian Revolt* (Stanford: Stanford University Press, 2006).

70 For a detailed history, see Lorenz M. Lüthi, *The Sino-Soviet Split* (Princeton: Princeton University Press, 2008).

71 See Roderick MacFarquhar and Michael Schoenhals, *Mao's Last Revolution* (Cambridge: Harvard University Press, 2006).

72 See Ben Kiernan, *The Pol Pot Regime: Race, Power, and Genocide under the Khmer Rouge, 1975–79* (New Haven: Yale University Press, 2008).

73 See Leslie Holmes, 'Afghanistan and Sino-Soviet relations', in Amin Saikal and William Maley (eds.), *The Soviet Withdrawal from Afghanistan* (Cambridge: Cambridge University Press, 1989) pp. 122–141.

74 See Ezra F. Vogel, *Deng Xiaoping and the Transformation of China* (Cambridge: Harvard University Press, 2011).

75 See Henry Kissinger, *On China* (London: Allen Lane, 2011).

76 See Zhao Hong, 'China's Afghan policy: The forming of the "march west" strategy?', *Journal of East Asian Affairs*, vol. 27, no. 2, Fall-Winter 2013, pp. 1–29; Zhu Yongbiao, 'China's Afghanistan policy since 9/11: Stages and prospects', *Asian Survey*, vol. 58, no. 2, March–April 2018, pp. 281–301.

77 Peter Simpson, 'China Begins Scramble for Afghanistan's Oil Reserves', *The Telegraph*, 27 December 2011.

78 For a comprehensive overview, see John F. Shroder, *Natural Resources in Afghanistan: Geographic and Geologic Perspectives on Centuries of Conflict* (Waltham: Elsevier Inc., 2014).

79 See Jessica Donati, 'China Seeks Greater Role in Afghanistan with Peace Talk Push', *Reuters*, 11 November 2014.

80 See *"Eradicating Ideological Viruses": China's Campaign of Repression against Xinjiang's Muslims* (New York: Human Rights Watch, 9 September 2018); Joanne Smith Finley, 'Securitization, insecurity and conflict in contemporary Xinjiang: Has PRC counter-terrorism evolved into state terror?', *Central Asian Survey*, vol. 38, no. 1, 2019, pp. 1–26.

81 See Matthew Hall, *The Shanghai Cooperation Organisation: A Partner for Stabilising Afghanistan?* (Canberra: Shedden Papers, Centre for Defence and Strategic Studies, Australian Defence College, 2009).

82 See Mikhail Myakgov, Peter C. Ordeshook and Dimitri Shakin, *The Forensics of Election Fraud: Russia and Ukraine* (Cambridge: Cambridge University Press, 2009); Graeme Gill, *Building an Authoritarian Polity: Russia in Post-Soviet Times* (Cambridge: Cambridge University Press, 2015).

83 See Amy Knight, 'The Crime of the Century', *New York Review of Books*, vol. 66, no. 5, 21 March 2019, pp. 51–52.

84 See Amin Saikal and William Maley, 'From Soviet to Russian foreign policy', in Amin Saikal and William Maley (eds.), *Russia in Search of its Future* (Cambridge: Cambridge University Press, 1995) pp. 102–122.

85 See Bobo Lo, *Russia and the New World Disorder* (Washington, DC: Brookings Institution Press, 2015).

86 Kirill Nourzhanov, 'Russia's Afghanistan policy after 2014: Staying at an arm's length and preparing for the worst', in Amin Saikal and Kirill Nourzhanov (eds.), *Afghanistan and Its Neighbors after the NATO Withdrawal* (Lanham: Lexington Books, 2016) pp. 163–178 at p. 171.

87 See Lawrence Freedman, *Ukraine and the Art of Strategy* (New York: Oxford University Press, 2019) pp. 58–59, 168.

88 Special Counsel Robert S. Mueller III, *Report on the Investigation into Russian Interference in the 2016 Presidential Election* (Washington, DC: Department of Justice, March 2019) vol. I, p. 1.

89 See Andrew Higgins and Mujib Mashal, 'Taliban Peace Talks in Moscow End With Hope the U.S. Exits, If Not Too Quickly', *The New York Times*, 6 February 2019.

90 See 'Shoigu: IG usilivaetsia v Afganistane dlia dal'neishei ekspansii v Tsentral'noi Azii', *TASS*, 30 April 2019.

91 Ekaterina Stepanova, 'Russia's policy on Afghanistan', in Marlene Laruelle (ed.), *The Central Asia-Afghanistan Relationship: From Soviet Intervention to the Silk Road Initiative* (Lanham: Lexington Books, 2017) pp. 89–113.

92 See Svante E. Cornell and S. Frederick Starr, *Modernization and Regional Cooperation in Central Asia: A New Spring?* (Washington, DC: Silk Road Paper, Silk Road Studies Program, Central Asia-Caucasus Institute, American Foreign Policy Council, November 2018); Peter Frankopan, *The New Silk Roads: The Present and Future of the World* (London: Bloomsbury, 2018) pp. 52–73.

93 See Timur Dadabaev, 'Afghanistan in 2018: Shifts in domestic, regional, and global dynamics', *Asian Survey*, vol. 59, no. 1, January–February 2019, pp. 114–123 at pp. 118–120.

94 See Walter C. Ladwig III, *The Forgotten Front: Patron-Client Relationships in Counterinsurgency* (Cambridge: Cambridge University Press, 2017).

95 See Gerrit W. Gong, *The Standard of 'Civilization' in International Society* (Oxford: Oxford University Press, 1984); Brett Bowden, *The Empire of Civilization: The Evolution of an Imperial Idea* (Chicago: University of Chicago Press, 2009).

96 See Stephen D. Krasner, *Sovereignty: Organized Hypocrisy* (Princeton: Princeton University Press, 1999).

97 See Robert H. Jackson, *Quasi-states: Sovereignty, International Relations and the Third World* (Cambridge: Cambridge University Press, 1990); Michael Barnett, 'The new United Nations politics of peace: From juridical sovereignty to empirical sovereignty', *Global Governance*, vol. 1, no. 1, Winter 1995, pp. 79–97.

98 See Minton F. Goldman, 'President Bush and Afghanistan: A turning point in American policy', *Comparative Strategy*, vol. 11, no. 2, 1992, pp. 177–193.

99 See Gutman, *How We Missed the Story.*

100 See David Halberstam, *The Best and the Brightest* (New York: Ballantine Books, 1992); Townsend Hoopes, *The Limits of Intervention* (New York: David McKay Co. Inc., 1969); Bernard Brodie, *War and Politics* (New York: Macmillan, 1973) pp. 113–222.

101 See David Halberstam, *The Making of a Quagmire* (New York: Random House, 1965).

102 See Thurston Clarke, *Honorable Exit: How a Few Brave Americans Risked All to Save Our Vietnamese Allies at the End of the War* (New York: Doubleday, 2019).

103 See David L. Phillips, *Losing Iraq: Inside the Postwar Reconstruction Fiasco* (Boulder: Westview Press, 2005); George Packer, *The Assassins' Gate: America in Iraq* (New York: Farrar, Straus and Giroux, 2005); Larry Diamond, *Squandered Victory: The American Occupation and the Bungled Effort to Bring Democracy to Iraq* (New York: Times Books, 2005); and Ahmed S. Hashim, *Insurgency and Counter-Insurgency in Iraq* (Ithaca: Cornell University Press, 2006).

104 *Hard Lessons: The Iraq Reconstruction Experience* (Washington, DC: Special Inspector General for Iraq Reconstruction, 2009) p. 326.

105 Robert Burns, 'Mullen: Afghanistan Isn't Top Priority', *The Washington Post*, 11 December 2007.

106 Robert M. Gates, *Duty: Memoirs of a Secretary at War* (New York: Alfred A. Knopf, 2014) p. 569.

107 *Remarks by President Trump on the Strategy in Afghanistan and South Asia* (Washington, DC: Office of the Press Secretary, The White House, 21 August 2017).

108 See Barnett R. Rubin, Humayun Hamidzada, and Abby Stoddard, *Through the Fog of Peace Building: Evaluating the Reconstruction of Afghanistan* (New York: Center on International Cooperation, New York University, 2003) p. 19.

109 See Clancy Chassay, 'Afghanistan: Corruption and Incompetence Cripple Reconstruction Effort, Say Aid Workers', *The Guardian*, 19 February 2009;

110 Maria Abi-Habib and Matthew Rosenberg, 'Task Force to Take on Afghan Corruption', *The Wall Street Journal*, 18 June 2010.

111 For a summary of the Special Inspector General's concerns, see *Special Inspector General for Afghanistan Reconstruction: Stabilization: Lessons from the U.S. Experience in Afghanistan* (Arlington: SIGAR, May 2018).

112 Thomas Gibbons-Neff and Julian E. Barnes, 'Under Peace Plan, U.S. Military Would Exit Afghanistan Within Five Years', *The New York Times*, 28 February 2019.

113 See Sarah Feldman, 'Where U.S. military personnel is stationed abroad', *Statista: The Statistics Portal*, 13 March 2019.

114 For Khalilzad's reflections on this period, see Zalmay Khalilzad, *The Envoy: From Kabul to the White House, My Journey Through a Turbulent World* (New York: St Martin's Press, 2016).

115 See Coll, *Directorate S*, p. 365; George Packer, 'The longest wars: Richard Holbrooke and the decline of American power', *Foreign Affairs*, vol. 98, no. 3, May–June 2019, pp. 46–68.

116 See Joshua Partlow, *A Kingdom of Their Own: The Family Karzai and the Afghan Disaster* (New York: Alfred A. Knopf, 2016) pp. 19–22.

117 Michael Howard, 'An unhappy successful marriage: Security means knowing what to expect', *Foreign Affairs*, vol. 78, no. 3, May–June 1999, pp. 164–175 at p. 164.

118 *Interview with Ambassador John Gunther Dean* (Arlington: Foreign Affairs Oral History Project, Association for Diplomatic Studies and Training, 6 December 2000) p. 115.

119 Frank Snepp, *Decent Interval: The American Debacle in Vietnam and the Fall of Saigon* (London: Allen Lane, 1980).

120 See Rod Nordland, 'U.S. Exit Seen as a Betrayal of the Kurds, and a Boon for ISIS', *The New York Times*, 19 December 2018.

121 For some critical reflections on this process, see William Maley, 'Goftuguha bara-i saleh-i Afghanistan', *Etilaatroz* (Kabul), 9 February 2019.

122 Zalmay Khalilzad, 'Afghanistan: Time to Reengage', *The Washington Post*, 7 October 1996.

123 Mujib Mashal, 'U.S. and Taliban Agree in Principle to Peace Framework, Envoy Says', *The New York Times*, 28 January 2019.

124 See Telford Taylor, *Munich: The Price of Peace* (New York: Doubleday, 1979) p. 38.

125 Mark Lander, 'U.S. Diplomat Is Focus of Afghan Leaders' Anger Over Peace Talks With Taliban', *The New York Times*, 15 March 2019.

126 See Karen DeYoung, 'Afghan Official says any U.S. deal with the Taliban would "dishonor" American troops as relations sink', *The Washington Post*, 14 March 2019.

127 See Ron Nordland and Mujib Mashal, 'Afghan National Security Chief Is Sidelined in His Own War', *The New York Times*, 30 March 2019.

128 For a review of the literature on domestic drivers of conflict, see Antonio Giustozzi with Niamatullah Ibrahimi, *Thirty Years of Conflict: Drivers of Anti-Government Mobilisation in Afghanistan 1978–2011* (Kabul: Afghanistan Research and Evaluation Unit, January 2012).

129 Barnett R. Rubin and Andrea Armstrong, 'Regional issues in the reconstruction of Afghanistan', *World Policy Journal*, vol. 20, no. 1, Spring 2003, pp. 31–40 at p. 31.

130 See Stephen John Stedman, 'Spoiler problems in peace processes', *International Security*, vol. 22, no. 2, Fall 1997, pp. 5–53.

131 Nishank Motwani and Srinjoy Bose, 'Afghanistan: "Spoilers" in the regional security context,' *Australian Journal of International Affairs*, vol. 69, no. 3, 2015, pp. 266–284.

132 Erin Cunningham, 'While the U.S. wasn't looking, Russia and Iran began carving out a bigger role in Afghanistan', *The Washington Post*, 13 April 2017. The then Taliban leader, Mullah Akhtar Mansour, was killed by a US drone strike in May 2016 while returning from a covert visit to Iran: see Carlotta Gall and Ruhullah Khapalwak, 'Taliban Leader Feared Pakistan Before He Was Killed', *The New York Times*, 9 August 2017.

133 Pervez Musharraf, *In the Line of Fire: A Memoir* (London: Simon & Schuster, 2006) p. 203.

134 Christopher Clary, 'Trump singled out India to do more in Afghanistan. That could easily backfire', *The Washington Post*, 24 August 2017.

135 Jon Boone, 'Musharraf: Pakistan and India's backing for "proxies" in Afghanistan must stop', *The Guardian*, 13 February 2015.

136 See Vahid Brown and Don Rassler, *Fountainhead of Jihad: The Haqqani Nexus, 1973–2012* (New York: Oxford University Press, 2013).

137 For more on the Islamic State-Khorasan Province and its relationship with the Taliban, see Niamatullah Ibrahimi and Shahram Akbarzadeh, 'Intra-*Jihadist* Conflict and Cooperation: Islamic State-Khorasan Province and the Taliban in Afghanistan', *Studies in Conflict and Terrorism* (forthcoming, 2019).

138 Lara Logan, 'Kabul under siege while America's longest war rages on', *CBS News*, 3 June 2018. For a listing of terrorist groups reportedly active in Afghanistan, see *Operation Freedom's Sentinel: Lead Inspector General Report to the United States Congress January 1, 2019 – March 31, 2019* (Washington, DC: Department of Defense, 2019) p. 25.

139 See Ian Clark, *Globalization and Fragmentation: International Relations in the Twentieth Century* (Oxford: Oxford University Press, 1997) pp. 16–26; Ian Clark, *Globalization and International Relations Theory* (Oxford: Oxford University Press, 1999) pp. 33–51.

140 See Anne-Marie Slaughter, *A New World Order* (Princeton: Princeton University Press, 2004); Anne-Marie Slaughter, *The Chessboard and the Web: Strategies of Connection in a Networked World* (New Haven: Yale University Press, 2017).

141 David Singh Grewal, *Network Power: The Social Dynamics of Globalization* (New Haven: Yale University Press, 2008) p. 292.

142 James H. Mittelman, *Whither Globalization? The Vortex of Knowledge and Ideology* (New York: Routledge, 2004) p. 4.

143 For a review of these debates, see Mauro F. Guillén, 'Is globalization civilizing, destructive or feeble? A critique of five key debates in the social science literature', *Annual Review of Sociology*, vol. 27, August 2001, pp. 235–260.

144 See Carolyn Chisadza and Manoel Bittencourt, 'Globalisation and conflict: Evidence from Sub-Saharan Africa', *International Development Policy/Revue internationale de politique de développement*, vol. 10, no. 1, 2018.

145 See Nita Rudra and Jennifer Tobin, 'When does globalization help the poor?', *Annual Review of Political Science*, vol. 20, 2017, pp. 287–307.

146 Hayatullah Mohammadi, *Tasir-e jahanishodan bar farhang dar Afghanistan* (Kabul: Entesharat-e Farhang, 2014).

147 Jonathan Mendel, 'Afghanistan, networks and connectivity', *Geopolitics* vol. 15, no. 4, 2010, pp. 726–751 at p. 744.

148 Anna Paterson and James Blewett with Asif Karimi, *Putting the Cart Before the Horse? Privatisation and Economic Reform in Afghanistan* (Kabul: Afghanistan Research and Evaluation Unit, November 2006).

149 'Taliban blackbans the Internet', *CNN*, 13 July 2001.

150 See *Social Media in Afghanistan: Users and Engagement* (Kabul: Altai Consulting and Internews, October 2017).

151 Javed Hamim Kakar, '$2.3bn invested in Afghanistan's IT sector, says Abdullah', *Pajhwok Afghan News*, 30 October 2018.

152 Ann J. Procter, *Afghanistan's Fourth Estate: Independent Media* (Washington, DC: Peacebrief no.189, United States Institute of Peace, August 2015).

153 Niamatullah Ibrahimi, Musab Omer and Mohammad Irfani, *Social Media and Articulation of Radical Narratives in Afghanistan: A Research and Policy Paper* (Kabul: Afghanistan Institute for Strategic Studies, November 2015).

154 *Afghanistan in 2018: A Survey of the Afghan People* (Kabul: The Asia Foundation, 2018) pp. 151–154.

6

CONCLUSION

In June 2019, a major cross-national study ranked some 163 states and territories according to their level of peacefulness. For Afghans, the results were sobering: 'Afghanistan is now the least peaceful country in the world, replacing Syria, which is now the second least peaceful. South Sudan, Yemen, and Iraq comprise the remaining five least peaceful countries'.[1] Afghanistan thus presents a paradoxical image to the wider world. Nearly two decades have passed since the overthrow of the Taliban regime, and Afghanistan during that period has acquired a new constitution and witnessed four presidential election processes and three legislative elections. Even more significantly, the forces of globalisation have powerfully reshaped Afghan society: the bulk of the population is now strikingly youthful and linked to the wider world in ways that no previous Afghan generation could claim to have experienced. Yet at the same time, Afghanistan and Afghans have been haunted for much of this period by a profound and pervasive sense of uncertainty and insecurity. The vast changes in the political order since the turn of the century have not been fully consolidated or institutionalised, and many Afghans retain a feeling that they are teetering on the edge of a precipice.[2] Under the circumstances, that ordinary people have a craving for peace is perfectly understandable. Yet at the same time, powerful factors and forces continue to militate against its being achieved. In the following remarks, we draw together some of the key points elaborated in this book to show why this is the case – and, indeed, why a reckless rush to pursue a 'peace process' or secure a 'peace agreement' could end up fuelling further conflict.

The future trajectory of Afghan politics will be determined by many different factors, including the positioning of actors in the wider world over which Afghanistan may have quite limited influence. Nonetheless, there are a range of domestic factors which the analysis in this book suggests are likely to be of continuing importance. One relates to the precise shape that the neopatrimonial system in Afghanistan takes in the future. The ubiquitous character of political networks has compromised the aspiration to develop a legal-rational political order, and has also affected the legitimacy of governments, although not necessarily of the constitutional system as a whole. But that said, there are a range of manifest defects in the constitutional and political systems which do require attention if Afghanistan's problems are to be effectively addressed. The high degree of centralisation of formal power has been at the expense of creativity and innovation, and the weakness of the Parliament compared to the Presidential Palace has deprived the system of the kinds of checks and balances that often make a political system work more smoothly. At the same time, the very weakness of the Parliament has led to its preoccupation with petty issues, most spectacularly in recent times, the highly ethnicised dispute over who should be the speaker of the *Wolesi Jirga*.[3] A serious factor contributing to this weakness has been the operation of the Single Non-Transferable Vote electoral system that militates against the development of effective political parties, but can encourage the use of ethnic symbolism to structure voting blocs within a legislature. Finding ways of invigorating political parties is an important challenge for Afghanistan's future. Unfortunately, an unintended consequence of the way in which the constitutional and political systems have taken shape in Afghanistan has been the creation of quite strong incentives for the practice of electoral fraud. This has led some to regret that Afghanistan moved so quickly to the use of mechanisms of electoral choice, which are inherently divisive and function best in political systems that are already consolidated; or even to argue that Afghanistan should suspend the holding of elections for the time being. But once a country starts holding elections, it is very difficult to stop without producing further adverse consequences, and this is one of the dilemmas that Afghanistan now confronts. The abandonment of electoral processes would leave the people of Afghanistan staring into a constitutional abyss. And ultimately, for all their problems, free and fair elections still offer the best mechanism for changing rulers without bloodshed.[4]

Of course, if some 'power sharing agreement' were struck with the Taliban, Afghanistan would find itself veering very much into the unknown as far as its political system was concerned. The existing constitutional and political systems would likely be very early victims. Parties with totalitarian visions tend to share power, if at all, only *tactically*; and are prone to employ what the Hungarian communist dictator Mátyás Rákosi called 'salami tactics', in which one moves to eliminate one's more moderate competitors slice by slice. This occurred in a range of Eastern European countries after the Second World War – Hungary being a prime example[5] – and more recently in the 1990s in Cambodia.[6] The most predictable consequence of such a development in Afghanistan would be refugee outflows in very large numbers.

In the economic sphere, much will depend on whether Afghanistan can succeed in moving further towards a civil economy. The substantial scale of Afghanistan's opium economy in *value* terms can lead one to lose sight of the fact that in *volume* terms, it is only a small part of Afghanistan's economy. Afghanistan produces a vastly greater tonnage of cereal crops than of the opium poppy, and the bulk of the workforce is employed in the normal activities of production and exchange that one associates with the operation of markets. Nonetheless, how Afghanistan's market system evolves will depend upon developments in a range of different spheres. One important sphere relates to property rights, and this in turn is linked to the wider question of the future of the 'rule of law' in Afghanistan. Property deeds, in the absence of a system of law which allows the rights that they confer to be enforced, are little more than pieces of paper. The most highly successful market economies are typically those in which property rights carry weight because in the event of a dispute, they can be given effect by an independent judiciary. Afghanistan is far from having such a system at the moment.[7] Another important sphere relates to finance. Some societies have historically been held back economically by the absence of structures such as joint stock companies that can facilitate entrepreneurship and the mobilisation of savings.[8] Furthermore, the Kabul Bank crisis cast a long shadow over the development of Afghanistan's banking system and highlights the importance of effective regulation as a device for instilling confidence in new economic mechanisms. This, of course, is far easier said than done, and there is a fine line to be trodden between on the one hand setting the scene for bank failures and the grief that such failures can cause for depositors, and on the other hand creating a moral hazard problem where those in charge of institutions act recklessly because they do not believe that they will be allowed to fail.

In contrast to President Karzai, President Ghani came to office with a very clear sense that economic progress in Afghanistan would be heavily dependent upon the enhancement of the ability of Afghans to trade with the wider world. His vigorous efforts to open transport corridors to more remote parts of the wider world formed part of the strategy, but it is, of its nature, a strategy that, if successful, will generate its main returns in the long run. And much will depend on the entrepreneurial spirit of ordinary Afghans. In sharp contrast to the 1950s and 1960s when state-driven economic development was seen in many countries as the wave of the future, there is now a much greater recognition of the danger that states will end up 'picking losers' rather than 'picking winners'. The state has a more important role to play in developing infrastructure that can facilitate private economic activity, but even here, it is important to remember that a neopatrimonial political system can significantly distort resource flows and, at worst, end up littering the landscape with white elephant infrastructure projects.

As we noted earlier in this book, Afghans have a long history of engaging with the wider world, contrary to romanticised images of Afghanistan as an isolated or hermit realm. In the political sphere, however, Afghan governments have relatively few resources to ensure that Afghanistan can control its own fate. As a result, its social and political future is heavily dependent on factors beyond Afghans' control. And for ordinary Afghans, this can make life seem like a voyage on a vessel with a drunken captain. For this very reason, it is important for Afghanistan to invest in the enhancement of its diplomatic capacities, since it cannot safely rely on the wider world either to understand the complexities of Afghanistan's environment or be motivated to respond to those complexities with appropriate policy settings. Diplomatic engagement is not a magic solution to this problem, but it is a relatively cost-effective tool with which Afghanistan can seek to ensure that its interests and priorities are not wholly neglected when policies towards West Asia are being determined. This also depends, however, on a minimal capacity on the part of the Afghan government to generate strategies to which Afghan diplomats can be tasked to give effect. This has been a weakness in recent years: key ministers have too often been preoccupied with domestic politics, leaving diplomats without instructions as to how to respond to opportunities for advancing Afghanistan's interests that may arise in the course of their day-to-day work.

The Soviet politician Trotsky once remarked that the road to Paris and London 'might lead through Kabul, Calcutta and Bombay'.[9] A modern variant of this claim might hold that the road to stability in Kabul leads through Washington, Tehran and Islamabad, and it is not a comforting thought. The advent of the Trump Administration has left key US policy decisions in the hands of the most erratic and unpredictable president in living memory – and furthermore, a president whose key counsellors have shown little direct interest in Afghanistan, but appear to be obsessed with Iran, to the extent that the US Secretary of State even blamed Iran for a bombing in Kabul for which the Taliban had already claimed responsibility.[10] There are many risks for Afghanistan in such circumstances. An Iran under attack might look for theatres of operation in which it could strike against the deployed forces of the attacker; and a United States looking for active support from regional allies might be prepared yet again to turn a blind eye to meddling in Afghanistan as the price to be paid for such support. But perhaps the greatest danger for Afghanistan from such an environment is its sheer unpredictability. There are simply too many variables at play for Afghanistan to have much capacity to shape its own future in the midst of larger events, and further disorder in Afghanistan could be catalysed by actions taken elsewhere even if that was not the intention of those who decided to act.

As insecurity continues to blight daily life in many parts of Afghanistan, much discussion has focussed on the use of a 'peace process' to overcome the problem.[11] In certain circumstances negotiations can solve problems, but not in all.[12] On the contrary, a negotiation process may be kept alive to distract a party from pursuing other options. This has a long history. On 27 May 1940, British Prime Minister Churchill warned of being lured into an indirect negotiation with Germany: 'The whole of this manoeuvre was intended to get us so deeply involved in negotiations that we should be unable to turn back'.[13] Likewise, in the 1980s, the USSR promoted the idea of negotiations over Afghanistan when it had no intention of making any concessions with respect to its presence in the country.[14] Furthermore, the very spectacle of negotiations can demoralise footsoldiers and unsettle people with reason to fear that 'negotiation' might be a euphemism for surrender.[15] Nonetheless, the Trump Administration from September 2018 embarked on a process of engagement with the Taliban. Several factors appeared to drive the push for a negotiated 'solution'. Almost certainly one of them was a desire on the part of the Trump Administration to divest itself of burdensome foreign commitments before the 2020 presidential election. Some Americans may also have adhered to the (naïve) belief that the Taliban could be a useful partner in confronting a terrorist group such as Islamic State.[16] Yet another motivation may have been a conviction that the war was 'unwinnable'. It is debatable, however, whether this was the most useful way of conceptualising the challenges that Afghanistan posed. A RAND study captured the nature of the problem:

> That there is no military solution to the war in Afghanistan has become a commonplace. But this is, at best, only half true. Winning may not be an available option, but losing certainly is. A precipitous departure, no matter how rationalized, will mean choosing to lose.[17]

What the authors did not say was that the main losers would most likely be Afghans.

On 7 September 2019, the US process of engagement with the Taliban unravelled spectacularly, when President Trump called it off in a volley of Twitter messages, and two days later he pronounced the process 'dead'.[18] The proximate cause was a bombing in the Shash Darak district of Kabul which killed an American soldier, and for which the Taliban claimed responsibility. At a deeper level, however, the entire process was beset with serious defects.[19] It had been heavily criticised by a group of former US ambassadors to Afghanistan and other eminent US diplomats even before President Trump aborted it.[20] The Afghan government had been excluded from the negotiations at the behest of the Taliban, and bitterly resented the way in which it had been undermined by its US ally. The Taliban, by contrast had been given the precious reward of a seat at the table with the Americans together with all the gains in status that flowed from it, but had steadfastly refused either to deal directly with the Afghan government, or to cease their attacks. The US most unwisely persisted with its discussions even when the Taliban claimed responsibility for a terrorist attack on 8 May 2019 on the Kabul office of Counterpart International, a civilian aid agency funded in part by USAID. And after long stating that 'nothing is agreed until everything is agreed', the US had abruptly shifted ground,[21] with US negotiator Zalmay Khalilzad stating that a process of direct negotiations between the Afghan government and the Taliban, up to that point a central part of the package, would occur 'after we conclude our own agreements'.

In the light of this failure, any future attempt to craft a political settlement in Afghanistan is likely to prove a veritable minefield. There is little credible evidence to suggest that the Taliban have turned into power-sharers; or abandoned any of their core values; or that *in power*, they would be much different from what they were when last they held state power.[22] There is also the question of the motives of

Pakistan as the Taliban's main backer. On 25 January 2019, a well-connected US observer, Dr Barnett Rubin, tweeted that the 'Trump Administration got Saudi Arabia and UAE to give Pak $12 bn to bring TB to the table'.[23] If it took such an enormous sum to secure Pakistani cooperation up to that point, would Pakistan, and specifically its military, continue to cooperate if lubricants of this kind and on such a scale were no longer available? Finally, a negotiation process can have the paradoxical effect of incentivising violence, by prompting actors to seize as much territory as they can before negotiations reach a critical phase. Such a process also runs the risk of triggering fragmentation if political actors conclude that they will serve their interests better by acting unilaterally rather than collectively.[24]

Here, it is worth recalling a grim Soviet anecdote from the 1950s. A man went to his rabbi to ask if there would be a war. '"There will be no war," replied the rabbi, "but there will be such a struggle for peace that no stone will be left standing"'.[25] This highlights the importance of thinking about 'peace' in a more nuanced fashion than one often encounters in media discussion of Afghanistan, and on closer examination, it proves to have what Richard Caplan has called a 'highly heterogeneous character'.[26] Peace means different things to different people and is accorded different value according to the form it takes. By employing a very narrow definition, for example, one might argue that Hitler brought 'peace' to Warsaw when his forces overran it in late September 1939 and the guns fell largely silent – but unsurprisingly, such a claim sticks in the throat. Afghans yearn for peace, yet the crucial question is what kind of peace is realistically on offer. The historian Jonathan Lee has supplied a characteristically forceful assessment:

> The only political solution offered by the international community boils down to a power-sharing agreement with the Taliban, Hikmatyar and other radical Islamic *jihad*ists. For Afghans, especially Shi'as, Hazaras, Uzbeks and women such a coalition is even more frightening than the continuation of the insurgency.[27]

In these unhappy circumstances, a certain nostalgia can easily colour one's view of Afghan history. Yet there is little to be gained from seeking to return to some 'golden age' from Afghanistan's past. Whilst it is true that Afghanistan between 1929 and 1978 was a relatively peaceful country – a French diplomat even called it the 'Switzerland of Asia'[28] – this was also a period in which forces and tensions developed that contributed powerfully to the collapse in the late 1970s from which Afghanistan has never recovered. Furthermore, for many Afghans during that period, the 'gold' on offer was fool's gold rather than a precious metal. The famine of the early 1970s was a chilling marker of the failure of the Afghan state to serve the needs of all Afghans equally. The observation of the economist Amartya Sen that 'No famine has ever taken place in the history of the world in a functioning democracy' is worth remembering.[29] Furthermore, numerous social groups have good reason to recall the days of 'peace' as a period of social marginalisation and struggle.

Afghanistan's prospects are *shaped* by its past, but not determined by it. But it is also here that at least a skerrick of hope lies. Whilst any Afghan under the age of 50 is unlikely to have much memory of 'peace', the future of Afghanistan will increasingly be in the hands of a younger generation of globalised Afghans with very different ways of seeing the world from their elders.[30] This is not without risk: young people who have grounds to feel that the world has abandoned them can easily become embittered or even radicalised. Nonetheless, it might offer Afghanistan an escape route, of sorts, from decades of sorrow and misery. It is young Afghans who, in Dylan Thomas's memorable words, can rage against the dying of the light.

Notes

1 *Global Peace Index 2019: Measuring Peace in a Complex World* (Sydney: Institute for Economics & Peace, 2019) p. 2.
2 See William Maley, 'Afghanistan on the Brink', *The Diplomat*, vol. 2, no. 5, December 2003–January 2004, pp. 10–11; William Maley, 'Afghanistan on a Knife-Edge', *Global Affairs*, vol. 2, no. 1, 2016, pp. 57–68.
3 Mujib Mashal and Jawad Sukhanyar, 'Long, Rowdy Feud in Afghan parliament mirrors wider fragility', *The New York Times*, 19 June 2019.
4 For a discussion of the value of free and fair electoral processes, see Adam Przeworski, *Why Bother with Elections?* (Cambridge: Polity Press, 2018); Jørgen Elklit and Michael Maley, 'Why Ballot Secrecy Still Matters', *Journal of Democracy*, vol. 30, no. 3, July 2019, pp. 61–75.
5 See François Fejtö, *A History of the People's Democracies: Eastern Europe Since Stalin* (Harmondsworth: Penguin, 1974).
6 See John M. Sanderson and Michael Maley, 'Elections and liberal democracy in Cambodia', *Australian Journal of International Affairs*, vol. 52, no. 3, November 1998, pp. 241–253.
7 See William Maley, *Transition in Afghanistan: Hope, Despair and the Limits of Statebuilding* (London: Routledge, 2018) pp. 129–145; William Maley, 'State strength and the rule of law', in Srinjoy Bose, Nishank Motwani and William Maley (eds.), *Afghanistan – Challenges and Prospects* (London: Routledge, 2018) pp. 63–77.
8 See Timur Kuran, *The Long Divergence: How Islamic Law Held Back the Middle East* (Princeton: Princeton University Press, 2010).
9 Isaac Deutscher, *The Prophet Armed: Trotsky: 1879–1921* (Oxford: Oxford University Press, 1954) p. 457.
10 See Siobhán O'Grady, 'The Taliban claimed an attack on U.S. forces. Pompeo blamed Iran', *The Washington Post*, 16 June 2019.
11 For careful overviews, see Omar Sadr, *Political Settlement of the Afghanistan Conflict: Divergent Models* (Kabul: Afghan Institute for Strategic Studies, March 2019); Rani D. Mullen, *Afghanistan: Time for Peace?* (Singapore: South Asian Scan no. 2, Institute of South Asian Studies, National University of Singapore, April 2019).
12 See Thérése Pettersson, Stina Högbladh and Magnus Öberg, 'Organized violence, 1989–2018 and peace agreements', *Journal of Peace Research* (forthcoming, 2019).
13 Tim Bouverie, *Appeasing Hitler: Chamberlain, Churchill and the Road to War* (London: The Bodley Head, 2019) pp. 408–409.
14 See Amin Saikal, 'The Afghanistan crisis: A negotiated settlement?', *The World Today*, vol. 40, no. 11, November 1984, pp. 481–489.
15 See Thomas Gibbons-Neff, Taimoor Shah and Najim Rahim, '"What kind of peace talks are these?": On the front lines of a 17-year war', *The New York Times*, 17 July 2019; Michael Hirsh, 'Ryan Crocker: The Taliban will "Retake the Country"', *Foreign Policy. com*, 28 January 2019; Ryan Crocker, 'I was ambassador to Afghanistan. This deal is a Surrender', *The Washington Post*, 29 January 2019.

16 See Niamatullah Ibrahimi and Shahram Akbarzadeh, 'Intra-*Jihadist* conflict and cooperation: Islamic State-Khorasan Province and the Taliban in Afghanistan', *Studies in Conflict and Terrorism* (forthcoming, 2019). Indeed, a danger that should be recognised is that a substantial group of Taliban could actually defect to Islamic State in the event of a 'peace settlement'.

17 James Dobbins, Jason H. Campbell, Sean Mann and Laurel E. Miller, *Consequences of a Precipitous U.S. Withdrawal from Afghanistan* (Santa Monica: RAND Corporation, January 2019) p. 2.

18 See Peter Baker, Mujib Mashal and Michael Crowley, 'How trump's plan to secretly meet with the Taliban came together, and fell apart', *The New York Times*, 9 September 2019; Michael D. Shear, 'Trump declares Afghan peace talks with Taliban "Dead"', *The New York Times*, 9 September 2019.

19 See William Maley, 'Caution rather than haste needed in the Afghanistan peace process', *Australian Outlook*, 21 August 2019; Kate Clark, *Trump Ends Talks with the Taleban: What Happens Next?* (Kabul: Afghanistan Analysts Network, 8 September 2019).

20 See James Dobbins, Robert P. Finn, Ronald E. Neumann, William Wood, John Negroponte, Earl Anthony Wayne, Ryan Crocker, James Cunningham and Hugo Llorens, 'U.S.-Taliban negotiations: How to avoid rushing to failure', *The Atlantic Council*, 3 September 2019.

21 Mujib Mashal, 'Confusion over Afghan-Taliban talks further complicates peace process', *The New York Times*, 27 July 2019.

22 For a revealing discussion, see Ashley Jackson, *Perspectives on Peace from Taliban Areas of Afghanistan* (Washington, DC: Special Report no. 449, United States Institute of Peace, May 2019).

23 For an elaboration of this point, see Barnett R. Rubin, 'Everyone wants a piece of Afghanistan', *Foreignpolicy.com*, 11 March 2019.

24 See Srinjoy Bose, William Maley and Nishank Motwani, 'Afghanistan: ceasefires and cascade effects', *Australian Outlook*, 21 August 2018; Dipali Mukhopadhyay, 'The Afghan stag hunt', *Lawfare*, 25 February 2019.

25 Vladimir Bukovsky, 'The peace movement and the Soviet Union', *Commentary*, vol. 73, no. 5, May 1982, pp. 25–41 at p. 36.

26 Richard Caplan, *Measuring Peace: Principles, Practices, and Politics* (Oxford: Oxford University Press, 2019) p. 25.

27 Jonathan L. Lee, *Afghanistan: A History from 1260 to the Present* (London: Reaktion Books, 2018) p. 683.

28 René Dollot, *L'Afghanistan: histoire, description, moeurs et coutumes, folklore, fouilles* (Paris: Éditions Payot, 1937) p. 15.

29 Amartya Sen, *Development as Freedom* (New York: Anchor Books, 1999) p. 16.

30 See Yukitoshi Matsumoto, 'Young Afghans in "transition": Towards Afghanisation, exit or violence', *Conflict, Security and Development*, vol. 11, no. 5, November 2011, pp. 555–578; Anna Larson and Noah Coburn, *Youth Mobilization and Political Constraints in Afghanistan: The Y Factor* (Washington, DC: Special Report no. 341, United States Institute of Peace, January 2014); Srinjoy Bose, Nematullah Bizhan and Niamatullah Ibrahimi, *Youth Protest Movements in Afghanistan: Seeking Voice and Agency* (Washington, DC: Peaceworks, United States Institute of Peace, January 2019).

BIBLIOGRAPHY

Barfield, Thomas J., *Afghanistan: A Cultural and Political History* (Princeton: Princeton University Press, 2010).

Bashir, Shahzad, and Robert D. Crews (eds.), *Under the Drones: Modern Lives in the Afghanistan-Pakistan Borderlands* (Cambridge: Harvard University Press, 2012).

Billaud, Julie, *Kabul Carnival: Gender Politics in Postwar Afghanistan* (Philadelphia: University of Pennsylvania Press, 2015).

Bizhan, Nematullah, *Aid Paradoxes in Afghanistan: Building and Undermining the State* (London: Routledge, 2018).

Bizhan, Nematullah, *Building Legitimacy and State Capacity in Protracted Fragility: The Case of Afghanistan* (London and Oxford: LSE-Oxford Commission on State Fragility, Growth and Development, 2018).

Bose, Srinjoy, Nematullah Bizhan and Niamatullah Ibrahimi, *Youth Protest Movements in Afghanistan: Seeking Voice and Agency* (Washington, DC: Peaceworks, United States Institute of Peace, January 2019).

Bose, Srinjoy, Nishank Motwani and William Maley (eds.), *Afghanistan – Challenges and Prospects* (London: Routledge, 2018).

Braithwaite, Rodric, *Afgantsy: The Russians in Afghanistan 1979–89* (London: Profile Books, 2011).

Brown, Vahid, and Don Rassler, *Fountainhead of Jihad: The Haqqani Nexus, 1973–2012* (New York: Oxford University Press, 2013).

Centlivres-Demont, Micheline (ed.), *Afghanistan: Identity, Society and Politics Since 1980* (London: I.B. Tauris, 2015).

Chayes, Sarah, *The Punishment of Virtue: Inside Afghanistan after the Taliban* (New York: Penguin, 2006).

Coll, Steve, *Ghost Wars: The Secret History of the CIA, Afghanistan and Bin Laden, from the Soviet Invasion to September 10, 2001* (London: Penguin, 2005).

Coll, Steve, *Directorate S: The C.I.A. and America's Secret Wars in Afghanistan and Pakistan* (New York: Penguin Press, 2018).

Crews, Robert D., *Afghan Modern: The History of a Global Nation* (Cambridge: Harvard University Press, 2015).

Crews, Robert D., and Amin Tarzi (eds.), *The Taliban and the Crisis of Afghanistan* (Cambridge: Harvard University Press, 2008).

Dalrymple, William, *Return of a King: The Battle for Afghanistan* (London: Bloomsbury Publishing, 2013).

Donini, Antonio, Norah Niland and Karin Wermester (eds.), *Nation-Building Unraveled? Aid, Peace and Justice in Afghanistan* (Bloomfield: Kumarian Press, 2004).

Dorronsoro, Gilles, *Revolution Unending: Afghanistan, 1979 to the Present* (New York: Columbia University Press, 2005).

Dupree, Louis, *Afghanistan* (Princeton: Princeton University Press, 1980).

Edwards, David B., *Heroes of the Age: Moral Fault Lines on the Afghan Frontier* (Berkeley & Los Angeles: University of California Press, 1996).

Edwards, David B., *Caravan of Martyrs: Sacrifice and Suicide Bombing in Afghanistan* (Oakland: University of California Press, 2017).

Farrell, Theo, *Unwinnable: Britain's War in Afghanistan 2001–2014* (London: The Bodley Head, 2017).

Fry, Maxwell J., *The Afghan Economy: Money, Finance, and the Critical Constraints to Economic Development* (Leiden: E.J. Brill, 1974).

Gall, Carlotta, *The Wrong Enemy: America in Afghanistan, 2001–2014* (New York: Houghton Mifflin Harcourt, 2014).

Giustozzi, Antonio, and Mohammed Isaqzadeh, *Policing Afghanistan: The Politics of the Lame Leviathan* (London: Hurst & Co., 2013).

Giustozzi, Antonio, *The Army of Afghanistan: A Political History of a Fragile Institution* (London: Hurst & Co., 2016).

Giustozzi, Antonio, *The Islamic State in Khorasan: Afghanistan, Pakistan and the New Central Asian Jihad* (London: Hurst & Co., 2018).

Green, Nile (ed.), *Afghan History Through Afghan Eyes* (London: Hurst & Co., 2015).

Green, Nile (ed.), *Afghanistan's Islam: From Conversion to the Taliban* (Oakland: University of California Press, 2017).

Gutman, Roy, *How We Missed the Story: Osama Bin Laden, the Taliban, and the Hijacking of Afghanistan* (Washington, DC: United States Institute of Peace Press, 2013).

Hanifi, Shah Mahmoud, *Connecting Histories in Afghanistan: Market Relations and State Formation on a Colonial Frontier* (Stanford: Stanford University Press, 2008).

Harpviken, Kristian Berg, and Shahrbanou Tadjbakhsh, *A Rock Between Hard Places: Afghanistan as an Arena of Regional Insecurity* (London: Hurst & Co., 2016).

Hussain, Rizwan, *Pakistan and the Emergence of Islamic Militancy in Afghanistan* (Aldershot: Ashgate, 2005).

Ibrahimi, Niamatullah, *The Hazaras and the Afghan State: Rebellion, Exclusion, and the Struggle for Recognition* (London: Hurst & Co., 2017).

Ibrahimi, Niamatullah, Musab Omer and Mohammad Irfani, *Social Media and Articulation of Radical Narratives in Afghanistan: A Research and Policy Paper* (Kabul: Afghanistan Institute for Strategic Studies, November 2015).

Jalali, Ali Ahmad, *A Military History of Afghanistan: From the Great Game to the Global War on Terror* (Lawrence: University Press of Kansas, 2017).

Jamal, Ahmad Shuja, *The Fatemiyoun Army: Reintegration into Afghan Society* (Washington, DC: Special Report no. 443, United States Institute of Peace, March 2019).

Johnson, Robert, *The Afghan Way of War: How and Why They Fight* (New York: Oxford University Press, 2011).

Johnson, Thomas H., *Taliban Narratives: The Use and Power of Stories in the Afghanistan Conflict* (London: Hurst & Co., 2017).

Kalinovsky, Artemy M., *A Long Goodbye: The Soviet Withdrawal from Afghanistan* (Cambridge: Harvard University Press, 2011).

Leake, Elisabeth, *The Defiant Border: The Afghan-Pakistan Borderlands in the Era of Decolonization, 1936–1965* (Cambridge: Cambridge University Press, 2017).

Lee, Jonathan L., *Afghanistan: A History from 1260 to the Present* (London: Reaktion Books, 2018).

Maley, William (ed.), *Fundamentalism Reborn?: Afghanistan and the Taliban* (London: Hurst & Co., 1998).

Maley, William, *Rescuing Afghanistan* (London: Hurst & Co., 2006).

Maley, William, *The Afghanistan Wars* (New York: Palgrave Macmillan, 2009).

Maley, William, *Transition in Afghanistan: Hope, Despair and the Limits of Statebuilding* (London: Routledge, 2018).

Maley, William, and Susanne Schmeidl (eds.), *Reconstructing Afghanistan: Civil-military Experiences in Comparative Perspective* (London: Routledge, 2015).

Mansfield, David, *A State Built on Sand: How Opium Undermined Afghanistan* (London: Hurst & Co., 2016).

Marsden, Magnus, *Trading Worlds: Afghan Merchants Across Modern Frontiers* (London: Hurst & Co., 2016).

Martin, Mike, *An Intimate War: An Oral History of the Helmand Conflict* (London: Hurst & Co., 2014).

Mason, Whit (ed.), *The Rule of Law in Afghanistan: Missing in Inaction* (Cambridge: Cambridge University Press, 2011).

Mousavi, Sayed Askar, *The Hazaras of Afghanistan: An Historical, Cultural, Economic and Political Study* (London: Curzon Press, 1998).

Mukhopadhyay, Dipali, *Warlords, Strongman Governors and the State in Afghanistan* (New York: Cambridge University Press, 2014).

Mullen, Rani D., *Afghanistan: Time for Peace?* (Singapore: South Asian Scan no. 2, Institute of South Asian Studies, National University of Singapore, April 2019).

Murtazashvili, Jennifer Brick, *Informal Order and the State in Afghanistan* (Cambridge: Cambridge University Press, 2016).

Paliwal, Avinash, *My Enemy's Enemy: India in Afghanistan from the Soviet Invasion to the US Withdrawal* (London: Hurst & Co., 2017).

Partlow, Joshua, *A Kingdom of Their Own: The Family Karzai and the Afghan Disaster* (New York: Alfred A. Knopf, 2016).

Rahimi, Mujib Rahman, *State Formation in Afghanistan: A Theoretical and Political History* (London: I.B. Tauris, 2017).

Rashid, Ahmed, *Taliban: Militant Islam, Oil and Fundamentalism in Central Asia* (New Haven: Yale University Press, 2010).

Roy, Olivier, *Islam and Resistance in Afghanistan* (Cambridge: Cambridge University Press, 1990).

Rubin, Barnett R., *The Fragmentation of Afghanistan: State Formation and Collapse in the International System* (New Haven: Yale University Press, 2002).

Saikal, Amin, *Modern Afghanistan: A History of Struggle and Survival* (London: I.B. Tauris & Co., 2012).

Saikal, Amin, and William Maley (eds.), *The Soviet Withdrawal from Afghanistan* (Cambridge: Cambridge University Press, 1989).

Saikal, Amin, and Kirill Nourzhanov (eds.), *Afghanistan and Its Neighbors after the NATO Withdrawal* (Lanham: Lexington Books, 2016).

Schetter, Conrad (ed.), *Local Politics in Afghanistan: A Century of Intervention in the Social Order* (London: Hurst & Co., 2013).

Shahrani, M. Nazif (ed.), *Modern Afghanistan: The Impact of 40 Years of War* (Bloomington: Indiana University Press, 2018).

Shahrani, M. Nazif, and Robert L. Canfield (eds.), *Revolutions and Rebellions in Afghanistan: Anthropological Perspectives* (Berkeley: Institute of International Studies, University of California, 1984).

Shroder, John F., *Natural Resources in Afghanistan: Geographic and Geologic Perspectives on Centuries of Conflict* (Waltham: Elsevier Inc., 2014).

Sinno, Abdulkader H., *Organizations at War in Afghanistan and Beyond* (Ithaca: Cornell University Press, 2008).

Stenersen, Anne, *Al-Qaida in Afghanistan* (Cambridge: Cambridge University Press, 2017)

Strick van Linschoten, Alex, and Felix Kuehn, *An Enemy We Created: The Myth of the Taliban/Al-Qaeda Merger in Afghanistan, 1970–2010* (London: Hurst & Co., 2012).

Thier, J. Alexander (ed.), *The Future of Afghanistan* (Washington, DC: United States Institute of Peace, 2009).

Thompson, Edwina A., *Trust Is the Coin of the Realm: Lessons from the Money Men in Afghanistan* (Karachi: Oxford University Press, 2011).

Wimpelmann, Torunn, *The Pitfalls of Protection: Gender, Violence, and Power in Afghanistan* (Oakland: University of California Press, 2017).

INDEX

Printed in Germany
by Amazon Distribution
GmbH, Leipzig